MASKED
DEPRESSION

MASKED

DEPRESSION

EDITED AND INTRODUCTION BY

Stanley Lesse M.D., MED. Sc. D.

Editor-in-Chief, American Journal of Psychotherapy
President, Association for the Advancement of Psychotherapy
Neurological Institute of the Presbyterian Hospital of New York
Faculty of Neurology, College of Physicians
and Surgeons, Columbia University
New York, New York

Jason Aronson, *New York*

jm po 1553 job 493 x5026

First Aronson Edition
© 1974 Jason Aronson, Inc. New York

Library of Congress Cataloging in Publication Data

Lesse, Stanley.
    Masked depression

    Includes bibliographies.
        1. Depression, Mental. 2. Psychology, Pathological.
I. Title. DNLM: 1. Depression. 2. Depression—
Therapy. WM207 L638m
RC537.L47 616.08 73-17744
ISBN 0-87668-122-4

Contributors

Irving Bieber, M.D.

Clinical Professor of Psychiatry, New York Medical College, New York City

Jacob Chwast, Ph.D.

Director, Mental Health Consultation Services, The Educational Alliance, New York City

Norman L. Farberow, Ph.D.

Director, Suicide Prevention Center, Los Angeles, California

Alvin I. Goldfarb, M.D.

Associate Clinical Professor of Psychiatry, Mount Sinai Medical School, New York City

Max Hayman, M.D.

Director, Alcohol and Drug Dependence Center, Compton Foundation Hospital, Compton, California

Stanley Lesse, M.D., Med. Sc.D.

Editor-in-Chief, American Journal of Psychotherapy

Robert E. Litman, M.D.

Professor of Psychiatry, University of Southern California School of Medicine, Los Angeles, California

Arnold M. Ludwig, M.D.

Professor and Chairman, Department of Psychiatry, University of Kentucky College of Medicine, Lexington, Kentucky

James F. Masterson, M.D.

Professor of Clinical Psychiatry, Cornell University Medical College, New York City

Julien Mendelwicz, M.D.

Senior Research Fellow, Department of Medical Genetics, New York State Psychiatric Institute, New York City

Donald I. Meyers, M.D.

Director of Experimental Psychiatry, The Henry Ittleson Center for Child Research, New York City

Hilde L. Mosse, M.D.

Assistant Clinical Professor of Psychiatry, New York Medical College, New York City

Marvin K. Opler, Ph.D.

Professor of Social Psychiatry, State University of New York, Buffalo, New York

Rose Spiegel, M.D.

Training Analyst, William Alanson White Institute, New York City

Norman Tabachnick, M.D.

Director, Suicide Prevention Center, Los Angeles, California

James M. Toolan, M.D.

Assistant Professor of Clinical Psychiatry, University of Vermont College of Medicine, Burlington, Vermont

Howard Wishnie, M.D.

Staff Psychiatrist, United States Public Health Service, Clinical Research Center, Lexington, Kentucky

Carl I. Wold, Ph.D.

Associate Clinical Professor of Psychiatry, University of Southern California School of Medicine, Los Angeles, California

To
Reds and Dad
with admiration, gratitude, and love

Contents

Preface

The subject of masked depression and depressive equivalents presents us with a paradox. While it represents one of the more common clinical syndromes seen in the United States and probably in western Europe, only a relative handful of clinicians has a meaningful awareness or understanding of it. This book is the first to view masked depression and depressive equivalents in broad perspective and to examine its numerous aspects in detail.

My interest in this subject is attributable to my training and clinical association with both neurology and psychiatry. It began in the early 1950s, when I was simultaneously on the attending staff of the Neurological Institute of the Presbyterian Hospital of New York and resident, research fellow, and then senior research psychiatrist, in that order, at the New York State Psychiatric Institute.

As a young attending neurologist-psychiatrist my practice consisted largely of referrals of "problem patients" from the more senior members of the Neurological Institute. Many of these patients had atypical facial pain and chronic low back syndromes, persistent headaches, and other continuing discomforts, despite negative workups. Also, because I had dual "board" accreditation in neurology and psychiatry, I was called in consultation at the Columbia-Presbyterian Medical Center by attending physicians from various departments to investigate patients who had persistent pain problems or who had clinical findings that did not follow classical or typical patterns.

With increased experience, it soon became evident to me

that in many of these patients the prime etiology was not organic; rather, the "somatic" complaints were commonly hypochondriacal or psychosomatic manifestations of underlying depressions.

A thorough review of the literature revealed a tremendous void with regard to the overall subject of masked depression. During the early and mid-1950s I also noted that my more senior colleagues in both the organic and psychiatric specialties had either no awareness or only a token appreciation of this syndrome.

In 1956 I published a paper entitled "Atypical Facial Pain Syndromes of Psychogenic Origin: Complications of Misdiagnosis" (*Journal of Nervous and Mental Diseases* 124:346–51). This was the first of my publications to deal with an aspect of the masked depression syndrome. It is interesting, now, to recall that the paper was rejected by two general mass-circulation, medical journals with comments reflecting the editors' diagnostic skepticism.

In order to gain a fuller understanding of the masked depression syndrome, I worked in various specialty clinics in the Presbyterian Hospital of New York from the mid-1950s through the early 1960s. In addition, I ran a special facial pain clinic for several years; and I saw hundreds of patients in private practice who had this syndrome. I found that 50 percent or more of hospital clinic patients in their forties, fifties, and sixties had variations of the masked depression syndrome. In addition, a very significant number of patients in this age group admitted to our hospital had masked depressions.

During the late 1950s I also became sharply aware that the symptoms masking depression were not limited to hypochondriasis or psychosomatic disorders, with or without histrionic flavoring. It became very obvious that various behavior patterns could also mask even severe underlying depressions. I observed patients in whom severe depressions were masked by alcoholism, drug habituation, latent or active homosexuality, rage responses, delinquency, learning disorders, bulimia, accident-proneness, sexual problems such as impotence, frigidity, and dyspareunia, and on through a long list. I reported that masked depression was common among executives; indeed, it probably represents the most common single serious ailment seen in junior or senior executives.

I am not implying that most patients are either overtly or covertly depressed. I am not designating this post–World War II period as the "era of depression," as some observers have suggested. I am, however, urgently indicating that depressive disorders, very often of severe proportions, are commonly masked. Indeed, this syndrome is one of the most common disorders seen in Western medicine. It rivals in frequency depressions of the more classic variety.

Despite the frequency of its occurrence, masked depression is rarely diagnosed at or near its inception. Years usually pass before its existence is recognized, after an expensive and painful process of elimination or after the underlying depression finally becomes overt. I found it truly sobering to discover that 42 percent of my patients with this problem had suicidal preoccupations or drives by the time I first saw them (see Chapter 4).

The greatest danger with regard to this syndrome lies in the clinical scotoma which exists in all branches of the medical and psychological sciences. Textbooks and handbooks of general medicine and psychiatry make little or no reference to it. Resident psychiatrists are rarely exposed to a formal awareness of it, since their teachers themselves are seldom aware of its existence. No school of medicine, dentistry, psychotherapy, or psychology offers definitive instruction in the subject.

It is my sincere hope that this book will stimulate a poignant awareness of masked depression and depressive equivalents. Beyond this, I hope it will serve as a reference source for clinicians, teachers, and students alike, whether they are primarily trained in the physical or the psychologic aspects of the health sciences. I anticipate that this book will be the first of several on this subject, since the symptoms or behavior patterns that mask depression vary sharply from culture to culture.

Each of the authors who has contributed to this book was carefully chosen for his or her extensive expertise with regard to a specific aspect of the problem. Each chapter represents a unique contribution, for which I am most deeply appreciative.

Professional people who flitter about lecturing, preparing conferences or preparing manuscripts are a very preoccupied and demanding group. There surely should be a very special reward for their long suffering spouses, who wittingly or unwittingly almost inevitably find themselves drafted to give assistance in these undertakings.

I would like to thank my wife Margie for her patient assistance and consistent encouragement in the preparation of the many talks, conferences, and papers dealing with masked depression that eventually resulted in this book.

July 10, 1973   Stanley Lesse

MASKED DEPRESSION

PART I

Depressive Equivalents and the Multivariant Masks of Depression

STANLEY LESSE

Depression may be hidden behind many facades. The term "depression" as commonly used by laymen usually refers only to a mood, which in psychiatric circles is more specifically labeled as sadness, dejection, despair, gloominess, despondency, or melancholy. If such a mood pattern is not noted overtly, then the layman does not consider the patient to be depressed. Unfortunately, this sort of scotoma frequently occurs among physicians too, and even among psychiatrists. The depressive affect and even many depressive syndromes may be so masked that the physician may be unaware of the fact that a serious psychiatric disorder is at hand until a massive, full-blown depression erupts and dominates the clinical picture. The type of practice in which one is engaged will in great measure determine the frequency with which the masked depression syndrome will be encountered and to some degree the nature of the masking process.

Terminologies and Concepts

The literature dealing with masked depression is sparse, to say the very least, despite the frequency with which these syndromes are observed in all cultures. The literature that does exist on the subject deals primarily with those depressive syndromes that are initially manifested clinically as psychosomatic disorders or hypochondriacal complaints referred to various organ systems.

Recently, however, reports have highlighted the fact that depressions may also be disguised by various types of "acting out" or behavioral disturbances. These behavioral masks may take the form of antisocial acts, impulsive sexual behavior, compulsive gambling, temper outbursts, destructiveness, sadistic or masochistic acts, compulsive work or behavior patterns, accident-proneness, histrionic dramatizations, and more. Less commonly, referential or delusional patterns may be discerned as masking processes. The depressive masking may also take the form of acute or chronic alcoholism or bulimia. Finally, it may manifest itself in the form of narcotics addiction, barbiturate habituation, the use of stimulant drugs, and the use of psychedelic agents such as lysergic acid or mescal derivatives.

The various terms used to designate the processes that mask depressive syndromes have been used interchangeably, particularly the most common ones: masked depression, depressive equivalent, and affective equivalent. In some ways this multiple labeling may be one cause of the limited awareness of this ubiquitous clinical problem.

It would be appropriate at this time to evaluate these labels and to determine just what each of them means. When is it appropriate to speak of masked depression, depressive equivalent, or affective equivalent? If it is found that specific differentiating criteria reveal no basic differences between the processes designated by the various labels, then it would be logical to narrow the number of labels to one or perhaps two, which would be either interchangeable or indicate specific limiting characteristics.

Most commonly, these terms indicate that if one probes behind the psychosomatic disorders, hypochondriacal symptoms, or various behavioral patterns one will find a depressive core from which a depressive affect will eventually become overt. Usually the depressive core rises to the surface spontaneously with the passage of time in a manner comparable to an iceberg that may rise to the surface under certain climatic conditions.

In this type of process, therefore, the psychosomatic or hypochondriacal symptoms or behavioral disturbances are indeed masking an active depression with the depressive core existing just beneath the surface. In these instances, as will be illustrated in a number of chapters, the underlying depressive affect can be readily uncovered by a perceptive investigator.

These patterns are by far the most common masked depressive processes, but they are not the only ones; there are other situations in which the terms "masked depression" and particularly "depressive equivalent" may be appropriate. Experienced physicians have frequently observed that many individuals who demonstrate hypochondriacal patterns early in life go on to develop overt depressive reactions. This pattern is often observed in women who develop overt depressions in the involutional period. It may also be seen in pre-involutional women, particularly those who have endogenous types of depressive reactions. I have also noted that women with histories of hypochondriacal trends are most susceptible to postpartum depressions. Physicians who treat a large number of patients with psychosomatic disorders have long been aware that these patients, especially in late middle age and later, are prone to develop depressive reactions.

I do not mean to imply that everyone who has a psychosomatic disorder or who is hypochondriacal or who has a behavior disorder is depressed or is inevitably destined to develop a depression. I would like to emphasize, however, that patients with these symptoms and behavior patterns appear to be particularly prone to develop depressive reactions, especially in their forties and after.

Even when very careful psychopathologic and psychodynamic investigations are conducted, a number of patients in whom one can observe psychosomatic disorders, hypochondriacal symptoms, or various chronic behavior patterns do not reveal an underlying depressive affect on initial examination or for a period of time afterward. Sooner or later, however—and it may be years later—some of these patients may spontaneously and even precipitously demonstrate overt depressions, at times of massive proportions. In other instances, repeated clinical evaluation will eventually discern an underlying depressive affect despite the fact that previous examinations have failed to elicit the underlying depressive core.

When this happens, one might be within good clinical bounds to state that the psychosomatic problems, hypochondriacal symptoms, and various behavior disorders may indeed have masked the underlying depressions or served as depressive equivalents. The depressive equivalents may be viewed as parts of a clinical spectrum having certain psychobiologic and psychodynamic origins with features in common. In this conceptualization, depressive or affective equivalents are considered as parts of a continuum that may or may not eventually manifest themselves as an overt, phenotypically manifested, full-fledged depression.

In other words, I am suggesting that in some patients psychosomatic disorders, hypochondriacal manifestations, and various behavior disorders may actually be different dimensions of depression, but nonetheless true depressive manifestations in which the usual depressive affect is not overt as defined by our current clinical and laboratory techniques. With the advent of improved clinical and biochemical procedures, these symptoms and syndromes eventually may be demonstrated to be true depressive equivalents in some individuals.

Unfortunately, only a very limited group of psychiatrists and psychotherapists has been sharply aware that psychosomatic disorders, hypochondriacal complaints, and abnormal behavioral patterns are common precursors or predisposing or forecasting manifestations of true depressive reactions. Yet after being exposed to a large number of these patients, one can become sensitive and expert in detecting hidden depression and recognizing those patients in whom these symptoms and behavior patterns are true masking phenomena. This diagnostic capability is most important, for, as we shall see in later chapters, failure to be sensitive to masked depressive syndromes not uncommonly results in the precipitous emergence of massive, overt depressive reactions, which at times are accompanied by suicidal acts.

Multivariant Masking Patterns

The clinical patterns serving as masking veneers may vary in accordance with one or more factors, such as age, sex, ethnic and cultural background, socioeconomic and sociophilosophic milieus, heredito-congenital processes, ontogenic development, and the nature and amount of treatment received.

All of these factors, individually or in combination, determine the quality and intensity of the masking syndrome or symptoms. These various factors will be considered in depth in subsequent chapters. Here let us take a panoramic clinical view of the vast array of masking processes and equivalents that pose a serious challenge to even the most serious and sensitive diagnosticians and therapists.

Masked Depression in Infancy and Childhood

Depression often goes unrecognized in children and adolescents because it tends to be hidden in symptoms not readily identified with this type of psychologic problem when it occurs in adults (9). When viewed from the standpoint of depressive symptomology as seen in adults, all depressive reactions seen in infants and in most children would fall into the category of masked depression. Toolen has noted that "one of the reasons that suicidal attempts have been overlooked in children and adolescents is the erroneous concept that youngsters do not experience depression. It is true they do not exhibit the signs and symptoms of adult depressive reactions, but rather other symptoms" (32).

In infancy and early childhood, deprivation reactions and depressive elements may be associated with developmental retardation as described by Spitz, who termed this symdrome "anaclitic depression" (30). This syndrome occurs in infants and small children who are deprived of mothering. It is most commonly seen in infants raised in understaffed or negligent institutions. These children demonstrate physical, intellectual, and emotional retardation. Initially they are capable of active protest, but finally they become apathetic, show decreased physical and mental activity, and reject those who approach them. As they advance into childhood and, later, adolescence, these youngsters find it very difficult to establish effective relationships with playmates or parental surrogates.

During my visit to the Pavlov Institute in Leningrad in 1956, I observed similar reactions produced experimentally in dogs (16). It was noted, for example, that when puppies one month old—the age when the "awareness reflex" appears —were given an electroshock whenever they were about to eat, they gradually retreated to the corners of their cages, withdrew from their keepers and the laboratory researchers, lost hair and body weight, and become markedly apathetic. It is significant that even after the environment was made much more pleasant, these little animals, who had been traumatized at a very early stage in their development, never attained a more normal pattern.

While growth failure (26) and impaired personality development (11) that occur as a response to maternal deprivation have been stressed, the existence of true depressive elements in children too frequently goes unrecognized, with the result that little attention is given to a corrective psychiatric approach to the problem (9).

In some departments of child psychiatry one can still hear

protests against the concept of childhood depression. Happily, a few more flexible child psychiatrists are beginning to recognize the clinical nuances indicating the presence of depressive reactions in some young patients.

Among older children, "acting out" behavior patterns and sociopathic manifestations are more likely to mask underlying depressions (32). These may take the form of disobedience, temper tantrums, truancy, or running away.

In a smaller group of children, depressive reactions take the form of being "loners," or an apparent inability to form any empathetic relationships. Some of these children have been mistakenly diagnosed as childhood schizophrenics.

School phobia (1) or underachievement in school (29) also may be the dominant characteristic of an underlying depression. The depressions masked by school failures may not be immediately evident to either the parents or the teachers. These unrecognized depressions are often aggravated by inappropriate punitive actions on the part of the parents or the school.

Unfortunately, if these children are not correctly diagnosed by the psychiatrist or psychotherapist to whom they are frequently referred, inappropriate psychotherapeutic techniques may actually cement the depressive process. In such unfortunate situations the underlying depressive process not infrequently mushrooms and becomes increasingly overt as childhood changes into pubescence. As these children become young adults, a number of them are finally correctly diagnosed as having endogenous depressions.

While hypochondriacal and psychosomatic problems camouflaging depression are most commonly seen in adults, they also occur in children (14). They are relatively frequent in adolescents. In children they may take the form of headaches, tics, choreiform movements, abdominal complaints, nausea, and vomiting. More complicated psychosomatic problems, such as asthma and migraine headaches, may sometimes mask underlying depression during the latter part of the first decade of life or in early adolescence.

In an opposite vein, symptoms such as suicide attempts, usually considered diagnostic of depression in adults, are considered by some observers as not necessarily indicative of depression in children, but rather a possible example of impulsive anger or rebellion (9, 10).

Depressions may also be masked in retarded children, particularly those in whom the intellectual retardation is not profound. These children are very frequently rejected by their parents, siblings, and peers. While their feelings of inadequacy and hopelessness may lead to overt depression, the depression may be masked by irritability and outbursts of rage directed at authority figures. These behavior patterns encourage further rejection and ensure a hostile environment for the retarded child. If the child's rage is stifled by punishment, it then may be directed toward younger children, small animals, or even inanimate objects (10). Masked depressive reactions such as these are often misdiagnosed and mismanaged, particularly in large institutions.

Masked Depression among Adolescents

Many of the depressive equivalents described for the older child may also be found in the young adolescent. School phobia and underachievement in school may conceal underlying depressions in this group as well as among older adolescents. Among high school and college students, depressions are frequently manifested by changing courses, failure to take examinations, and dropping out of school. Other such students change from full-time to part-time schooling. The threat of graduation, laden as it sometimes is with fears of unknown responsibilities, may be associated with depressive reactions.

Rejections and failures associated with dating and early sexual contacts are also associated with depressive reactions. Among older adolescents, automobile accidents, often with tragic consequences, may be acting-out expressions of severe underlying depressive reactions.

During the 1930s, 1940s, and early 1950s, depressive reactions associated with excessive alcohol intake were noted on college campuses in a significant group of students. This symptom is less common now; but increasing numbers of depressive reactions, both masked and overt, have been precipitated by an excessive use of marihuana, barbiturates, amphetamines, psychedelic drugs, cocaine, and narcotics. In some ethnic groups, the commonest cause of death among adolescents is overdosages of drugs. Some psychologic autopsies suggest deliberate rather than accidental overdosage.

While there has been a great deal of confusion with regard to the effects of marihuana, there is a considerable body of experience indicating that certain sensitive adolescents who use marihuana frequently enough to be called "hopheads" by their friends smoke excessively in an attempt to compensate for underlying depressive manifestations. Their depressive reactions may become overt when they stop smoking marihuana for even a brief time. I have known a few depressed patients in whom the excessive use of marihuana after the onset of the depression significantly modified the clinical manifestations of the depression without diluting its itensity. Indeed, one patient attempted suicide in the middle of a "high."

I noted earlier that psychosomatic disorders and hypochondriacal problems masking depression are relatively frequent among adolescents. This is particularly true of older adolescents.

I have commonly recorded histories of adolescent hypochondriasis in adults diagnosed as having endogenous depressions. Frequently, if one probes carefully, a history of intermittent depressive reactions associated with the hypochondriacal complaints will be discovered. In some instances, in accordance with the diagnostic criteria described earlier, adolescent hypochondriasis may very definitely be considered as true masked depression. In other instances, even after intensive investigation of the hypochondriacal adolescent, no definitive depressive reaction can be elicited.

What is the difference between the individual who is

hypochondriacal but does not manifest any underlying depressive reaction and the adolescent who is hypochondriacal and covertly clinically depressed? The psychodynamic patterns do not enable one to differentiate between these two groups, and our biochemical methods are too primitive at the present time to be of any help in the matter. Some investigators (4, 25) suggest that there may be heredito-congenital explanations. The evidence for these suggestions is not yet very convincing.

MacCurdy was one of the first observers to stress the characteristics of masked depression in adolescents. In 1925 he stated, "Depression is so frequently seen in the youth of both sexes that the term 'adolescent depression' would not be out of place" (24). He emphasized that depressions were commonly diagnosed by symbolic outlets, with only a general background of depression by adult standards. These observations were also emphasized by Aichhorn in 1935 (2).

More recently, Chwast has pointed out that depressive reactions may be masked by delinquent behavior among adolescents from lower socioeconomic backgrounds (3). He observed that among adolescent offenders, evidences of depression are commonly hidden behind sociopathic behavior patterns. His findings parallel observations made among adult criminals by many psychiatrists and psychologists (28).

Chwast (3) found frequent evidence of overt or covert depression among 121 adolescents from lower socioeconomic environments referred by police juvenile officers. Almost 50 percent of his patients manifested signs of depression. Depression appeared to occur more commonly among girls than boys. He also noted that it appeared more often among older adolescent offenders than among those aged thirteen or under.

The usual patterns associated with so-called neurotic depressions are relatively rare among adolescents. Among some delinquents the sociopathic acting out serves to ward off a decompensating schizophrenic defense mechanism. Fighting and destructive behavior may also be seen as attempts to combat depressive manifestations that threaten to become overt. The gang relationships of many delinquents represent a search for "significant others" to compensate for a lack of meaningful attachments. Stripped of gang contacts, some of these culturally deprived young people are immobilized by feelings of inadequacy, hopelessness, and even overt depression.

Masked Depression in Adults

Hypochondriasis and Psychosomatic Disorders

In our culture, hypochondriacal complaints and psychosomatic disorders referred to various organ systems are the clinical patterns that most frequently mask underlying depression (13, 20). Ironically, although this syndrome rivals in frequency true overt depression, it is insufficiently appreciated by both psychiatrists and nonpsychiatrists. There are several reasons for this. The nonpsychiatrists usually record "physical" complaints with literal eyes without probing beneath the surface to detect the affect associated with the complaints.

It is usually only after months or years of repeated physical and laboratory examinations, and after the failure of multiple medical and even surgical procedures, or after the rapid mushrooming of a severe, undisguised depressive affect, that the psychiatrist is called upon as a consultant. Nevertheless, physicians who specialize in organic medicine find that patients with masked depressions account for many if not most of the depressions with which they are confronted.

Psychiatrists also are often only remotely aware of this syndrome, and nonmedical psychotherapists are almost completely oblivious of its existence. Very few psychiatrists receive anything approaching a clear appreciation of this diagnostic process during their residency training. And relatively few psychiatrists maintain sufficient contact with internal medicine or neurology to be sharply aware of what constitutes a reliable history of true organic deficits.

Psychiatrists find that the masked syndrome is seen in a more limited number of depressed patients. Hochstetter, a psychiatrist, observed for example, masked depression in only 27 of 258 patients (10.5 percent) with depressive syndromes (13). At the other extreme, neuropsychiatrists who are called in as consultants in large medical centers may see this syndrome more frequently. For example, of 324 patients that I saw during a two-and-a-half-year period who I diagnosed as being depressed, 100 (30.9 percent) had masked depressions (20).

The hypochondriacal and psychosomatic symptoms were referred to many organ systems (cardiovascular, respiratory, gastrointestinal, genito-urinary, endocrine, and otolaryngological), various joints and aspects of the osseous system, and the central and peripheral nervous system. This syndrome was found to be an ailment of middle age, with 88 percent of the patients being between thirty-six and sixty-four years; and of these, more than two-thirds were women.

There is a considerable delay between the onset of illness and formal neuropsychiatric consultation. In an earlier study of a hundred patients with masked depressions, I reported that more than three-quarters of the patients had been ill for more than one year, more than two-thirds for more than two years, and almost one-third for more than five years by the time they were seen in formal neuropsychiatric consultations, when the correct diagnosis was finally made. These figures are important, because the prognosis in patients with masked depression is in great measure dependent upon the duration of illness. If a correct diagnosis is made early and appropriate treatment is instituted promptly, very satisfactory therapeutic results may be obtained.

In another study, I found that excellent or good results were obtained (as evaluated by the amelioration of presenting symptoms and the degree of social and vocational adaptation) in slightly more than half of the patients who had been ill for one year or less (17). In contrast, only one in four patients who had been ill for two years had good or excellent results. The prognosis in patients who were ill for more than two years was relatively poor.

Masked depressions very frequently are not of minor proportions. At times the underlying depression may precipitously explode in a suicidal gesture. Hochstetter noted that two-thirds of his patients with depressive equivalents were preoccupied by suicide (13). In an earlier study I noted that 42 of 100 patients with masked depressions studied in a two-and-one-half-year period were similarly preoccupied (20). These figures indicate that by the time patients with masked depressions are referred to a psychiatrist, the depressions may be very severe and the patients may require urgent or even emergency treatment.

Hypochondriacal complaints and psychosomatic disorders that serve to mask depression may take various forms. They may occur purely as expressions of underlying depression, without any organic lesions present. On the other hand, this syndrome may be superimposed upon a true organic deficit, and the organic lesion may be of major or minor proportions. These combinations tax the diagnostic and therapeutic ingenuity of all physicians, psychiatrists and nonpsychiatrists alike.

Drug Dependence

I previously noted that in our culture drug dependence is one of the more common masks of depression in adults and with increasing frequency in older adolescents. The term "drug dependence" is now being used by the World Health Organization to replace terms used earlier, such as "drug addiction," "drug abuse," and "drug habituation." It can be defined as "a state of psychic or physical dependence, or both, on a drug arising in a person following administration of that drug on a periodic or continuous basis" (6). While public attention has recently been focused upon problems secondary to narcotics addiction (because this type of drug dependence is most commonly associated with major crime in large cities), the excessive use of alcohol remains the most frequently encountered drug abuse. Nine million persons in this country are estimated to be chronic alcoholics. If one includes in the conceptualization of chronic alcoholism those persons who daily require several drinks at lunchtime, after work, and in the evening in order to function vocationally and socially, then the total number of alcoholics assumes truly massive proportions. The annual economic losses to business and industry due to excessive drinking total billions of dollars. The economic deprivation and emotional traumas suffered by the families of alcoholics are legendary.

Chronic alcoholism frequently serves to mask underlying depressive episodes. Suicidal acts commonly may occur when a chronic alcoholic sobers up after a bout of heavy drinking (21). In some debilitated drinkers the continued imbibing of alcohol itself properly may be viewed as an attempt at suicide.

The lowering of the ego boundaries which occurs with excessive intake of alcohol may permit unbridled development of feelings of hopelessness, rejection, and overwhelming retroflex rage, alone or in combination. Precipitous, massive depressive reactions may occur in these states. Or overwhelming guilt feelings may dominate the patient after a debauch, and a profound depressive reaction that had been masked by alcohol may rapidly emerge. The inhibition of sexual performance so commonly associated with alcoholism may precipitate an impulsive suicidal act when the patient sobers up.

I have noted with increasing frequency many similar reactions during and following the use of hallucinogenic agents. Lysergic acid has been used by a large number of adolescents and young adults in an attempt to escape the here and now—to attain an illusory utopia. For some of these patients the psychedelic drug serves to mask underlying depressive syndromes. Several weeks may pass after the patient has been "on a trip" before a covert depressive reaction may precipitously become overt. However, if one follows these patients day by day, the underlying depression is readily observable shortly after they have taken lysergic acid.

An increasing number of suicide attempts under the influence of LSD have been reported. Many of these attempts occur under bizarre circumstances. A number of these unfortunate individuals have histories indicating previous depressive reactions. Most have had depressive reactions within a schizoid personality matrix.

Dependence upon the various narcotic preparations may also conceal depressive syndromes. This phenomenon is particularly frequent among persons from lower socioeconomic groups, but it is also a problem among artists, musicians, and other entertainers. Patients with histories of masked depression in adolescence who enter the arts or entertainment fields appear to be susceptible to drug dependence in adult life. Narcotics addiction may sometimes be seen as an attempt to cope with an underlying endogenous depression. Some of the suicide attempts that are made when addicts are taken off narcotics may be ascribed to the emergence of massive depressive reactions that had been masked by the addiction.

Amphetamine-dependent persons not infrequently have a depressive matrix. Rapidly mounting depressive reactions very commonly result from the withholding of amphetamines from chronic users. Amphetamines are dispensed frequently and in large quantities to depressed patients in an attempt to ameliorate the depression. When a depressive reaction is profound, these drugs may merely serve to mask it, and if the psychiatrist is not wary, a precipitous increase in the depressive process may occur, at times accompanied by suicidal reactions. The severity of the depressive syndrome may actually increase while the patient is on amphetamines, and the therapist may be quite unaware of the continuing exacerbation.

Barbiturate habituation has become a progressively more common problem. Like the amphetamines, barbiturates are overproduced to a degree that must be considered a sociological hazard of major proportions. If the pharmaceutical houses were bent intentionally upon mass destruction, they could not cause greater harm than they have done by their unconscionable overproduction of barbiturates, which flow through illicit channels to the streets to cause psychosocial pollution, death, and worse. (Yes, there *are* fates worse than death.) Barbiturate dependence is often seen in combination with amphetamine dependence; the patients alternate the drugs, or even take them in combination. When these drugs are abruptly withdrawn from habitual users, grand mal seizures may ensue, and these are not uncommonly followed by depressive reactions.

The introduction of the tranquilizing and antidepressant drugs into our psychiatric armamentarium has produced an entirely new clinical psychiatric population made up of severely depressed patients who formerly would have been hospitalized or given ambulatory electroshock treatment. A large number of inadequately treated patients have underlying depressions masked to varying degrees. This is confusing, particularly to nonpsychiatric physicians. Many psychiatrists are called upon to treat suicidal patients who have been treated with antidepressant drugs and tranquilizers for periods of time. Some psychiatrists have been lulled into a false sense of security by the early results obtained among severely depressed, even suicidal patients following the use of these preparations. In some patients the depressive affect may be only blunted and the psychiatrist may prematurely relax his vigilance, at times with tragic results (21). The extensive use of the psychotropic drugs has been paralleled by the appearance of a large group of such patients; they pose a difficult therapeutic problem.

In similar fashion, electroshock therapy may on occasion merely blunt or mask a severe depressive reaction, particularly if the frequency or number of treatments is inadequate. This is particularly true among patients in whom the depressive affect is part of a broader schizophrenic syndrome.

Geriatric Patients

Organic mental reactions caused by neoplastic processes,

vascular deficits, metabolic abnormalities, degenerative or infectious diseases, or traumas may mask underlying depressive disorders in any age group. Depressive reactions concealed by organic brain deficits are particularly prominent among geriatric patients, most commonly secondary to cerebrovascular insufficiency or so-called primary degenerative processes. Patients who demonstrate fluctuations in the intensity of an organic mental syndrome deserve very close scrutiny. When they are in a marked state of confusion, one commonly notes a decrease in the intensity of a depression, even of suicidal impulses. As they regain relative clarity and insight into the nature and intensity of their problems, however, a depression deepening toward suicide may occur (21).

Hypochondriacal complaints and psychosomatic disorders may also mask depressions in this group. I have previously reported on this syndrome in senior executives prior to and following retirement (19). In this older age group underlying depressive mechanisms also may be hidden behind patterns of irritability, marked obsessive-compulsiveness, or a marked increase in psychomotor activity.

The elderly patient is too frequently taken at face value. If evidences of depression are not obvious, it is more than likely that masked depressive elements will not be persistently sought out. It is a very sobering fact that suicide rates increase sharply among elderly patients.

Masked Depression Considered as a Heredito-congenital Process

As I noted previously, a number of authors have proposed that there is evidence that some masked depressions, particularly those masked by hypochondriacal or psychosomatic disorders, may be linked to genetic factors. This was the conclusion of Da Fonseca from a study of sixty probands (6). He studied twins and close relatives, and found that within close family constellations there was an unusually high frequency of certain somatic and psychosomatic syndromes, particularly syndromes resembling rheumatism, asthmatic attacks, peptic ulcers, and certain dermatoses.

Again, the overall clinical evidence documenting the genetic link in patients with masked depression is not yet clear-cut beyond the realm of speculation. But the material currently at hand indicates that further studies in this direction are definitely warranted.

Masked Depression in Relation to Cultural and Ethnic Background

Depression may appear in radically different clinical guises, in part dependent upon local custom, educational level, degree of religiosity and superstition, regional mythology, and the like. So far the transcultural investigation of depression on an organized basis has been very limited. During the past few years, however, a number of psychiatrists have described in some detail how depressive reactions in different countries may vary widely from those considered typical in the Western world. A series of papers entitled "The Theory and Practice of Psychiatry in Different Cultures" in the *American Journal of Psychotherapy* describes a wide variety of depressive reactions noted in a number of countries. More recently, I have reported that in developing countries the types of depressive reactions seen in traditional rural communities may differ radically from those observed among families living in highly industrialized urban centers (22). This tendency was particularly noticeable in Japan and India, but to a lesser degree it may also be noted in Thailand. The transcultural study of masked depression deserves more intensive investigation, since it could be a vehicle for significant progress in our comprehension of the relationships between individual psychodynamics and sociodynamics.

In sum, the masks of depression are so multivariant and are influenced by so many factors that generations of serious psychiatrists and psychologists have been unaware of the frequency of these syndromes, even though they rival overt depression in frequency. This entire subject poses a major diagnostic and therapeutic challenge to all who practice in the health sciences.

References

1. Agras, S. The Relationship of School Phobia to Childhood Depression. *Amer. J. Psychiat.* 116:533, 1959.
2. Aichhorn A. *Wayward Youth.* New York: Viking Press, 1935.
3. Chwast, J. Depressive Reactions as Manifested among Adolescent Delinquents. *Amer. J. Psychother.* 21:574, 1967.
4. Cohen, M. B.; Baker, G.; Cohen, R. A.; Fromm-Reichmann, F.; and Weigert, E. V. An Intensive Study of Twelve Cases of Manic-Depressive Psychosis. *Psychiatry* 17:103, 1954.
5. Eddy, N. B.; Halbach, H.; Isbell, H.; and Seevers, M. H. Drug Dependence: Its Significance and Characteristics. *Bull. W.H.O.* 32:721, 1965.
6. Da Fonseca, A. F. Affective Equivalents. *Brit. J. Psychiat.* 199:464, 1963.
7. Freud, S. Mourning and Melancholia. In *Collected Papers* 4:152–72. London: Hogarth Press, 1950.
8. Friedman, A. S.; Cowitz, B.; Cohen, H. W.; and Granick, S. Syndromes and Themes of Psychic Depression. *Arch. Gen. Psychiat.* 9:504, 1963.
9. Glasser, K. Suicide in Children and Adolescents. In *Acting Out: Theoretical and Clinical Aspects,* ed. L. E. Abt and S. L. Weiseman. New York: Grune & Stratton, 1965.
10. Glasser, K. Masked Depression in Children and Adolescents. *Amer. J. Psychother.* 21:565, 1967.
11. Goldfarb, W. Effects of Psychological Deprivation in Infants and Subsequent Stimulation. *Amer. J. Psychiat.* 102:18, 1945.
12. Hallucinogen Use "Near Epidemic." *California Medical Tribune* 8:1, May 1, 1967.
13. Hochstetter, W. Depressive Syndromes. *Proc. Virchow Med. Soc. N. Y.* 18:116, 1959.

14. Keeler, W. R. Children's Reactions to the Death of a Parent. In *Depression*, ed. P. Hoch and J. Zubin. New York: Grune & Stratton, 1954.
15. Kreitman, N.; Sainsbury, P.; Pearce, K.; and Costain, W. R. Hypochondriasis and Depression in Out–patients at a General Hospital. *Brit. J. Psychiat.* 111:607, 1965.
16. Lesse, S. Current Clinical and Research Trends in Soviet Psychiatry. *Amer. J. Psychiat.* 114:1018, 1958.
17. Lesse, S. Automatic Faciocephalgia: A Psychosomatic Syndrome. *Trans. Amer. Neurol. Ass.* 86:224, 1961.
18. Lesse, S. Masked Depression: A Diagnostic and Therapeutic Problem. *Dis. Nerv. Syst.* 29:169, 1968.
19. Lesse, S. Psychodynamic Mechanisms of Emotional Illness in Executives. *Int. J. Soc. Psychiat.* 7:24, 1966.
20. Lesse, S. Hypochondriasis and Psychosomatic Disorders Masking Depression. *Amer. J. Psychother.* 21:607, 1967.
21. Lesse, S. Apparent Remissions in Depressed Suicidal Patients. *J. Nerv. Ment. Dis.* 144:291, 1967.
22. Lesse, S. The Psychosocial Future of Man: Golden Age or Stereotypy. *Proceedings of the International Future Research Conference, Tokyo, April 1970.* Tokyo: Kodanska, 1971.
23. Lewis, N. D. C., and Hubbard, L. D. The Mechanism and Prognostic Aspects of the Manic Depressive Schizophrenic Combinations. In *Proceedings, Association for Research in Nervous and Mental Diseases*, ed. W. A. White, T. K. Davis, and A. M. Franz, 9:539. Baltimore: Williams & Wilkins, 1931.
24. MacCurdy, J. T. *The Psychology of Emotion*. New York: Harcourt, Brace, 1925.
25. Mendlewicz, J. The Nature of Affective Equivalents in Relation to Affective Disorders. Paper presented at Fifth World Congress of Psychiatry, Mexico City, December 1971.
26. Patton, R. G., and Gardner, L. I. *Growth Failure in Maternal Deprivation*. Springfield, Ill.: Charles C. Thomas, 1963.
27. Pletnef, S. Zur Frage der somatischen Cyclothymie. *Z. Klin. Med.* 107:145, 1928.
28. Schmideberg, M. The Psychological Treatment of Adult Criminals. *Probation* 25:45, 1946.
29. Silverman, J. S.; Fite, M. W.; and Mosher, M. M. Clinical Findings in Reading Disability Children: Special Cases of

Intellectual Inhibitions. *Amer. J. Orthopsychiat.* 29:298, 1959.

30. Spitz, R. A., and Wolf, K. M. Anaclitic Depression: An Inquiry into the Genesis of Psychiatric Conditions in Early Childhood. *Psychoanal. Stud. Child* 2:313, 1946.
31. Stekel, W. *Nervoses Angstzustaende und Ihre Behandung.* Vienna: Urban & Schwarzenberg, 1924.
32. Toolen, J. M. Suicide and Suicidal Attempts in Children and Adolescents. *Amer. J. Psychiat.* 118:719, 1962.

2

Cultural Variations
of Depression
Past and Present

MARVIN K. OPLER

Masked depression is one of the most prevalent disorders in modern American society, yet it is perhaps the most neglected category in the psychiatric literature. One difficulty has been that in early stages, depression can appear as hypochondriasis or as a psychosomatic disorder. The psychosomatic manifestations are more prevalent in modern Western societies. This fact and the consequent difficulty of diagnosis have been pointed up in classic papers by Lesse (10, 12). With brilliant insight Lesse called one of these papers "Depression sine Depression." In addition, a famous paper by Diethelm on treatment of depressions points out that depression is all too frequently regarded as a simple and easily stereotyped condition, whereas in reality the clinical picture often changes radically in conjunction with changes in the patient's environment and his adjustment to them (2).

A related difficulty in recognizing the importance and prevalence of masked depression has been the lack of a cross-cultural perspective that would take into account the hypomanic forms of depression, the acting-out defenses frequently encountered, and all the other "multivariant masks of depression," in Lesse's apt phrase (11). The psychodynamics of the acting-out and hostility defenses as masks of depression have been described by Spiegel (21). Yet students are still ordinarily being taught simply that depressions run the gamut from normal grief and reactive depression to the much over-emphasized categories of depressive state, manic-depressive state, and involutional depression. This studied inattention to a massive problem is now being challenged, in this book and elsewhere—for instance, in Lesse's work on hypochondriasis and psychosomatic disorders as masks for depression (9). Dr. Phyllis Greenacre, a psychoanalyst, has clearly indicated that abandonment in infancy and later gaps in mothering which interfere with the development of parent-child trust often lead to depressive states later in life (4, 5). It remains for the anthropologist or specialist in social psychiatry who has encountered masked depression in many cultural settings to add that it may be found in many cultures of the world, across remote continents and in exotic settings. Because mother-child relationships are made difficult in many cultures, women, especially those past the age of childbearing, become particularly vulnerable, since they, unlike the vast majority of men, have played the roles of both the mothered and the mothering person. I therefore believe that our culture, among others, has created major stress for women in the middle years of life (18).

Confusional States

One need not read beyond the Introduction of my book *Culture and Social Psychiatry*, to hear about "confusional states" with underlying masked depression, catathymic outbursts, and driving, compulsive imitations and mannerisms, both slavish imitations and negativistic rebellion. Both imitative and negativistic behavior occur, for example, in arctic hysteria, and in the famous *imu* illness of the Ainu of Hokkaido. Actually, arctic hysteria has a very wide distribution outside the arctic, often in tropical settings like Malaysia, and practically all articles about it note that it is not hysteria as we know it in Europe and the United States. Nor can one fail to see the fantastic similarities between catatonic mannerisms in medieval reports and the slavish imitations or negativistic behaviors of arctic hysteria, so called, and *imu* illness (16). Persons who wish to learn more about masked depression and its cognate or related forms in nonliterate societies would do well to read J. C. Carothers' atrociously named book *The African Mind in Health and Disease* (1), a gold mine of material on Africa. Carothers writes repeatedly of "confused mental states" among African patients who exhibit either slight depressive tendencies or agitated euphoria. Masked depression in our own society also often includes confusional periods.

The behavior of a woman past middle age in the Luya tribe of Kenya is pertinent. The Luya live in dispersed settlements but frequently come together at district markets. The woman's problem was episodic; that is, she was normal most of the time. But occasionally she surprised her neighbors or groups at the marketplaces by noisily creating a disturbance: talking loudly and rapidly, and excitedly imitating the behavior of young girls—something she was never known to do during her "normal" periods. When she was in a hypomanic state she also showed sexual excitement. Sometimes her acting out took more highly symbolic forms (16; see Introduction).

It is difficult, of course, to place such a case confidently within the context of the typical psychiatric diagnostic nomenclature of the United States or Europe. In my experience, psychiatrists often omit the confusional factor in modern cases. It is not surprising, then, that they tend to maximize confusion when they hear of it among primitive peoples. Carothers is only one of many writers who tend to use prejudicial terms like "confused mental states" and "catathymic outbursts" as labels rather than using them descriptively in a careful psychodynamic style of diagnosis. People of other cultures are sometimes viewed as strange or exotic to begin with and some investigators therefore have difficulty in identifying their symptoms with those they encounter in our own society (17).

When cross-cultural psychiatric and epidemiological work has been done with clearer vision, better diagnostic and descriptive views prevail. In a paper to be published in the *International Journal of Social Psychiatry*, Dr. Joseph Hartog of the Department of International Health (Psychiatry), University of California at San Francisco, describes almost one hundred Malay psychiatric patients who exhibited neurotic and borderline manifestations of depressive behavior, acting out, and psychosomatic illnesses. Some of these patients were urban and some rural, so of course varying economic pressures were included in their life stresses. One is impressed by the frequency of an absent parent or inadequate parental relationships in the early lives of these patients. Surely these phenomena are part of the syndromes with which we are dealing here, and again we see masked depression threading its way through a sample of people deprived of adequate mothering (6). In the Indonesian syndrome of *latah*, as it is found in female patients of Java, we encounter a similar style of acting out by women in their middle years.

Non-literate Cultures

In each individual case the diagnostic and therapeutic challenges of masked depression are probably also based on the uniqueness of the illness configuration. That is to say, not all cases have the same environmental background or degree of seriousness. In nonliterate cultures it has frequently been noted that the "lighter" disorders are more open to spontaneous remission or to shamanistic and priestly curing practices (16). The lady in Kenya whom I discussed earlier is such a case of spontaneous remission; true, she rather suddenly and periodically "gets worse," but then the episode passes and she stays well for a long period. Her attacks do not always appear annually, so she may not be subject to the "anniversary phenomenon" so ably described by Dr. Josephine Hilgard (7).

Masked depression obviously runs the gamut from these mild disorders through disturbances of moderate seriousness to more markedly severe and recalcitrant cases. Since Carothers and other authors constantly find spontaneous remissions in the literature dealing with primitive societies, it would seem that masked depression tends to occur in its least severe form in most nonliterate cultures. There are some mild and moderate cases in our modern urban culture, but we also find severe disturbances of affect (17).

In our culture, psychosomatic warnings often signal that basic problems of affect are being displaced to autonomic system organic functioning. Asthma is such a culprit. The bronchial spasm is a substitute for the sobbing affect that the individual cannot bring himself to disclose. Migraine headache is another frequent signal of depressed affect that the proud individual cannot own up to simply because this would be damaging to his self-esteem (14). So one puts on a cheerful face but complains of headaches privately, often only to closest associates or to the psychiatrist if the person is in treatment. Nonliterate cultures typically do not utilize such psychosomatic syndromes.

Naturally, any discussion of a continuum of this sort is statistical in nature, and therefore cannot cover every possible case. One may, for example, find very severe masked depression in a nonliterate culture, particularly one that has been influenced heavily by European conquerors. And in modern societies one does encounter some cases of spontaneous remission of disorders that must be categorized as merely neurotic, and even lightly so in the scale of disturbance. But to plot the continuum we must focus chiefly on the central tendencies as they appear statistically:

1. Simple and open confusion is more characteristic of primitive or nonliterate peoples. This may be so because confusion constitutes a frank "cry for help" in a culture in which the family or the kin group may quickly seek shamanistic or priestly cult intervention. In the modern scene, where people tend to feel far more guilty (and needlessly so) about psychiatric disorders, the guilt-ridden individual is ordinarily reluctant to show such dependent attitudes. Instead, he puts

on a brave front for public consumption and carries through with almost obsessive determination. People in modern societies may therefore mask depression by doing a splendid job in their work roles, or in the jobs of housewife and mother, or in their social relationships.

2. The hostility factor remains fairly central in the total syndrome, but the targets of hostility in nonliterate cultures are often in the plural, whereas in the modern scene, as Dr. Rose Spiegel rightly points out, the chief target of hostility is often clearly the most important or the "love object" of the individual (21). This can be accounted for by the fact that nonliterate cultures have more diffuse patterns of authority and succorance. In the modern society, the spouse, the parent of the opposite sex, or some other person very close to the individual is the prime focus of affect, and therefore becomes the target.

3. The diffusion of hostility among various persons in nonliterate societies versus the focus on a single person in the modern scene, or two or three at most, is paralleled by differences in acting out. Consider, for example, the widespread practice of child adoption among the Eskimo of the Arctic and the Ute Indians of Colorado and Utah. In each case, children are often adopted out of the nuclear family to relatives who want or need a child. In such circumstances object relations become diffused, and enactments of hostility likewise have a broad focus. When a Malaysian runs amok, there is obviously a very diffuse pattern of violent aggression toward anyone the individual finds in his path.

4. In the nonliterate cultural scene, acting out usually occurs in the presence of relatives or neighbors. No one runs amok in a crowd of strangers. Women who are carried away by the *latah* syndrome of Indonesia will act out by uttering obscenities that are sometimes puns on phrases commonly used in polite conversation. Over teacups they will talk of vaginas and penises, and then blush scarlet. But in our culture there is much more constriction in this acting-out factor of masked depression. I recall one woman who, during the stage of trans-

ference, phoned her therapist and used obscene language, completely out of character, in a conversation marked by vituperative haranguing. But usually the acting out will show more constriction, and hence less release or catharsis.

5. Because our culture emphasizes guilt, the hypomanic answer is to project it upon another, often the same person who is the target of hostility. Thus freed from the confines and strictures of our culture, the individual may indulge in recreational, social, or sexual acting out. Finding new friends, going on a spree, or behaving in ways that were forbidden during adolescence may form the substance of the acting out. This indulgence in new life styles contrasts markedly with the simple cathartic procedures of our primitive cousins. The narrow focus of hostility and acting out among the sufferers of masked depression in our culture may be one reason psychoanalysts are constantly confronted with the same shifts in life patterns—the woman who walks out on her marriage and flees to some distant part, the shy fellow who suddenly becomes socially agressive to the point of making a nuisance of himself.

One woman who was depressed after giving birth to a highly defective child fled to a distant town, where the baby died a natural death, whereupon she returned home in good remission. Another wife took a plane trip across the continent and stayed awhile in a West Coast city, but that was not enough so she fled again to Hawaii; after a brief period of acting out, she too returned. Of course, acting out need not involve travel at all. Buying sprees, immersing oneself in one's job, writing voluminously, sexual promiscuity—all these and more will do as well.

And so there is an evolutionary continuum of defensive confusion, anger, and acting out, from relatively frank and direct behavior in nonliterate cultures to increasing disguise and distortion in modern societies.

A second continuum deals with the formation of depression, from mild beginnings to more serious dimensions. Of course, no two cases are exactly alike, just as no two individuals are alike. All of us have distinctive cultural backgrounds and individual experiences. But still we can sketch in the possible stages in a continuum from very mild depression to serious disturbance.

Hypothetical Projection

Dr. Phyllis Greenacre (4, 5) found that persons who developed serious manic-depressive psychosis had lacked proper mothering in early infancy. The related work of Dr. René Spitz on anaclitic depression in infants also discloses a lack of adequate mothering (22). And the massive theoretical model of Erik Erikson begins with a first layer of *either* basic trust or basic mistrust laid down in the infant personality in its earliest stage (3). Now, for theoretical purposes only, let us hypothesize a case that bears no resemblance to anyone living or dead, as writers of fiction are careful to say:

An illegitimate child was born of a very young immigrant mother in the city of Atlantisville, capital of Atlantis. In Atlantisville there was a large garment industry in which the mother had to struggle to earn her livelihood at a time when that industry was not yet strongly organized. The Atlantisville boss, who is the villain of this hypothetical situation, told the mother that she could bring the infant to the sweatshop provided she kept him quiet; otherwise she would lose her job. Obviously, when this hypothetical infant was hungry or uncomfortable, his cries were smothered. One can assume that there was also a great deal of compensatory loving bestowed upon this infant at home after work. Some ingredients of basic mistrust and some incomplete ingredients of Spitz's anaclitic depression might come to the surface in the early life of such a child. The mothering of this infant is by no means wholly lacking, but there are residues of conflict.

Such a person may in fact be well equipped to endure such later stresses as Atlantisville life may impose; for example, at his lower socioeconomic level he may have to go to work early, say at fourteen. An adolescent deprived of the typical leisure of the fun-loving years will feel he has missed something. We all know that deprivations such as these have led to shocking increases in suicide among adolescents in recent years (8).

Adolescents also express their loneliness in gangs, in communes, and in drug-using recreational parties. In our hypothesized case, a further sense of deprivation can be built up from the conflict of being traumatized in the sweatshop but loved at home. These, then, are some imagined ingredients that could go into a single life history and contain certain hazards for later life adjustments. If the Atlantisville youth were separated from this highly symbiotic relationship with his mother, and if he had no siblings, he would be likely to feel the loss intensely, although the depth of his feeling might be unconscious and hence unrecognized.

Now let us suppose further that this now independent and seemingly emancipated person gave every evidence of being well adjusted. He might suddenly develop asthma in his twenties. There are many cases of late-developing asthma in persons who undergo separation from parents following intensely symbiotic relationships (13). To make this fictional account more clinically hazardous, we could add that the mother died rather suddenly, and that well-meaning but inept and psychologically ill-informed relatives tried to shield the young man from knowledge of her illness and subsequent death. This too could be traumatic for the person in his twenties.

Thus far, our young man would be rated "well" in the Midtown Manhattan Mental Health Research Study, conducted by the Cornell University Department of Psychiatry from 1952 on (23). In the statistical continuum of the Ridit Scale, utilized by Dr. Irwin Bross as statistical consultant to that study, this person in his twenties, with only one psychosomatic ailment (asthma), would be rated 1 on a continuum from 0 to 12, which is in fact one of the better ratings for personality adjustment in the Midtown Study (23).

In our hypothesized case, the decade of the thirties imposed other trauma. Still his adjustment was marked by cheerfulness, optimism, and an energetic attack on life's problems. The Midtown rating would continue to be 1, although the Achilles' heel in this mythological account might begin to show in some slight hypochondriacal interest in maintaining optimum health and vigor. If other serious traumas followed, the manner of coping might involve psychosomatic or hypomanic responses, and might well be tied to many admirable traits of character attuned to achievement and constructive behavior. Masked depression often has hypomanic defenses as well as hypochondriacal ones. Such cases could hardly be called serious in any culture.

Although the sex ratio for masked depression favors females, we should not forget that many men in their forties and fifties begin to evidence such syndromes as Don Juanism, ordinarily translated as "playing around," as a defense against their advancing years. Other men, close to retirement, begin to assess their achievements in life with feelings of loss of self-esteem because they unfortunately have not measured up to past ideals and great expectations.

Among women an analogue to this development is the "empty nest" syndrome. Great numbers of women in their late forties and early fifties find their children launched in colleges or careers and hence no longer a major concern at home. Studies of depression in women list the "empty nest" syndrome as a common trauma, and it has even been noted in studies of suicidal tendencies in women (18). I have noted that mother-daughter symbioses may reach levels of intense importance at such times, especially for the mother; so much so that events in the daughter's life may be fraught with symbolic significance for the mother. When we remember that the mother-daughter relationship is psychoanalytically of great importance for the female, the early infancy model I have used surely strengthens such later symbiotic effects either positively or negatively depending on whether the mother experienced traumatic inadequacies in *her* early mother-child relations. Much also can depend on whether the daughter later experiences good or bad luck in her own maturing relationships.

The first continuum can be called, paraphrasing Lesse, multivariant masks of depression *in cultural evolution*. The second continuum refers to the development of depressive syndromes or individual types of depression, from mild to serious. We know, of course, that the descriptive accounts for both continua will be overlapping, since sociocultural events, or sociodynamics, can be reflected in psychodynamics (15). Because the so-called primitive or nonliterate cultures of the world, especially nomadic peoples like the Ute and Eskimo, require vigor and mobility, they also lend themselves to cathartic behavior when they are faced with psychological stresses. One notes that the same themes are often seen in their art, in their spirited dances, and in their vigorous musical styles. People who have seen displays of Eskimo masks, for example, are struck immediately by their vigor and almost zany imaginativeness. Ruth Benedict, in her *Patterns of Culture*, called hypomanic societies like the Ute and Eskimo and Apache "Dionysian"; low-keyed and placid societies, such as the Pueblo Indians of the Southwest, she called "Apollonian." While such dichotomies are admittedly oversimplifications, Benedict's characterizations serve well to point up the contrasts between two major types of society and the personalities formed by them.

Midtown Manhattan Study

I would like now to turn to our own society and explore some major discoveries made in the course of the Midtown Manhattan research. When we studied hospitalized Italo-Americans, we noted that hospital personnel, purely out of habit, labeled Italian schizophrenics as "paranoid reaction" in type. Irish-American patients were given the same label. Hospitals and psychiatrists made no distinction in nomenclature. Yet, as we studied carefully selected samples of such groups for a period of two years, we found that the Italian male patients were really schizo-affective. When we consulted the Italian literature, we found that Italian hospitals had high rates of manic-depressives. So while the labeling was right for the Irish, it was dead wrong for the Italians.

When we studied the samples with thirteen carefully designed tests, including the Rorschach, TAT, Wechsler-Bellevue, and Bender-Gestalt, we found by chi-square tests that the Italian differed from the Irish like day from night. My colleagues and I have written abundantly of the controlling Irish-American mother and her dominating role in the family; and we noted the forceful effect of domineering fathers on the Italian male patients in our sample (16, 20).

What about Italian mothers who had strongly symbiotic relationships with their daughters? Among the second generation of Italian women we found that the affective disorders often had deeply depressive overtones. In contrast to the hypochondriasis of the males, the female samples showed all manner of psychosomatic symptoms: migraine, asthma, dysmenorrhea, obesity beginning in adolescence. The Italian-American female epidemiology is also replete with relatively high suicide rates and such depressive signals as postpartum psychoses (14).

Failures in Diagnosis

One may wonder why masked depression has been missed so often in the writings of American psychiatrists, when its epidemiology is so widespread and touches so many social problems. Probably one factor is the curious way in which courses in psychiatry have been taught in medical schools. Often such courses have utilized chronic cases from state hospitals to teach differential diagnosis. Year after year one would see the same obsessive-compulsive lady, the same classic type of sociopathic male. Such recalcitrant cases from the back wards tend to be stereotypes. Depression would be seen only in deeply depressed and moribund psychotics. In other words, the touch of reality represented by patients who might have many assets in addition to their liabilities was missed amid the distortions that come from failure to recognize that nearly all cases begin on simple and often neurotic levels, and are the results of a complexity of forces.

Another factor, I believe, is an unwillingness to use a continuum of psychological development running either from wellness to illness or from more serious to less. But patients are people, let us remember, and it is people who suffer reverses or who move forward toward a greater stability. It is psychiatric nihilism to suppose that depressions of all manner and variety—and especially masked depressions, which have so much psychic zest—cannot be dealt with in therapy optimistically and energetically. As Rose Spiegel has pointed out, the psychiatrist must be willing to take a good deal of buffeting as the substitute target during countertransference in cases of this sort (21). But he can be assured that much can be done to alleviate masked depression, if only he studies the in-depth and infantile materials most carefully. I am therefore very much opposed to the here-and-now tactics of Rogerian psychotherapy in such cases, and to the do-it-yourself school of Gestalt therapy, which has become a fad among the youth of today.

Therapeutic Suggestions

A further argument against therapeutic nihilism in the approach to masked depression is the very vitality of the patients themselves. Child and youth in masked depression contrast markedly with schizophrenics in their tight hold on reality. Both in nonliterate cultures and more occasionally in the modern world, these people show a happy, pasted-on cheerfulness that cannot be missed by those who observe them in their hypomanic phases. Often they have been the resourceful, energetic, and optimistic persons in whom one places the greatest confidence. Among other endearing traits, one could add an intensity of interest in helping others (which unfortunately may manifest itself as manipulating others' lives). When, therefore, the discomfort of the negative psychological processes begins, they bear their psychosomatic ailments valiantly, as if these were ordinary humdrum organic accidents or defects. While psychosomatic flare-ups (cover-ups, really) like migraine or asthma may be uncomfortable, they are put down as natural consequences of other extraneous environmental factors, ranging from noxious pollens in the air all the way to flaws in life style, in choice of friends, or in marital relationships.

Even as the psychodynamic process continues in therapy, psychiatrists are urged to build upon the cheerful, energetic, vital, and problem-solving abilities of the patient. As hostility grows toward the targeted love object, or as it develops in countertransference with the therapist, one has the impression that a great deal of negative affect must be discharged, much to the discomfort of the love object, or the therapist, or the community of appalled neighbors in the more primitive scene. One must not forget, therefore, that the patient's vitality, which can lead to spontaneous remission in primitive societies, is to be viewed as an asset—one of the many endearing assets of this highly striving and coping personality.

This vital type of patient does indeed have brief confusional and excited states. When such patients are not forced to cover up their symptoms, as prideful people do in our society, they may frankly tell a friend or neighbor that they really cannot understand why they "have to" attack the target or love object, be it friend, spouse, or therapist.

As I have pointed out in *Culture and Social Psychiatry*, in primitive patients' neurotic or borderline psychotic processes may be listed under such terms as brief confusional and excited states, often accompanied by an underlying hysteriform or hysterical derangement. I have listed some of the prominent types, such as arctic hysteria, Malaysian *latah* and running amok, and the *imu* illness of Hokkaido. Hysterical disorders are, of course, very simply and clearly expressive of an underlying conflict, almost in a naive way from the viewpoint of the sophisticated modern. The modern case, with its greater sophistication, uses deeper disguises and more personally damaging methods for coping with problems. The psychosomatic derangement, for example, damages the organism in some selective way. In the nonliterate scene, the hysteric, however temporarily lame, halt, or blind, can be easily and readily restored to proper functioning through the psychosocial intervention of the shaman or the curing cult. In the same way, primitive practitioners *do* cure or find channels for the possible spontaneous remission of their temporarily disturbed patients (17).

It is somewhat harder to achieve such remissions in the deeply depressed patients of our culture, but in the masked depression syndrome, once one has looked beneath the cheerful disguises or psychosomatic cover-ups, I believe that the prognosis can be optimistic. Whereas disorders in primitive society tend to express people's problems openly and directly, with a minimum of disguises, the individual in our urban culture has been taught to disguise his difficulties, to cover them up, to secret them, as it were, in his own diary or his own desk drawer, out of some false sense of pride. Thus both patients with masked depression and psychiatrists tend to overlook such syndromes. The Protestant ethic damages us in ways that occur less readily among the more honest and direct persons in primitive societies.

References

1. Carothers, J. C. *The African Mind in Health and Disease.* WHO Monograph no. 17. Geneva: World Health Organization, 1953.

2. Diethelm, O. Treatment of Depressions. *J. Ment. Sc.* 104:537, 1958.
3. Erikson, E. H. Growth and Crises of the Healthy Personality. In *Personality*, ed. R. S. Lazarus and E. M. Opton, pp. 167–213. London: Penguin Books, 1967.
4. Greenacre, P. Considerations Regarding the Parent-Infant Relationship (1960). In *Emotional Growth*, pp. 199–224. New York: International Universities Press, 1971.
5. Greenacre, P. The Influence of Infantile Trauma of Genetic Patterns (1967). In *Emotional Growth*, pp. 260–99. New York: International Universities Press, 1971.
6. Hartog, J. Ninety-six Malay Psychiatric Patients: Characteristics and Preliminary Epidemiology. *Internat. J. Soc. Psychiat.*, in press.
7. Hilgard, J. Anniversary Depression Phenomena.
8. Jacobs, J. *Adolescent Suicide.* New York: Wiley, 1971.
9. Lesse, S. Hypochondriasis and Psychosomatic Disorders Masking Depression. *Amer. J. Psychother.* 21:607, 1967.
10. Lesse S. Masked Depression: A Diagnostic and Therapeutic Problem. Dis. Nerv. Syst. 29:169, 1968.
11. Lesse, S. The Multivariant Masks of Depression. *Amer. J. Psychiat.* 124:35, 1968 (supplement).
12. Lesse, S., and Mathers, J. Depression sine Depression (Masked Depression). *New York State J. Med.* 68:535, 1968.
13. McDevitt, J. B., and Settlage, C. F., eds. *Separation-Individuation.* New York: International Universities Press, 1971.
14. Opler, M. K. Ethnic Differences in Behavior and Health Practice. In *The Family: A Focal Point in Health Education*, ed. I. Galdston, pp. 173–95. New York: International Universities Press, 1961.
15. Opler, M. K. Cultural Induction of Stress. In *Psychological Stress*, ed. M. H. Appley and R. Trumbull, pp. 209–241. New York: Appleton-Century-Crofts, 1967.
16. Opler, M. K. *Culture and Social Psychiatry.* New York: Aldine-Atherton Press, 1967.
17. Opler, M. K. The Social and Cultural Nature of Mental Illness and Its Treatment. In *An Evaluation of the Results of the Psychotherapies*, ed. S. Lesse. Springfield, Ill.: Charles C. Thomas, 1968.

18. Opler, M. K., and Small, S. Mouchly. Cultural Variables Affecting Somatic Complaints and Depression. *Psychosomat.* 9:261, 1968.
19. Selye, H. The Concept of Stress in Experimental Physiology. In *Stress and Psychiatric Disorder*, ed. J. M. Tanner, pp. 69–74. Oxford: Blackwell Scientific Publications, 1960.
20. Singer, J. L., and Opler, M. K. Contrasting Patterns of Fantasy and Motility in Irish and Italian Schizophrenics. In *Personality*, ed. R. S. Lazarus and E. M. Opton, pp. 370–80. London: Penguin Books, 1967.
21. Spiegel, R. Anger and Acting Out: Masks of Depression. *Amer. J. Psychother.* 21:597, 1967.
22. Spitz, R. Hospitalism. In *The Psychoanalytic Study of the Child* 1:53–73. New York: International Universities Press, 1945.
23. Srole, L.; Michael, S.; Langner, T.; Opler, M. K.; and Rennie, T. A. C. *Mental Health in the Metropolis.* New York: McGraw-Hill, 1962.

3

A Genetic Contribution Toward an Understanding of Affective Equivalents

JULIEN MENDELWICZ

Affective disorder is one of the most frequent diagnoses, but it cannot be said to represent a clear-cut psychiatric entity. Recently the group of primary affective disorders has been subdivided into bipolar or manic-depressive illness and unipolar or recurrent depressive illness on the basis of clinical, genetic, and biological differences.

Unipolar vs Bipolar

This separation was based on the clinical history of the patients (10), and was initially supported by family history studies that indicated that relatives of bipolar patients had bipolar and unipolar illness, whereas relatives of unipolar patients tended to have only unipolar illness (15, 23). Some clinical features that differentiate bipolar from unipolar illness are an earlier age of onset, increased prevalence of postpartum disorder, and an increase in suicidal behavior in bipolar patients.

Biological differences were first reported by Perris (15), who noted that bipolar patients in remission had a decreased threshold to visual stimuli in comparison with unipolar patients. Studies performed at the National Institute of Mental Health reported that bipolar patients had an "augmenting" pattern and unipolar patients a "reducing" pattern of average cortical evoked response (2). The urinary excretion of 17-hydroxycorticosteroids was reduced in depressed bipolar patients in comparison with unipolar patients (5). In addition, erythrocyte catechol-o-methltransferase activity was lower in women with unipolar illness than in women with bipolar illness (3).

Some authors, following Kraepelin's formulation, have proposed that the concept of affective illness be enlarged to include such entities as endogenous melancholia, anxious thymopathy, and certain forms of asthenia (11). Baruk (1) suggested that certain periodic algias may constitute true equivalents of manic-depressive psychosis. Pitts and Winokur (17) have demonstrated the genetic link between manic-depressive illness and alcoholism. Da Fonseca (4) performed a family study on sixty twins with affective disorder. On the basis of genetic evidence he proposed to classify some cyclical psychosomatic syndromes as affective equivalents. The syndromes described were periodic, resistant to treatment, and associated with mood changes. They also showed spontaneous remission. This large concept of affective equivalents is based upon the notion that many depressive syndromes may be manifested clinically as hypochondriac or psychosomatic disorders. Affective equivalents might thus be perceived as part of a continuum at one end of the depressive spectrum.

Genetic Study

To help clarify the nature of the relation between depressive equivalents and affective disorders, we undertook a genetic study based upon the distribution of depressive equivalents in patients and their first-degree relatives. Our patient population is composed of a carefully worked-up group of sixty patients with affective disorders attending the Lithium Clinic at the New York State Psychiatric Institute. This group has been further subdivided into two distinct subgroups: thirty patients with manic-depressive illness (so-called bipolar illness) were matched for sex with thirty patients with recurrent depression only (unipolar illness). The bipolar and unipolar groups are equally divided between male and female (fifteen of each).

The age span of the bipolar group is 25 to 57 years; the mean age is 31.8 years. This group contains 118 first-degree relatives (61 females and 57 males). The age span of the unipolar group is 25 to 69 years; the mean age is 43.7 years. This group contains 124 first-degree relatives (72 females and 52 males). Both groups of patients are comparable in socioeconomic background (most of them upper middle class) and ethnic origin.

The purpose of this study is to determine whether manic-depressive (bipolar) illness can be distinguished from unipolar depressive disease on the basis of affective equivalents in the patients and their families.

Our definition of affective equivalents includes two main groups of disturbances:

1. *The group of psychosomatic disorders of an episodic nature.*
(a) Musculo-skeletal: rheumatoid arthritis, neuralgic and lumbago crisis.
(b) Respiratory: periodic asthma, tuberculosis.
(c) Gastrointestinal: duodenal ulcer, periodic gastric pains, colitis.
(d) Dermatological: eczema, erythema, psoriasis, neurodermatitis, dermatitis.
(e) Iatrogenic: drug photosensitivity, generalized drug rashes, urticaria, skin flushes, erythema.
(f) Cardiovascular: heart condition, hypertension.
(g) Endocrinological: thyroid conditions, obesity.
(h) Genitourinary: pelvic pain and others.

2. *Manifest behavioral disturbances revealing underlying depressive reactions.*
(*a*) Periodic and chronic alcoholism, drug dependence, compulsive gambling, suicidal behavior.

Methodology

The diagnoses of bipolar and unipolar illness were made separately by two investigators. All the above syndromes were studied in patients and their first degree relatives. The family study method has been used. This screening method is based on the use of a structured questionnaire. Data are obtained by personal interviews with index cases, all the available first-degree relatives, and the spouses of the patients. The family study method is used because it is known to be more reliable than the family history method (family history data collected from the proband only) (18). Differences between these two groups of patients and their relatives were evaluated by use of the chi-square test. The frequency of alcoholism in relatives was expressed in terms of morbid risk. Morbid risk is defined as an estimate of the probability that a relative will develop the condition at some time during his life if he survives the period at risk.[1]

---

1. We used the Weinberg abridged method (22) for calculating the morbid risk in realtives. In the formula

$$\text{Morbidity risk} = \frac{a}{b - bo - 1/2\ bm}$$

a is the number of affected individuals, *b* the number of individuals examined, *bo* the number of individuals who have not reached the period at risk, and *bm* the number of individuals currently passing through that period. In this formula, the denominator expresses the number of people at risk. The period at risk for alcoholism was taken as twenty to fifty years of age.

Results

Incidence of Psychosomatic Syndromes

TABLE 1   Distribution of Psychosomatic Syndromes in Patients and Their First-Degree Relatives

| | BIPOLAR | | UNIPOLAR | | P VALUE |
	First-Degree Relatives (N = 118)	Patients (N = 30)	First-Degree Relatives (N = 124)	Patients (N = 30)	
Total disorders	26 (22%)	22	54 (43.5%)	26	<.001
Musculoskeletal	1	—	9	6	
Respiratory	—	—	3	1	
Gastrointestinal	1	5	12	4	
Duodenal ulcer	—	4 (13%)	1	—	
Others	1	1	11	4	
Dermatological	2	1	8	3	
Iatrogenic	1	6 (20%)	4	1 (3%)	
Cardiovascular	9	—	8	6	<.05
Heart	2	—	7	3	NS
Hypertension	7	—	1	3	<.01
Endocrinological	11	10 (33%)	3	2 (6%)	<.001
Thyroid	6	4 (13%)	1	1 (3%)	
Obesity	5	6 (20%)	2	1 (3%)	
Genitourinary	1	—	7	3	

Table 1 presents the incidence of psychosomatic syndromes in both groups of patients and their relatives. Unipolar patients suffer from a wide range of physical complaints involving many different systems. Psychosomatic syndromes as a whole are slightly less common in bipolar patients; however, four conditions emerge as being possibly associated with manic-depressive illness. These are duodenal ulcer (present in 13 percent of bipolar patients versus none in unipolar patients), iatrogenic reactions (20 percent of bipolar patients versus 3 percent of unipolar patients), thyroid dysfunction (13 percent of bipolar patients versus 3 percent of unipolar patients), and obesity (20 percent of bipolar patients versus 3 percent of unipolar patients). For both groups, psychosomatic syndromes seem to occur especially in middle-aged and elderly women. The sexual distribution of psychosomatic syndromes for the entire sample is female, 63 percent; male, 37 percent.

The familial prevalence of psychosomatic syndromes as a whole is significantly higher in unipolar patients ($x^2 = 13.6375$, $df = 1$, $p < .001$). There are two exceptions, however: cardiovascular conditions are significantly more prevalent in the families of bipolar patients ($x^2 = 3.0136$, $df = 1$, $p < .05$), and this difference is due to the higher incidence of hypertensive syndromes ($x^2 = 9.6296$, $df = 1$, $p < .01$). Endocrinological conditions (thyroid, obesity) are also significantly more common in the relatives of bipolar patients ($x^2 = 13.9722$, $df = 1$, $p < .001$).

The high prevalence of one disease in a family may be due to the interaction of learning and identification processes with genetic factors. Kallmann (9) showed bipolar patients to be prone to cardiovascular complications. We cannot confirm this finding in our study. However, the finding of a higher incidence of hypertensive relatives in the bipolar group should be noted because hypertension may be a symptom or an equivalent of mood dysfunction. In depressed patients with functional hypertension, the hypertension often disappears with recovery of depression. Moreover, depression sometimes develops in hypertensive patients who are treated with sedatives and tranquilizers, especially the rauwolfia derivatives. Those drug-induced depressions usually occur in patients with past histories of affective illness or, as in our study, with family histories of affective illness. These drugs may unmask already present but unrecognized mood disorders.

An interesting finding is the higher prevalence of thyroid dysfunction (insufficiency in most cases) in both patients and relatives of the bipolar group. Mental stress has been shown to alter thyroid function (21) and to be associated with thyroid antibody production (7). Thyroid disease has also been related to object loss and depression (12). Recently some authors (6, 19) have observed the emergence of transitory goiters in manic-depressive patients treated with lithium carbonate. They have asked whether this alteration in thyroid function is directly due to lithium or any drug treatment, is a consequence of dietary insufficiency, or is perhaps related to manic-depressive illness. It is impossible to answer this question before comparing the incidence of goiter in a manic-depressive population with its incidence in the general population. However, our data support the last hypothesis, that is, that there may be a biological relationship between thyroid metabolism and manic-depressive illness.

Most of the affective equivalents manifested as psychosomatic syndromes in our patients occur in middle-aged or elderly women and have a tendency to recur. These patients often present organic functional troubles, but their overinvolvement and the physician's nonrecognition of this syndrome makes them subject to multiple investigations. The iatrogenic factor may then enhance the patient's hypochondriac fixation (13).

Alcoholism

There are few studies on the specific relation between affective disorder and excessive drinking habits. Table 2 analyzes the distribution of alcoholism among the patients and their relatives. Bipolar patients suffer more from alcoholism, although the difference between the groups is below statistical significance ($x^2 = 1.5711, df = 1, p < 20$). The sex distribution for alcoholism in both groups showed a predominance of females. A striking difference appears in the nature of alcoholism. Bipolar patients show primarily an episodic type of alcoholism, while unipolar patients tend to suffer from chronic alcoholism and other dependencies ($x^2 = 4.7059, df = 1, p < .05$). Increase of alcohol ingestion by the bipolar patients appeared during both the depressed and

TABLE 2   Distribution of Alcoholism in Patients and Their First-Degree Relatives

	BIPOLAR		UNIPOLAR		P VALUE
	First-Degree Relatives	Patients	First-Degree Relatives	Patients	
Alcoholism	7	9 (7 F, 2 M)*	29	4 (4 F, 1 M)	<.20
Chronic	6	1 (1 F)	23	3 (2 F, 1 M)	
Episodic	1	8 (6 F, 2 M)	6	1 (1 F)	<.05

* F = female, M = male.

the high periods. Table 3 shows that alcoholism is more rare in the families of bipolar patients (the likelihood that their first-degree relatives will become alcoholics is 7 percent), while we find a higher incidence of chronic alcoholism and multiple drug dependence in the families of unipolar patients (the likelihood that their first-degree relatives will become alcoholics is 28 percent).

TABLE 3   Morbid Risk for Alcoholism* in First-Degree Relatives of Bipolar and Unipolar Patients

	BIPOLAR			UNIPOLAR		
	No. Ill	No. at Risk	Morbid Risk	No. Ill	No. at Risk	Morbid Risk
Alcoholism in first-degree relatives	7	92	7%	29	104	28%

* Weinberg abridged method.

We have already discussed in a previous study (14) the episodic nature of alcoholism in bipolar patients. The periodicity of episodic drinking habit has been linked to the cyclical nature of manic-depressive illness, but it is not yet clear whether there is a genetic or psychosomatic relation between the two conditions. In our bipolar patients, the drinking habit was generally not present before onset of the affective illness.

The course of alcoholism was initially episodic, although it was not always directly related to mood changes. After five to ten years, however, some of these patients developed a physiological and psychological dependence and their episodic drinking habits changed to chronic alcoholism.

Our genetic study reveals that relatives of the unipolar group suffer more from alcoholism combined with excessive use of nicotine, coffee, tea, analgesics, and barbiturates. Winokur and Pitts (24) reached the same conclusion: they indicated that fathers of patients with affective disorder show five times the prevalence of alcoholism that was seen in the fathers of a control group. Furthermore, unipolar patients have more relatives with alcoholism than bipolar patients. The affective disorder that is seen in relatives of alcoholic probands is usually only depressive disease (25). Therefore, one may conclude that if alcoholism is not inherited, it is certainly contagious.

Suicidal Behavior

Suicidal behavior is analyzed in Table 4. There is no significant difference in the incidence of suicide attempts in unipolar versus bipolar patients, but there is an appreciable frequency of suicidal behavior in both groups (30 percent for bipolar and 33 percent for unipolar patients). Suicide rates in first- and second-degree relatives of bipolar patients appear to

TABLE 4   Suicidal Behavior

	Bipolar Patients	Unipolar Patients	P Value
Suicide attempts* in patients	9 (30%)	10 (33%)	NS
Suicide in patients' first- or second-degree relatives	12 (3 F, 9 M)+	2 (2 M)	<.001

* One or more.
+ F = female, M = male.

be significantly higher than in the relatives of bipolar patients: 12 out of 30 bipolar patients reported a suicide in their first- or second-degree relatives for only two out of 30 unipolar patients ($x^2 = 7.54658$, $df = 1$, $p < .001$). Affective disorder has always been associated with high suicidal risk (14, 20). Guze and Robins (8) established on the basis of follow-up studies that the ultimate risk of suicide among such patients was between 14 and 16 percent, that is, approximately 30 times the risk in the general population. A high incidence of suicide in the relatives of bipolar patients has also been reported (16). Underlying depression may suddenly explode in a suicidal gesture; the self-destructive behavior might be its unique manifestation and thus be interpreted as a depressive equivalent.

To summarize, four psychosomatic conditions are more commonly associated with bipolar illness than with unipolar: duodenal ulcer, iatrogenic reactions, thyroid dysfunction, and obesity. Relatives of bipolar patients show a higher prevalence of hypertension, obesity, and thyroid dysfunction than do relatives of unipolar patients. Age and sex distribution reveal that most of the psychosomatic syndromes occur in middle-aged or elderly women. Bipolar patients suffer more from episodic alcoholism than do unipolar, but chronic alcoholism and drug dependence are more often diagnosed in the relatives of unipolar patients. The ultimate risk of suicide is higher in the relatives of bipolar patients than in unipolar patients. The equivalents described here may be masking affective disturbances in predisposed individuals. The homeostatic value of depression is then shifted toward physiological channels whose localizations are probably genetically determined. Affective equivalents could be genetically conceptualized in two different ways: one, as a different genetic subtype of affective disorder consistent with a model of heterogenic inheritance; two, as part of a continuum in a homogenic model of mood disturbances.

References

1. Baruk, H. *Troite de Psychiatrie*. Paris: Doin, 1959.
2. Buchsbaum, M.; Goodwin, F. K.; Murphy, D. L.; and Borge, G. Average Evoked Responses in Affective Disorders. *Amer. J. Psychiat*. 128:19, 1971.
3. Cohn, C. K.; Dunner, D. L.; and Axelrod, J. Reduced Catechol-o-methyltransferase Activity in Red Blood Cells of Women with Primary Affective Disorders. *Science* 170:1323, 1970.
4. Da Fonseca, A. F. Affective Equivalents. *Brit. J. Psychiat*. 109:464, 1963.
5. Dunner, D. L.; Gershon, E. S.; Goodwin, F. K.; and Bunney, W. E., Jr. Excretion of 17-Hydroxycorticosteroids in Unipolar and Bipolar Depressed Patients. *Arch. Gen. Psychiat*. 26:360, 1972.
6. Fieve, R. R., and Platman, S. R. Follow-up Studies of Lithium and Thyroid Function in Manic-Depressive Illness. *Amer. J. Psychiat*. 125:1443, 1969.
7. Goodman, M.; Rosenblatt, M.; Gottlieb, J.; Miller, J.; and Chen, C. H. effects of Age, Sex, and Schizophrenia on Thyroid Antibody Production. *Arch. Gen. Psychiat*. 8:518, 1963.
8. Guze, S. B., and Robins, E. Suicide and Primary Affective Disorders. *Brit. J. Psychiat*. 117:437, 1970.
9. Kallmann, F. J. Genetic Principles in Manic-Depressive Psychoses. In *Depression*, ed. P. Hoch and J. Zubin. New York: Grune & Stratton, 1954.
10. Leonhard, K. *Aufteitung der Endogenen Psychosen*, 2nd ed. Berlin: Springer Verlag, 1959.
11. Lopez-Ibor, J. J. *La Angustia vital*. Madrid: Paz Montalvo, 1950.
12. Mandelbrote, B. M., and Wittkower, E. D. Emotional Factors in Graves' Disease. *Psychosomat. Med*. 17:109, 1955.
13. Mendelwicz, J.; Shulman, C. C.; Deschutter, B.; and Wilmotte, J. Chronic Prostatitis: Psychosomatic Incidence. *Psychother. & Psychosomat*. 19:118, 1971.
14. Mendelwicz, J.; Fieve, R. R.; Rainer, J. D.; and Fleiss, J. L. Manic-Depressive Illness: A Comparative Study of Patients With and Without a Family History. *Brit. J. Psychiat*. 558:523, 1972.

15. Perris, C. A Study of Bipolar (Manic-Depressive) and Unipolar Recurrent Psychoses (I–X). *Act. Psychiat. Scand.* 194:1, 1966 (supplement).
16. Pitts, F. N., Jr., and Winokur, G. Affective Disorder: III. Diagnostic Correlates and Incidence of Suicide. *J. Nerv. & Ment. Dis.* 139:176, 1964.
17. Pitts, F. N., Jr., and Winokur, G. Affective Disorder: VII. Alcoholism and Affective Disorder. *J. Psychiat. Res.* 4:37, 1966.
18. Rimmer, J., and Chambers, D. S. Alcoholism: Methodological Considerations in the Study of Family Illness. *Amer. J. Orthopsychiat.* 39:760, 1969.
19. Shopsin, B. Effects of Lithium on Thyroid Function. *Dis. Nerv. Syst.* 4:237, 1970.
20. Stenstedt, A. A Study in Manic-Depressive Psychosis. *Acta Psychiat. Neurol. Scand.* 79:1, 1952 (supplement).
21. Toscano, M.; Van den Abeel, K.; and Mendelwicz, J. Approche biologique des affections psychiatriques: Analyse statistique. *In Proceedings: Congrès de Psychiatrie et de Neurologie de Langue Francaise,* 67th session. Brussels: Masson, 1969.
22. Weinberg, W. Zur Vererbung bei manisch-depressiven Irresein. *Zeitsch. Angewandte Anat. Konstitations Lehre* 6:388, 1920.
23. Winokur, G., and Clayton, P. Family History Studies:I. Two Types of Affective Disorders Separated According to Genetic and Clinical Factors. In *Recent Advances in Biological Psychiatry,* ed. J. Wortis. New York: Plenum Press, 1967.
24. Winokur, G., and Pitts, F. N., Jr. Affective Disorder: VI. A Family History Study of Prevalence, Sex Difference, and Possible Genetic Factors. *J. Psychiat. Res.* 3:113, 1965.
25. Winokur, G.; Reich, T.; Rimmer, J.; and Pitts, F. N., Jr. Alcoholism: III. Psychiatric Illness in 259 Alcoholic Probands. *Arch. Gen. Psychiat.* 23:104, 1970.

4

Hypochondriasis and Psychosomatic Disorders Masking Depression

STANLEY LESSE

While the masks of depression are multivariant, as was noted in Chapter 1, in our culture depressive syndromes in adults are most commonly masked clinically by hypochondriacal or psychosomatic disorders. These symptoms and signs may be referred to any organ system. This variation or phase of the depressive syndrome has been given many labels, such as *(a)* masked depression, *(b)* depression sine depression, *(c)* depressive equivalent, *(d)* affective equivalent, *(e)* occult depression, *(f)* latent depression, *(g)* hidden depression, and *(h)* depression in disguise.

This syndrome rivals overt depressions in frequency, however, it is appreciated insufficiently by psychiatrists and nonpsychiatrists alike, at times with tragic results. The depressive affect may be masked to the extent that the physician may be unaware that a serious psychiatric disorder is at hand until a massive, full-blown depression erupts and dominates the clinical picture.

Physicians without formal psychiatric training tend to record a patient's physical complaints with literal eyes, without probing to see whether the affect associated with the symptoms is secondary to a true physical deficit or whether it is a psychological expression mimicking an organic disorder. As a result, patients are often subjected to unnecessary and inappropriate treatment for long periods of time.

It may be stated without fear of exaggeration that from one-third to two-thirds of patients past the age of forty who are seen by general practitioners and other physicians who limit their practices to one of the recognized specialties other than psychiatry are victims of masked depressions, with the depressive syndromes masked by hypochondriacal or psychosomatic disorders. In the vast majority of instances, the etiology of the problem is incorrectly diagnosed. A great many therapies are employed, most of them inappropriate. When they do work, their efficacy may usually be ascribed to unintended or placebo effects.

Patients with masked depressions of this type are not limited to those attending physicians' private offices. They form a very high percentage of patients seen in hospital clinics, and a sizable proportion of general hospital beds are occupied by patients with masked depressions, particularly persons in the middle and older age groups. Unfortunately, many of these patients, after undergoing a multitude of laboratory examinations, are subjected to a variety of treatment procedures, some of them quite radical. In one report, one-third of patients with masked depressions had undergone unnecessary surgical procedures, some having as many a four operations (11).

As a general rule, only after months or years of repeated physical and laboratory examinations, after the failure of multiple medical and surgical procedures, is the psychiatrist called in as a consultant. As I have noted, it is not uncommon for the underlying depression to manifest itself precipitously in a suicidal attempt, and it may be the suicidal behavior that brings about an emergency psychiatric consultation. Hochstetter has reported that two-thirds of his patients with masked depression had suicidal preoccupations (10). These figures indicate that by the time these patients are seen by a psychiatrist, their depressions may be very severe, requiring urgent or even emergency therapy.

Psychiatrists are also insufficiently cognizant of this syndrome, for a variety of reasons. The various textbooks and handbooks of psychiatry make no more than passing reference to masked depressions or depressive equivalents. In none is there a realistic appreciation of these syndromes. Resident psychiatrists are rarely exposed to a formal awareness of this clinical pattern, usually because their own teachers often are unacquainted with this most important clinical entity. In part, this lack of awareness is a by-product of the growing schism between psychiatry and the various organic branches of medicine. Relatively few resident psychiatrists now have good training in the various medical specialties. Therefore, relatively few are poignantly aware of what constitutes a reliable history of true organic deficits.

And the situation is even more frustrating than this. To my knowledge there is no medical school that offers definitive courses to acquaint medical students with this very common clinical syndrome. This again may be ascribed to the fact that both psychiatric and nonpsychiatric instructors have no significant awareness of the multivariant masks of depression. And those branches of the health sciences allied with medicine—the schools of dentistry, psychology, and psychotherapy—are just as ignorant of the masked depression syndromes.

When one considers just how widespread the masked depression syndromes are, and how readily they can be diagnosed, the magnitude of this clinical scotoma staggers one's sensibilities.

Literature

As one might expect from what has just been said, there is relatively little in the psychiatric literature relating specifically to the masked depression syndrome, and for the most part that which is available is poorly documented clinically. Freud observed briefly that physical rather than psychic complaints may at times dominate the clinical picture in a depressed patient, so that "one is reminded of a somatic rather than a psychic disorder" (8). Stekel in 1924 (24) and Landauer in 1925 (12) stressed that repressed affects, including depression, may be disguised by physical equivalents. Pletnef pointed out in 1928 that physical complaints may be an integral part of the depressive syndrome, even when they appear dissociated from the underlying depressive affect (22).

Brill noted that in manic-depressive psychoses the mood swings may be represented at times by a fluctuation of physical complaints (3). Schick described several case histories in which somatic complaints represented phases of recurrent periodic depression (23). In 1956, I described a syndrome that I called "atypical facial pain of psychogenic origin," which indeed represented masked depressions with hypochondriacal and at times psychosomatic patterns masking the underlying depressions (14).

In 1959 Hochstetter reported that the masked depression syndrome occurred in 27 (10.5 percent) of the 258 depressed patients in his series (10). As I noted before, he found that 66 percent of the 27 patients showed overt suicidal tendencies. Four threatened suicide; two made serious attempts; one died.

In another study, a group of quarrulous, hypochondriacal, self-preoccupied, complaining, irritable, body-conscious patients were identified and the illnesses of these patients were said to represent a subtype of depression (9). A similar group was described earlier by other authors who found that the patients had psychodynamic structures that were "orally fixated and narcissistic in nature." This group constantly demanded immediate relief from their symptoms and utilized their complaints to attract attention (4).

In 1961, I reported that autonomic faciocephalgia, which is more commonly classified as "cluster headache," a syndrome that is related in many aspects to migraine headache, was a psychosomatic syndrome that in most instances masked an underlying depression, often of severe proportions (15). I later described a broad group of facial pain patterns that were either hypochondriacal or psychosomatic veneers of underlying depressions (16).

Kreitman et al., in 1965, reported a study of 120 patients who were referred to a general hospital clinic that was specifically organized to study hypochondriacal patients (11). Twenty-one, or slightly less than 10 percent of the patients, were diagnosed as having depressions. One-quarter had previous histories of overt psychiatric illnesses. Several more recent reports testify to a broad spectrum of syndromes by which the depressive reactions are masked (1, 2, 7, 13). In another paper, dealing with the psychodynamic mechanisms of emotional illness in executives, I reported that masked depression is commonly seen in executives in large corporations (17).

There have been studies attempting to demonstrate a genetic determination for depressive equivalents (5, 6, 21). In a number of instances, particularly since the advent of lithium carbonate as a treatment for manic-depressive problems, there have been allegations that a genetic relationship exists between this type of affective disorder and a number of psychosomatic problems.

In 1963 Da Fonseca found an unusually high frequency of certain somatic and psychosomatic syndromes among sixty probands who had suffered from affective disorders of an indigenous nature, their twins, and their first-degree relatives (5). In the family constellations of these patients he found that certain somatic and psychosomatic syndromes appeared with unusual frequency, especially syndromes resembling rheumatism, asthma, peptic ulcers, and certain dermatoses (6). These problems tended to run a cyclic course and were found to be correlated with alternation of moods. They often ended in spontaneous remission. It was Da Fonseca's impression that there was a greater heredito-congenital propensity in this type of problem than in psychoses generally.

At present the proof of a genetic linkage between certain types of depressive reactions and specific psychosomatic disorders appears very thin. Most of the criteria offered for the diagnosis of bipolar and unipolar depression would arouse a great deal of controversy if they were submitted to a broad group of psychiatric diagnosticians. In addition, the research patterns have not taken into consideration important clinical phenomena such as Wilder's Law of Initial Value (25). At this point in time, the biochemical studies relating to depressive reactions have been inconsistent in their results and replicability. Many of these biochemical studies have been poorly conceived and have been insufficiently correlated with the patient's clinical status.

Why do some patients who manifest psychosomatic problems and hypochondriasis develop depressive reactions, while others do not? The question has not been answered. Thus far, it appears that a number of factors may be involved. These are psychodynamic, genetic, and cultural in nature. At times it appears that all three may be involved in varying degrees. Many years ago, when reports on psychosomatic problems began to appear in the literature, a genetic implication with regard to the organ of expression was inferred as being related to a "locus minoris resistentiae." I have already noted in Chapter 1 that there are definite cultural differences in the clinical manifestations of depressive reactions.

In the study of the relationship between psychosomatic disorders and depressive reactions, one is brought back to the frequently discussed but still unanswered question as to the relationship between anxiety and depression. Are these both primary psychologic reactions to stress, or is depression a secondary defense mechanism against primary anxiety?

In a recent and very detailed monograph resulting from an eighteen-year research program in which I studied the components, development, and treatment of anxiety, I attempted to delineate specific psychodynamic patterns that could be related to specific psychosomatic disorders (20). Despite an intensive study of the 151 patients who made up the psychosomatic aspect of the investigation, I was unable to do so. I did find that the psychodynamic profiles of patients with various psychosomatic problems are very similar. In many ways they resemble the psychodynamic pattern seen in depressed patients. I noted that this may in part account for the fact that a history of psychosomatic disorders is obtained in a very large number of patients who finally manifest overt agitated depressions, particularly in middle and advanced age.

I observed that the personality profiles, ontologic development patterns, and parental background of patients with obsessive-compulsive difficulties, agitated depressions, and psychosomatic difficulties are quite similar. Almost all have rigid, mechanistic, obsessive-compulsive personality profiles. Life is seen in a polar fashion, black versus white, without many shades of gray interposed. One can find in almost every history a dominant, rigid, obsessive-compulsive, often rejecting, and on occasion sadistic parent. In such a family environment the child develops a negative image of himself, feels inadequate, and is self-derogatory.

I also observed that many of these patients become hypochondriacal and may manifest severe depressive reactions. Others may develop psychosomatic difficulties. Still others may show paranoid defense mechanisms. In addition, I called attention to the fact that phobic phenomena may also be a part of this mosaic of symptoms.

Type of Practice and Frequency of Occurence

The type of practice in which the physician is engaged will determine in great measure the frequency with which he will encounter the masked depression syndrome. Physicians specializing in organic medicine will find that patients with masked depression will account for many, if not most, of the depressions with which they are confronted. Most psychiatrists, as Hochstetter noted (10), see this syndrome in a more limited percentage of depressed patients. I have previously noted that the syndrome will be observed more commonly by neuropsychiatrists who are consulted frequently by internists and surgeons in large general hospitals (19).

At the present time there is no clinical information as to the frequency with which the masked depression patterns are seen by nonmedical psychotherapists.

Masked Depression: A Diagnostic Challenge

The masked depression syndrome may pose a sharp challenge to the physician's diagnostic acumen. It may occur simply as an expression of an underlying depression, without any organic process. Or the patient may have a true organic deficit with a masked depression superimposed. Thus a minor organic illness may be magnified to a great extent by this psychogenic overlay, and to the uninitiated may appear as a major organic disorder. Too often in such situations the physician mistakenly exaggerates the importance of the organic component and fails to recognize the psychogenic aspect of the problem. This usually leads to months or years of repeated clinical diagnostic and laboratory examinations by many physicians parallelled by multiple organic therapies. In these instances a massive iatrogenic overlay is often superimposed upon an already complicated situation.

On the other hand, a patient with a major organic lesion also may be plagued by hypochondriacal or psychosomatic complaints. In this instance, if the physician becomes preoccupied with the psychogenic aspects of the problem and fails to give adequate emphasis to the organic lesions, serious, even tragic consequences may result. Therefore, the ability to recognize and diagnose the masked depression syndrome as a separate entity and in relationship to true organic lesions is of major importance for psychiatric and nonpsychiatric physicians alike, and for psychotherapists who are not physicians.

In the main, this syndrome can be diagnosed readily by nonpsychiatric physicians early in the course of illness. There are usually definite symptoms and signs to alert the physician to the fact that he is dealing with a psychologically ill individual.

Clinical Studies

Between January 1963 and January 1970 I treated a total of

984 patients who had depressions of various types. Of these, 336 or 34.1 percent had masked depressions referred to various organ systems.

This percentage is in contrast to the 10.5 percent frequency of masked depression reported by Hochstetter (10). The relatively high frequency of masked depression noted in this study may be accounted for, at least in part, by the fact that I am both a psychiatrist and a neurologist, and am regularly called in consultation by a large number of specialists in a very large medical center. These consultations are frequently for the purpose of determining whether a patient's illness is organic or psychogenic in nature, or a combination of both.

The hypochondriacal and psychosomatic symptoms were referred to many organ systems, including the central and peripheral nervous systems, cardiovascular, respiratory, gastrointestinal, genito-urinary, endocrine, otolaryngologic, osseous, joint, and dental systems.

Sources of Referral

The sources of referral of my patients were of three types:

1. Physicians in various organic medical subspecialties and general practitioners (designated as "organicists").

2. Psychiatrists and psychotherapists.

3. Former patients.

Table 1 indicates the referrals from these sources.

Of the 599 depressed patients referred by various organicists, 285 (47.6 percent) had masked depressions. Only 13 (11.2 percent) of the 116 depressed patients referred by other psychiatrists or psychotherapists had the depression sine depression syndrome; 38 (14.1 percent) of the 269 depressed patients referred by former patients had this syndrome.

TABLE 1   Patient Referral Sources

Source	Total	Overt Depressions	Masked Depressions	Percent
Organicists	599	314	285	47.6%
Psychiatrists and psychotherapists	116	103	13	11.2
Former patients	269	231	38	14.1
TOTAL	984	648	336	

Age Distribution

In this study the patients' ages ranged from twenty-seven to seventy-eight years. Table 2, which breaks the age statistics down according to decades, presents a very significant picture.

TABLE 2   Age Distribution

Age	20–29	30–39	40–49	50–59	60–69	70–79
Number of patients	3	48	135	90	43	17

It was striking that there were only three (0.9 percent) patients under thirty. The vast majority of the patients at the time of my initial consultation were in their forties, fifties, or sixties. Only forty-eight (14.4 percent) were in their thirties, and 35 of these were between thirty-six and thirty-nine. At the other end of the spectrum, only seventeen (5.1 percent) were over seventy, and thirteen of these were seventy-three or under. Thirty-five of the forty-three patients who were in their sixties at the time of my initial consultation were between sixty and sixty-four.

On careful evaluation I found that 225, or 66.9 percent, of the patients with masked depression were between forty and fifty-nine, while 295, or 87.8 percent, were between the ages of thirty-six and sixty-four.

This syndrome, therefore, may be said to be in general an ailment of middle age. The literature offers little information as to age distribution, but reports by Kreitman (11) and Freedman (9) also suggest that this ailment is primarily one of middle age.

Sex Distribution

A striking disparity with regard to the sex ratio was noted in my study: 246 of the patients were women and only 90 were men. This represents a female:male ratio of 2.7:1 (16).

In summary, it would appear that the syndrome of masked depression is seen in the majority of instances in middle-aged women either shortly prior to, during, or following menopause.

Duration of Illness Prior to Neuropsychiatric Consultation

There was a considerable delay between the onset of the patient's illness and the initial neuropsychiatric consultation. In my experience only 18 percent of the patients were ill for less than one year. Of the remaining 82 percent who were ill for more than one year, 65 percent had been ill for more than two years. Even more striking was the fact that almost 32 percent had been ill for more than five years. I was truly astounded to find that 15 percent had been ill for more than ten years, while five percent had histories of fifteen or more years' duration.

These figures must be considered in the context that all of the patients had been studied and treated by at least one and usually many physicians for organic disease processes throughout their long periods of illness, with very little or no consideration for the possible presence of a psychologic disorder.

As I noted before, this syndrome may become extremely complicated at times, if the masked depression occurs in conjunction with a true organic deficit. In this study slightly more than one-third of the total number of 336 patients with masked depression had organic lesions that in some instances accounted for some of their symptoms and signs. However, it was clear from the character (that is, intensity, quality, duration, fluctuation) of the complaint, together with the results of the physical examinations and laboratory studies, that at best the organic factors accounted for only a small part of the clinical syndrome in most of the patients.

Some of the patients were referred to me for neuropsychiatric consultation by some specialists and general practitioners who were astute diagnosticians. They had found that the clinical patterns, while closely mimicking an organic process, did not follow the classic picture of a specific organic deficit or did not respond to therapies that were usually very effective for a given organic lesion. Unfortunately, a sizable number of the patients had been seen previously by psychiatrists who had been unable to recognize any psychiatric illness. Ironically, some of these same patients had suicidal preoccupations at the time they were interviewed by the psychiatrists. This psychiatric scotoma was more marked in nonmedical psychotherapists than it was in neuropsychiatrists. However, a number of patients had been incorrectly diagnosed by medical psychotherapists who for many years had had little or no contact with physical medicine.

General Clinical Characteristics

The vast majority of the patients with this syndrome were middle-aged women who presented their histories in a very definite, forceful manner. Marked circumstantiality to the point of logorrhea usually characterized the telling of these histories.

Since many if not most of these patients had been seen by one or more physicians or dentists and had been exposed to repeated examinations, multiple diagnostic tests, and various treatments, their histories were replete with medical jargon that had been gleaned from their multitudinous medical and dental contacts, and even from medical texts they frequently consulted.

Despite these painfully detailed, repetitious histories, the clinical descriptions were vague and did not represent classic descriptions of specific organic deficits. At best, the histories were suggestive of a more unusual organic process. Characteristically, these patients emphasized ad infinitum, in a fashion exaggerated far beyond that commonly seen in patients who have true organic lesions, the great suffering they had endured. Also, patients with masked depression were far more handicapped in their social and vocational performances than are patients with true organic illnesses, even those of severe proportions.

The patients' descriptions as well as the behavior demonstrated during the taking of the anamneses were colored by iatrogenic factors, which were secondary to multiple exposures to somatic therapies prior to the neuropsychiatric consultation. The duration and cost of this treatment enhanced the patients' hypochondriacal fixation upon their symptoms. At times the iatrogenic factors were so marked as to hopelessly restrict any effective therapeutic results.

It cannot be emphasized too strongly that the interview in its initial phases should be directed primarily to rooting out a true organic process. However, even the few clinical characteristics already described should alert the physician to the probability that the patient's difficulties, at least in part, are due to psychogenic problems and warrant intensive psychiatric evaluation. These patients, almost without exception, come with a rigidly held belief that their problems are organic in nature, and they usually become extremely hostile if any suggestion is made early in the examination that their problem may be "emotional" in origin.

The histories, therefore, must be taken in a gentle, patient fashion. Time must be allotted for the patients to relate the details of their problems, to expound upon their ailments and upon their expensively acquired knowledge of medicine, and to ventilate their hostility toward previous physicians or dentists. In other words, a careful psychiatric evaluation must be made, either without the patient's awareness or in such a way that it will not cause the patient to run from the examination and eventual treatment.

The intensity and pointedness of the psychiatrist's investigation may be broadened as he notes that he has gained the patient's trust and confidence. One might say that the intensity of one's questioning should be inversely proportionate to the degree of the patient's hostilities and resistances. Patients often respond very emotionally to probing comments such as "These long-standing discomforts must put you under a great deal of stress." In almost all instances one could depend upon the tearful response "Oh, if you only knew how much I have suffered!"

With gentle interrogation one could gradually piece together a characteristic picture. The patient routinely described an agitated state in which she was restless, paced the floor, and was plagued by constant feelings of tension and a gnawing anxiety. She complained of insomnia, anorexia, and persistent fatigue that was most marked in the morning. An inability to concentrate and a loss of interest in social and vocational activities were invariably noted. Everything was an effort. Even routine personal habits proved to be major chores. The patients often exclaimed that they were "losing their minds," and pointed to "poor memory" as evidence. The poor memory, in reality, was due to the fact that they were so preoccupied with themselves that they were often barely aware of what was going on about them.

During the interview the patients constantly referred back to their "physical illnesses," but with continued patience and gradually increasing pointedness I could usually obtain a statement to the effect that they were "feeling blue." Most patients, however, quickly followed this admission with the disclaimer "I'd be fine if only I was free of my physical problem."

Once the patient admits to being blue, it is relatively easy to detect the true intensity of the underlying depression. Many patients admitted to frequent crying spells. The presence of feelings of hopelessness could be elicited by such questions as "Do you ever feel as if you will never get better?" Another question that stimulated definite responses was "Do you ever feel as though you would like to go to bed and not wake up the next morning?" Very frequently this would elicit a statement to the effect that "life isn't bearable, if I must continue to suffer like this."

The marked intensity of the underlying depression was pointed up by the fact that more than two-thirds of my 336 patients with masked depressions in this series expressed feelings of hopelessness.

It is imperative that one determine whether suicidal preoccupations or drives are present. At this point I routinely pose the question "Have you ever had any thoughts of hurting yourself?" In an earlier report on 100 successive patients with masked depression, I noted that 42 percent of the patients had suicidal preoccupations of varying frequency and intensity (18).

In this current series of 336 patients with hypochondriacal complaints or psychosomatic syndromes masking depression, 151 or 44.5 percent had suicidal preoccupations of various frequencies and intensities. This is testimony par excellence to the fact that the depression sine depression syndrome very commonly masks depression of serious degree. This finding corroborates Hochstetter's observation that 18 (66 percent) of his 27 patients with masked depression had suicidal ideas, which they blamed upon "somatic symptoms that had become unbearable" (10).

Patients with masked depressions who have suicidal preoccupations invariably will remark, "If I must continue to suffer like this, I don't want to live." One must ascertain the

intensity and imminency of the suicidal drives in such patients. A number of the patients in my study were actively
contemplating suicide at the time of the initial interview.

A careful anamnesis usually revealed a close correlation
between the onset of the patient's symptoms and various
environmental traumas. They were more often than not incidents of minor proportions. To obtain this correlation one
requires a step-by-step account of the patient's life situation
prior to, during, and following the onset of the somatic symptoms. These traumas could be subtle or gross, acute or chronic.
They were related to vocational and social situations, sexual
problems, physical illness, economic pressures, menopausal
changes; indeed, they dealt with all sources of stress.

At times, a specific, impressive environmental trauma
could not be documented. In such cases, however, careful
interrogation elicited the information that for long periods the
patient had been under pressures more severe than that with
which she could satisfactorily cope. Many of these were conflicts that had their origins in childhood.

Personality Profile

The patients were characteristically very intelligent, capable, meticulous, hard-driving, usually aggressive personalities with a need to dominate their environments. One of
the most frequent traumas these patients described was the
real or imagined feeling that they could no longer control their
environments. Of course, the patients usually were unaware
of this need to dominate. Perfection was their aim.

In all instances the patients were found to be rigidly
inflexible in their management of everyday responsibilities.
These patients were usually very critical of others, but further
probing revealed that they were most critical and intolerant of
themselves. Unfortunately, they were often very overbearing
and thereby frequently alienated those around them. Without
fail one found that the aggressive, compulsive need to domi-

nate the environment was an attempt to compensate for lifelong feelings of inadequacy and self-derogation.

It was interesting to note the ninety male patients in this series were also very vigorous, aggressive, and perfectionistic in their vocational challenges. However, forty, or approximately 40 percent, were relatively passive at home in relation to more dominant, aggressive wives. As the wife of one of these male patients said, "He's a tiger in business but a pussycat at home."

While most of these patients reported they had many friends, I learned that in truth most of these so-called friends were often just working acquaintances. These women often became leaders in their communities without ever forming any true, close relationships. By the time patients came for psychiatric consultation, they were socially seclusive, were unable to function effectively vocationally, had no sexual desires, and often expressed fears of being alone.

The presence of guilt feelings associated with the decline from their usual high performance levels was another constant feature of this syndrome. Even more shattering to the patients was the awareness of their lack of desire to perform. There was a feeling of worthlessness associated with the lowered performance level. In their own eyes, they had lost stature and had no *raison d'être*.

It should be noted that the history-taking itself was often a very painful, tearful episode for the patients, and that by the end of the initial neuropsychiatric examination they were literally exhausted.

Family History

The patient usually came from a home in which one or both parents were described as having been very agressive and perfectionistic. In an earlier study I noted that 79 of 100 patients reported that the mother had been the dominant figure (18). In this current series of 336 patients, 82 percent reported that the mother was the dominant person in the home. At times some of these patients associated paternal shouting with aggressiveness, only to contradict this impression with the recollection that they always turned to their mothers for security, advice, and direction.

Frequently it was the mother who managed the family finances. She was often remembered as having been an "attentive martyr." On the other hand, the father was usually described as having been a rather passive, dependent personality who obviously and unsubtly was dominated by the mother. Maternal hypochondriasis or a history of migraine headaches, peptic ulcer, asthma, allergy, colitis, cystitis, severe menstrual difficulty, problems with obesity, periods of exhaustion, backaches, and on and on was not uncommon.

The mother also frequently had a history of phobias: cancer phobias, death phobia, claustrophobia, dirt phobias, animal phobias, agoraphobia. The patients also described referential trends in the mother.

Characteristically, there was evidence of a running conflict between the patient and the dominant parent. Some patients denied this in their initial interviews, but most of them reported it readily. The recollection of these conflicts was associated with a great deal of guilt.

Psychodynamic Development

The patient developed marked feelings of worthlessness and inadequacy as a child in response to the parents' real or imagined rejection. This negative image lingered and was projected in all of the patient's vocational and social relationships through the years. The patient unconsciously, and at times consciously, anticipated that her teachers, schoolmates, and other associates would have the same negative image of her that she had herself.

Such a patient literally spent her whole life compensating

for her feelings of inadequacy through a very high level of performance. However, at no time was she able to function in a fashion that led to lasting self-satisfaction and a relaxation in her struggle for self-recognition. This type of patient was obsessed with the mechanics of life and was intolerant of any failures on her part. Her compensatory attempts were highly intellectualized and she projected her dissatisfaction with herself upon others in the form of sharp criticism. This frequently led to a state of social bankruptcy.

The patient often presented a history of excessive fear and frustration in relationship to any physical ailment. This could be explained by the fact that physical ailments threatened to frustrate her driving efforts to prove herself to herself and to her world. If, in addition, one or both of her parents were hypochondriacs, she frequently mimicked the parents' complaints. For example, if a parent had been bowel conscious, the patient was bowel conscious; if the parent had headaches, the patient was head conscious and often had headaches; if the parent was preoccupied with his or her heart, the patient was cardiac conscious; if the parent had frequency attacks of dyspepsia, then the patient was stomach conscious.

As noted before, this type of patient is usually a most capable woman. Through her struggles against imagined adversity she frequently reaches far greater heights than the average person. By means of vigorous activity and by making great demands on herself she is usually able to compensate for her feelings of inadequacy until she enters the menopause or is post-menopausal. Menopause has a powerful symbolic meaning to many of these women. To some it represents the end of youth, the end of physical attractiveness. To others, since these women think in concrete mechanical terms, the end of their reproductive period fills them with terror, even though they have no desire for more children. They also associate the menopause with a loss of femininity. These factors, plus the biochemical changes that are inherent in the menopause, expose these patients to overwhelming stress.

Anger

The patients in my sample were without exception extremely angry persons. In most the rage was overt; in some it was covert.

Covert anger could result from either of two childhood circumstances. In both instances the child's early attempts to fight back had been overwhelmingly crushed. This situation was most commonly seen in patients who had been abandoned emotionally by their parents. This psychic abandonment led to fears of isolation and feelings of worthlessness and inadequacy. The child had initially reacted with anger to this type of deprivation, but soon became too frightened to express anger for fear of becoming completely isolated from the parents. These patients were unable to react with appropriate anger in later life, even when it was justified.

Covert anger also occurred when the parents were so hostile, domineering, critical, and sadistic that the patient was terrified by the aggressive, punitive atmosphere. In this environment, all attempts by the patient to protest against this massive psychic attrition had been met with overwhelming and crushing punishment. The parents of such patients had usually been martyrs who incessantly reminded the child how grateful she should be for the bounty she had received. The child was also constantly reminded that she had broken the most sacred of all rules: to honor her parents under any and all circumstances. Thus even repressed rage became guilt-linked and in a retroflex fashion self-punishment occurred in the absence of any overt anger.

As noted before, most patients with masked depressions were overtly hostile. The psychodynamic mechanisms in these patients paralleled in great measure those already described, with some important exceptions. The dominant parents of patients who in adult life manifested overt hostility had also been very aggressive, meticulous, and critical. Their negative attitudes had filled the child with anxiety and feelings of inadequacy and lack of worth. In this type of patient, in contrast to the patient who developed covert rage, the domineering, critical parent did not *completely* destroy the child's compensatory rage capacities and did not block the patient from expressing anger. Indeed, it was this compensatory mechanism that finally dominated the patient's personality. The patient literally spent her entire life in a futile attempt to attain a satisfactory level of self-recognition.

The psychopathologic processes and psychodynamics so briefly described in this chapter represent only a brief summary of the various patterns noted in patients with masked depression.

I cannot emphasize too forcefully that every one of these patients must have careful physical examinations and, when necessary, pertinent laboratory studies, for, as I stressed earlier, a masked depression *may* be superimposed upon a true organic illness of severe or minor proportions.

REFERENCES

1. Alcarin, R. Hypochondriasis and Depression in the Aged. *Gerontol. Clin.* 6:266, 1964.
2. Barduagni, S. Latent Depressive Syndromes in General Medicine (Study of 100 Cases). *Osped. Maggiore* 59:899, 1964.
3. Brill, A. A. *Lectures on Psychoanalytic Psychiatry*, Lecture 10. Boston: Knopf, 1946.
4. Cohen, M. B.; Baker, R. A.; Fromm-Reichmann, F.; and Weigert, E. V. An Intrinsic Study of Twelve Cases of Manic-Depressive Psychoses. *Psychiatry* 17:103, 1954.
5. Da Fonseca, A. F. Affective Equivalents. *Brit. J. Psychiat.* 109:464, 1963.
6. Da Fonseca, A. F. Basic Conceptual View points on Affective Equivalents. Fifth World Congress of Psychiatry. Mexico City, November 30, 1971.
7. Diamond, S. Depressive Headaches. *Headache* 4:255, 1964.
8. Freud, S. Mourning and Melancholia. In *Collected Papers*. London: Hogarth Press, 1924.

9. Freedman, A. S.; Cowitz, B.; Cohen, H. W.; and Granick, S. Syndromes and Themes of Psychic Depression. *Arch. Gen. Psychiat.* 9:504, 1963.

10. Hochstetter, W. Depressive Syndromes. *Proc. R. Virchow Society* 18:116–28. Basel: S. Karger, 1959.

11. Kreitman, N.; Sainsbury, P.; Pearce, K.; and Costain, W. R. Hypochondriasis and Depression in Out-Patients at a General Hospital. *Brit. J. Psychiat.* 111:607, 1965.

12. Landauer, K. Equivalente der Trauer. *Int. Ztschr. Psychoanal.* 11:178, 1925.

13. Lederer, W. Uprooting Depression Without Depression: Obesity and Other Psychosomatic Depressive Equivalents. *Nervenarzt* 36:118, 1965.

14. Lesse, S. Atypical Facial Pain Syndromes of Psychogenic Origin. *J. Nerv. Ment. Dis.* 124:535, 1956.

15. Lesse, S. Autonomic Faciocephalgia: A Psychosomatic Syndrome. *Trans. Am. Neurol. Assoc.*, 1961, pp. 224–26.

16. Lesse, S. Neurologic Aspects of Facial Pain. *Bull. N.Y. State Dental Soc. Anesthes.*, June, 1963, pp. 2–7.

17. Lesse, S. Psychodynamic Mechanisms of Emotional Illness in Executives. *Int. J. Soc. Psychiat.* 12:24, 1966.

18. **Lesse, S. Hypochondriasis and Psychosomatic Disorders Masking Depression.** *Am. J. Psychother.* 21:607, 1967.

19. Lesse, S. Masked Depression: A Diagnostic and Therapeutic Problem. *Dis. Nerv. Syst.* 29169, 1968.

20. Lesse, S. *Anxiety : Its Components, Development and Treatment.* New York: Grune & Stratton, 1970.

21. Mendelowicz, J. The Nature of Affective Equivalents in Relation to Affective Disorders. Fifth World Congress of Psychiatry, Mexico City, November 30, 1971.

22 Pletnef, S. Zur Frage der Sematischen Cyctothymie. *Ztschr. Klin. Med.* 107:145, 1928.

23. Schick, A. On a Physical Form of Periodic Depression. *Psychonal. Rev.* 34:432, 1947.

24. Stekel, W. *Nervose Angstzustaende und ihre Behandlung.* Vienna: Urban & Schwarzenberg, 1942.

25. Wilder, J. Stimulus and Response: The Law of Initial Value. Bristol: John Wright, 1967.

5

Anger and Acting Out as Depressive Equivalents

ROSE SPIEGEL

Anger and depression are nuclear elements of human anguish with the force of personae in the old morality plays. They are linked in a peculiar and special way, though it would be a mistake to say that one is equivalent to the other. By means of anger and acting out, the depressed person thrusts himself into the lives of others, even onto the larger social scene.

We have long been told that there is a strong connection between hostility, aggression, and depression, but our image of depression does not include open anger or rage.

Literature

Though there have been some significant dissenting voices, most psychoanalytic writers include hostility and aggression in the essential character, the psychogenesis, and the psychodynamics of depression. In the very first paper on depression in the psychoanalytic literature, Abraham (1) commented on hostility and ambivalence in depressives. Freud, in *Mourning and Melancholia* (5), interpreted the

melancholiac's self-reproaches as covert translations and introjections of hostility and ambivalence in reaction to the disap-
pointing love object.

Rado (10) elaborated on the theme of the depressive's
hostility and came to designate this element in
psychodynamics as "retroflexed rage," a much more vivid
affect term than "hostility." Melanie Klein (7) conceived of a
depressive phase in infancy, in which the infant experiences
hostility and aggressive wishes toward the parents with the
aftermath of a feeling of guilt. She presents this concept as
characteristic of all human beings, and also as her paradigm
for manic-depressive psychoses. Although Rado's theory of
the psychodynamics of depression has a similar ring to it, he
does not universalize a depressive position.

Associated with the concept of the depressive's hostility
is that of aggression. Among contemporary writers, Bonime
(4) takes the particularly stringent view that "depression is one
of the *forms* of expressing hostility," that depression is a
covert, manipulative expression of anger, involving "covert
punitiveness." I do not doubt that this may often be true, but I
do question whether it is necessarily and universally so.

It is noteworthy that all this literature on the intrinsic
nature of depression deals with hostility and aggression in
covert form, either as the purpose, so to speak, of the depression or as a theoretical component. Aggression is not viewed
as unmistakably manifested in expression or action, nor is
hostility considered to require the clear emotion of anger or
rage.

Jeanne Lampl–de Groot (9) presents other perspectives on
aggression and depression: (1) the existence of an erotic linkage between them, and (2) their working through in psychoanalysis.

Kolb (8) observes that when the depressive patient begins
to express open rage, or even projective behavior in response
to actions of the psychotherapist, he immediately thereafter
emerges from his depressive attack. Kolb believes that such a
clinical course supports the psychodynamic interpretation

that much of the depressive constellation is due to efforts at repression or suppression of rage.

From another methodological approach, that of Grinker's research group (6), we gain a still different perspective on depression and anger. In setting up the factors for subsyndromes of the depressions in ninety-six patients, these observers consistently ranked anger, whether as feeling or as behavior—shouting, using derogatory language, destroying objects, striking at people—as among the least typical manifestations of depression. Here again we find depression and openly angry behavior viewed as antithetical. The closest a subsyndrome came to anger was in their Factor 4, in which the "current behavior" of the patient was characterized by unappreciativeness, active anger, and provocativeness, with excessive demands and complaints made to the staff. In Factor 4 we find behavior that might well mask depression and be missed by the harassed hospital staff.

Coming closer to the topic of depression covered by anger and acting out is the suggestion made by Frank Ayd (2) that depression often underlies extremes of violence, such as the murder of an entire family topped off by suicide. Such extremes, however, are rarely encountered among the depressives we are called on to help in psychotherapy, though more often than our literature would indicate we do encounter rage/anger, aggression, and acting out in these patients.

We are here concerned with open and unmistakable anger/rage, observable by the proverbial man in the street; this open manifestation is actually the mask. The depression, contrary to our usual image, here is submerged. Clinically, the term "mask" has two meanings: (1) the directing of affect toward a misleading target, so that the underlying depression is missed and therapy may therefore miss the core of depression; (2) the psychodynamic use of rage as a defense against depression, even a masking from the patient himself that he is depressed.[1]

---

1. This introductory section is based on one of my earlier papers (11).

An important dissent from the view that hostility and aggression are basic to the underlying depression and its later open manifestation comes from Bibring (3), who does not consider them invariably present; nor do I. However, discussion of this point would take us away from the present concern.

The relationship of anger and rage to depression is many-faceted; at times it is part of self-healing, at others it is a consuming destruction of the self and others.

Anger and the Depressive Core

In order to explore anger as a depressive equivalent, it is necessary to focus on some aspects of the core of depression as carefully as though it were a molecule. The potential for anger and rage is implicit in the depressive core. The model of the trauma-provoking depression may be formulated as: "I have been abandoned, rejected, deserted, or betrayed by the world (a parent, you)." This inner formulation may be experienced simply as a statement or as an accusation directed at the (assigned) perpetrator of the trauma, not necessarily in actual language, but at least in attitude and mood.

The accent in open simple depression, then, is on loss and dejection. On the other hand, the accent can be more pointedly accusatory: "I have been wronged by a specific person, past or present; by you; by a group or society; or by life." We see here the opening for an aggressive or even delusional orientation and, depending on the intensity of the activation, the opportunity for anger and acting out as the depressive equivalent. In contrast, in the purely depressive the response is linked to oneself: "I was unworthy, therefore I was abandoned."

The accent also varies as to the perpetrator of the trauma of rejection. For instance: "I have been abandoned because of an interloper, who alienated your affections from me. If I get rid of the interloper—my sibling or my rival in love—you will love me again."

Anger and Depression - Opposites in Adaption

So much for the person's inner formulation of the trauma and its perpetrator. As we continue with our comparison of the functioning of depression and of anger, we shall see that anger refutes depression and that they are at opposite poles from the point of view of adaptation. A pivotal parameter of anger and depression is a sense of power. In open depression there is a feeling of a lack of power, of helplessness and ineptitude, though at times a sense of power may paradoxically appear in negative and covert form. But in the anger equivalent there may be a feeling, perhaps transient, of glory: "Now you (or society) will feel the power of my anger, the power of my actions."

In open depression the sense of powerlessness is accompanied by constricted communication and the feeling that one has not succeeded in reaching anyone, the feeling of being invisible, grayed out. Anger and acting out serve as defenses against this feeling. As one patient put it, "When I'm good and behaving properly, I am ignored. I decided to raise hell. People will have to know I'm here. You will have to relate to me when I'm bad and not doing all the nice things." Vindictiveness too is a psychodynamic: "No one cares how I suffer, so why should I care if anyone else suffers?"

Open anger/rage as a depressive equivalent is often misleading to the observer, because the underlying depression may be missed and therapy then will not engage the depressive core to resolve it.

Open anger/rage may be restricted to the verbal and expressional, and hurled irrationally and violently at some inappropriate target in the world at large, at an intimate, at the psychotherapist. Rage may be expressed in gross behavior, in violence to people, animals, or things. The clinical course may oscillate from depression to rage and back again, with only illusory relief.

When extreme, anger/rage acting out may have a paranoid quality, which then serves as a mask for depression. It is particularly abrasive in a marriage, when the hidden depression in one or both members is the basis for searing accusations, demands, and reproaches, at times leading to extramarital sexual relationships in which the new partner really serves as target for acting out as punishment of the spouse.

Though it often is the case that anger/rage directed outward is actually a reversal of anger directed at the self, it ain't necessarily so. The person may be suffering from the tension of the lack of discharge and not because qualitatively the anger is directed toward himself.

Some depressive people, even in the interim between flagrant depressions, just don't know how to relate other than by depressive anticipation of rebuff or by reproach intensifying to accusation and anger. They don't know how to give or accept tenderness.

The following two cases will illustrate a number of these points.

The Case of Eileen

Eileen, a writer about twenty-two years old, sought ambulatory psychotherapy after a brief hospitalization because she felt depressed and feared she might lose control and commit suicide.

Eileen's initial mood of depression and anxiety and her suicidal ideation diminished after several sessions, and she then declared in a light manner, "I feel so well I don't have anything to talk about. Is this resistance against coming here any more?" This slightly facetious manner and difficulty in dealing with the past in depth occurred fairly frequently throughout her psychotherapy.

After about two months in therapy her mood was good and even slightly elated. She was able to return to her writing and worked five hours a day. Writing, she said, was the one thing in life that mattered. She resented anything that came between her and writing. She felt pushed to produce because "I am a prodigy."

She had difficulty in getting close to people. Whenever her boy friend, Paul, talked of marriage, she would withdraw. There was no sex.

Her adoptive father was described as domineering, generous, and picturesque, with a frontier style of aggression that could lead to violence. Eileen felt her relationship with her parents was good, but she and her brother were harshly competitive. Her brother cheated her when they were children, though she didn't realize it till she reached her late teens. At that time she took solace in being much brighter than he.

She had had a similar episode of intense anxiety and depression and inability to function in school two to three years earlier. This episode lasted five or six months and necessitated dropping out of school. When she recovered, she left her family in Oklahoma and moved to New York City.

She had disliked school even in the elementary grades. The fierce competitiveness of her classmates, urged on by their ambitious mothers made her "very nervous" and uncomfortable; she felt she had "no identity."

She later cultivated an outer identity by means of which she exacted "respect," which she valued more than liking. She learned that she could get results by losing her temper, and she became demanding and commanding.

Her relationships with men alternated between a plunge into intimacy and withdrawal from the man-woman relationship to that of "friendship," and to several of the men she was supportive and helpful. She stated that to be remote and aloof was the only way to retain her appeal. The more she liked someone, the more she wanted to get out of the whole situation.

She was reluctant to marry and found reasons to consider each relationship unsuitable; sometimes she was brighter than he, or had more status or more money. Sometimes the young man had his own problem of aloofness.

Throughout therapy there was occasional suicidal ideation but no suicidal impulse or action. She permitted the thoughts, she said, in order to be able to report to the therapist. On the whole she showed distinct improvement in the two years of therapy. At the end of this time she received word of the grave illness of her father, flew back to Oklahoma, and became submerged in the emotional upheaval of his death and the massive practical problems of disposing of the estate among the members of the large family.

Several months after her father's death she received word of the suicide of a boy friend, Roger, and had feelings of self-doubt and guilt as to whether she could have been more helpful. Roger's suicide and the grief of his mother were very painful to Eileen.

Shortly after Roger's death she met John, a lawyer, at a party, and both became overwhelmingly infatuated. He had been a confirmed bachelor, about forty years old to her twenty-four, until this whirlwind relationship developed. Eileen did not want to work through in therapy what this relationship was, and no longer kept regular sessions. Soon they eloped.

It appeared that her grief at the loss of her father and of Roger contributed to an urgency to fill in the empty spaces with this new relationship. John provided an opportunity to act out in response to these traumas. Almost as soon as they were married, tensions mounted. John would call her at home during the day, and expected her always to be there. He would come home for lunch and want sex. She felt smothered. More and more she wanted to be alone to write, she said. She considered his calls and his lunch-hour demands evidence that he was suspicious of her. In a joint interview he appeared rather rigid, puzzled, and unable to accept her need to be left alone. When he saw the therapist for a short time alone, he confidentially reported that she drank heavily. She increasingly experienced him as not only a psychologic but a physical threat to her, and in great anxiety and rage moved to a hotel.

Almost immediately Eileen started divorce proceedings, which had considerable complexity both interpersonally and legally. The last I heard, the marriage was dissolved in great mutual hostility.

The course of therapy and the ensuing improvement had

been sharply altered with the death of Eileen's father and then of Roger. Her flight from grief (and perhaps depression) into the at first exuberant marriage with an older man was an acting out with a quality of elation. The swing into withdrawal, unacceptable to the husband, had progressively paranoid qualities, which simmered down with the tedious process of the divorce action.

The Case of Al

Al, in his mid-fifties, began therapy with me after a ten-month period of hospitalization. His difficulties dated back twenty-five years. At that time he had developed episodic severe abdominal cramps. After being seen by an internist, he was referred to a psychoanalyst for treatment because he complained of having great difficulty with his work and obsessive fear of failure. Since then he had been in psychoanalytic treatment with several psychoanalysts, with his presenting difficulty always centering around his inability to make responsible decisions in his work.[2] From time to time in the past twenty years his anxiety about decision-making verged on panic.

He gradually became incapacitated, unable to make decisions or take any action, and unable to tell anyone. Finally his anxiety grew so great that he felt his only recourse was to stop going to work. Since that time he had not worked at all and had felt completely helpless and hopeless about his ability to do anything for himself. In response to his wife's demands that he take some action aimed at resolving his difficulties, he agreed to hospitalization to avoid the possibility that she might leave him.

2. Inquiry into these therapeutic endeavors disclosed that much depended on the individual styles of the therapists and not only on their theoretical orientations, which were similar—an interesting side issue.

The diagnosis at the hospital was "depressive reaction in an obsessive-compulsive character disorder with borderline features," and the prognosis was "poor to guarded." It was noted that in some twenty years of treatment he had never established a deep emotional relationship with any therapist. At fifty-four, then, he faced the vacuum of his lapsed career with two and one-half years of inability to work, the knowledge of his self-doubts and trigger-sensitive rages, the apparently empty marriage.

At our initial interview he declared, "I have no motivation. To tell you the truth, I don't care if tomorrow never comes. I don't give a goddamn if I wake up tomorrow.

"I'm looking for a job, but that's halfhearted.

"I have very little satisfaction out of work and just a few occasions of pleasure out of my work. There have been moments of pleasure with my wife.

"I feel I am just marking time, waiting until I die."

When I asked if he had any feelings of anger, he said, "Of course I have. At the hospital. Most of the time I repressed it. I never got angry with my analyst; I needed her too much. Nor with my wife, except recently.

"When I left the hospital [glint of a smile], I was able to say to the psychiatrist, 'You're full of shit. You haven't helped me at all.'"

Al experienced his upbringing as having taken place in a two-generation matriarchy, with his father—good-natured, inept, a gambler—swept out of the household and divorced when Al was five. Al was given typical boy's gifts by his father, to the harsh mockery of mother and grandmother, and play with the various mechanical toys was contaminated by their denigration. He yearned for closeness with his mother and sought to cling to her, but she had read about the Oedipus complex and discouraged his demonstrativeness.

Later, in Al's relationships with girls, ardor was always followed by backing away, until he met and fell in love with his wife. Scholastically he was brilliant, but after being an honor student for three years at college, he fell behind.

Most of the time self-contained emotionally, he had outbursts of rage at work, and when he was with the army in the
Philippines he once "blew [his] top" at the ineptitude of a
native civil servant; he became so enraged that he felt his
words alone might destroy the man.

The expression of rage played an active role in his interpersonal and intrapsychic life. He was verbally scathing but
never threatened anyone physically. The force of his rage was
so great that his first and crucially important posthospital job
was in jeopardy. He attacked superiors who he thought were
inept or unethical, as well as subordinates who fumbled their
jobs. But he was respectful of competence and integrity. Together we scrutinized the drafts of his reports to his employer,
searching for derogatory comments that might jeopardize his
job.

Verbal rage spilled over into his social comments. He
found himself thinking, "Anyone who causes a disturbance
ought to be killed, and I want to be the one to do it. The student
agitators at Columbia—cut their tongues off, cut their heads
off; cut their tongues off and if that doesn't help, kill them.

"When the whites collect to kill the Negroes, kill the
whites. When the Negroes collect to throw rocks at the whites,
kill the Negroes. I would like to have the power just to look and
kill.

"Kill the muggers."

Then he said, "It's an intrusion of violence into my not-
knowing. I can't say it any better than that. It's as though I am
on a plane in which these things don't exist. I don't know
about them and suddenly these things intrude and it disturbs
me. . . . After I got sick, I had occasional fantasies of pushing
my wife out the window when she began asking questions I
didn't want to answer."

And he said, "I was not in any fights as a kid. [Pause.] I
just had the thought: My reactions to violence may be because
I am afraid to be violent and so I have the fantasy and the will to
be violent. Others can be violent; why [smile] should they
have all the fun?

"Maybe I am saying all this here, because you asked me and I can talk here as no place else. I have authority. I'd feel important if I'd kill a hundred thousand people. . . . If I were laid bare, whom would I kill? I don't know." Observing my notetaking, he laughed. "You're having a field day."

Let me interrupt the vividness of Al's discourse. My working conception of therapy in his case was based on a shift in emphasis from the diagnosis of a primarily obsessive-compulsive personality with a depressive decompensation to a primarily depressive personality whose obsessive-compulsive defenses had crumbled. This is far more than a semantic quibble.

Early in our work I told him my hunch that the depression was the basic, profound, and permeating condition. He said thoughtfully, "That strikes home. No one has ever said that to me before."

After about a year of therapy, a particularly insightful and enlightening session took place. It began with reference to his wife's pregnancy years earlier. When she became pregnant he fell into a prolonged depression, which persisted after she had an abortion.

"I don't remember feeling angry. I didn't want to slit her throat. *Now* I feel rage. 'How dare you do that to me, how dare you become pregnant!' I feel that more now than I did then. I just now started thinking of my work." (An interesting fleeting self-distraction.)

"You used the word 'rage,' so I thought 'rage,' and I thought 'pregnancy,' and I felt anger. [Pause.] Just now I felt anger, and then it disappeared, and the fantasy was I was sinking to my knees almost as if I was pleading or begging and there was a simulated physical movement down my leg, with that.

"And the thought 'beg' just came to my mind, and my eyes started to water, and I am just on the verge of crying, and thinking, 'Never in my life did I want to have to beg for something,' and the vague recollection of my childhood—six, seven, eight, and I didn't dare ask for anything, as I recollect now. And feeling, 'I don't know how to ask'; I had to whine, wheedle, or plead, and the words that I have for it now is that I was emasculated and I still am. And I am crying with it right now.

"And the tears are not necessarily for pity, but there's rage with them, acute despair, of not knowing what the hell really has any meaning or any value to me.

"When I put some grand music on, it is as though the music moves forward indomitably. It is as though it carries me along and I experience feelings I don't feel otherwise. Its thrust is of indomitability and it is going to reach its destination and do it beautifully on the way. [A momentary phone call.] I don't know what is going on now, a circling nowhere. I don't know if this unhappiness I feel now is a deep despair or something more paralyzing, or just not being able to express unhappiness.

"Just a thought that I am no good. And an almost simultaneous awareness. This is not reality, or fact, or what I mean. But the simultaneous awareness of inner reality, that this feeling of 'I am not good' is something else."

He gave details of his sexual fantasies and said he had a feeling that these fantasies themselves were creative.

"There are very few occasions in my life when I have the feeling of creativity, and here I do. A few times at work I felt creative. In the Y job I did. Before that, fifteen years ago, I did the job and felt creative. Most of the time I do the job and feel harried or frightened and uncertain.

"And the uncertainties I always felt were my fault, my failings. [Pause and laugh]. I was just thinking of Pandora's box. You pulled out the bung and out poured something."

In the case of Al also we see fluidity in the shift to and from anger and depression, in spite of the general impression one has of rigidity in depression. The usual inarticulateness of depression gave way to a sensitive and discerning revealing of himself; the rage gave way to a yearning for tenderness; the sense of powerlessness, to admiration of the power in Bach's music. The anger played many roles, both syntonic and dystonic, both organizing and alienating.

In the case of Eileen, the anger from which she borrowed a sense of strength and power more often was destructive to herself and others.

Clearly, the role of the equivalence of anger needs to be understood by both the patient and the therapist; and when anger or rage is dominant, the therapist should consider a relationship to depression.

References

1. Abraham, K. Notes on the Psychoanalytic Investigation and Treatment of Manic-Depressive Insanity and Allied Conditions. In *Selected Papers on Psychoanalysis*. London: Hogarth Press, 1911.
2. Ayd, F. J., Jr. *Recognizing the Depressed Patient*. New York: Grune & Stratton, 1961.
3. Bibring, E. The Mechanism of Depression. In *Affective Disorders*, ed. P. Greenacre. New York: International Universities Press, 1953.
4. Bonime, W. The Psychodynamics of Neurotic Depression. In *The American Handbook of Psychiatry*, ed. S. Arieti, vol. 3. New York: Basic Books, 1966.
5. Freud, S. Mourning and Melancholia. In *Collected Papers*, vol. 4. London: Hogarth Press, 1917.
6. Grinker, R. R., Sr., et al. *The Phenomena of Depressions*. New York: P. B. Hoeber, 1961.
7. Klein, M. *Contributions to Psycho-Analysis, 1921–1945*. London: Hogarth Press, 1948.
8. Kolb, L. Psychotherapy in Management of Depression. In *Aspects of Depressive Illness*, ed. D. C. Maddison and G. M. Duncan. Edinburgh & London: E. & S. Livingstone, 1965.
9. Lampl–de Groot, J. Depression and Aggression. In *Drives, Affects, Behavior*, ed. R. M. Loewenstein. New York: International Universities Press, 1953.

10. Rado, S. The Problem of Melancholia. *Int. J. Psycho-Anal.* 9: 420, 1928.
11. Spiegel, R. Anger and Acting Out: Masks of Depression. *Amer. J. Psychother.* 21:597, 1967.
12. Spitz, R. Aggression: Its Role in the Establishment of Object Relations. In *Drives, Affects, Behavior*, ed. R. M. Loewenstein. New York: International Universities Press, 1953.

6

Masked Depression in Relation to Work, Pleasure, and Sexuality

IRVING BIEBER

A depression is not only a disturbance of affect; it is a component of a complex attitudinal and behavioral constellation. In an overt case, both the patient and the psychiatrist are very much aware of the depression, and therapeutic decisions revolve around alleviating it.

In a masked depression, the patient may be quite unaware that he is depressed; or he may not feel depressed yet recognize signs and symptoms that he has come to identify as depression; or he may feel depressed yet be able to conceal it from others. A depression may be defended against in many ways, and it becomes a matter of semantics whether defenses are viewed as depression-avoidance maneuvers or as depression-masking maneuvers. The concept of "masked depression" seems more useful, because the clinical manifestations may be evoked in such cases without much difficulty. Masking may occur in any type of depression, acute or chronic.

Substantive differences among psychiatrists about the etiology and psychodynamics of depression abound. In my view, depression is a reaction to loss or threatened loss of something or someone highly valued—a loved one, a body part, an ability, a function, self-esteem, money, an artifact. The common denominator of all depressions is the high value placed upon the loss. Two types of depressive reactions occur. The first concerns the individual's conscious or unconscious belief that he has been responsible for the loss in some way, and could or should have prevented it. The second is a grief reaction, associated particularly with the loss of a loved one, when the bereaved harbors no conviction that he participated in bringing about the loss. Pure grief is not accompanied by guilt or hostility toward the lost one. Most depressive reactions met with in clinical practice concern the first category, in which the patient believes, often correctly, that he has played some part in the loss or threatened loss. Thus guilt feelings, self-recrimination, and loss of self-esteem usually accompany this type of depression.

The principle involving a sense of loss of something of value is operant in all depressions, including the so-called endogenous depression, often thought to result from metabolic disturbances. The physiological changes that occur in a depression are its concomitants, not its triggering mechanisms, and in each case the precipitant is a psychological one. Freud once pointed out that the two basic elements of human existence are love and work. The sense of loss that presages depression can usually be located in either or both of those areas.

Work and Depression

In order to maintain physical and psychological health, human beings require the type of stimulation that patterned, organized behavior provides. Probably most other mammals also require it. When productively organized behavior is plugged into socioeconomic systems, we term it work. When behavior is involved with experiencing pleasure per se, we term it play. The distinction is not a particularly good one, for work and pleasure articulate unless disrupted by deleterious influences. Each normal newborn has the developmental potential for organizing an extensive, complex repertoire of learned, intelligent behavior. Failure in developmental potentials may be due to a combination of parental and/or cultural understimulation, seen especially among the disadvantaged; or learning may become inhibited as a consequence of neurotic disorders. The psychological substratum for a depression is established when potentials are not developed or when they are developed, but are not available to the individual because of neurotic inhibition.

The inability to use one's inner resources, the reality situation permitting, is always a symptom of psychopathology, a symptom I have termed "work inhibition" (1). Two major psychodynamic constellations can be delineated: fears of failure and fears of success. It is readily apparent why people fear failure, but insight into fears of success requires psychological sophistication. In a paper written in 1904, "Those Wrecked by Success," Freud (5) first described this phenomenon, which he observed in the case of a young woman who had lived with her lover for many years. When the marriage she had tried to achieve became possible, she became hopelessly psychotic. Another case he reported was that of a schoolteacher who developed a severe depression after being promoted to a position he had long wished for.

The fear of success is a central dynamic in work inhibition (4); it is a salient component in the psychopathology of everyday life from early years on. The dynamics of this fear must be worked out for each individual, yet in most cases where fear of success is prominent, certain beliefs and attitudes are regularly discernible, such as apprehension about evoking jealousy and vindictiveness in others, especially power figures; guilt and concern about rejection by loved ones for surpassing them; and guilt that one's success will evoke feelings of inferiority and depression in colleagues, friends, siblings, or parents, especially the parent of the same sex, for this relationship embraces the dynamics of the Oedipus complex with its component of hostility.

Work, as we know it in our society, begins with school-ing. When the child enters first grade, his world becomes structured around the fulfillment of a variety of new expecta-tions outside the family milieu and among peers. Some chil-dren cannot meet academic demands because of maladap-tive, preschool social conditions, developmental defects, specific reading disabilities, perceptual disorders, or neuro-tic problems. These youngsters develop depressive reactions that are often manifested in behavior disorders or other symptoms such as apathy, daydreaming, and boredom, each an expression of a disinclination to participate in the learning process. When such children come from a disad-vantaged background, the parents may not be particularly concerned about a low level of school performance, and so these children do not experience the pressures for achieve-ment notable among upwardly mobile families. Disadvan-taged children are nevertheless depressed by school failure, but they are less likely to get the corrective attention needed.

A decline in the school performance of a normally de-veloping child is usually a signal that distressing psychological problems are blocking concentration and motivation. In fact, a drop in school performance may be the first observable sign of a depression. Sometimes a difficult teacher may account for it, but most often its determinants can be traced to psychologic disorders within the family and surfacing pathology in the child.

Once a child advances beyond the early grades, dysfunc-tion in school tends to occur most often in the first year of junior high school, the last year of high school, the first year of college, and the completion of college. In professional and graduate schools, work breakdowns seem to occur most fre-quently in the first half of the course, peaking again in the last year.

Characteristic of the identity crisis described by Erikson are severe work disorders and the absence of occupational goals. It is not uncommon for students to reach college without having any idea at all what subjects they are interested in or which general area they would like to work in someday. Psychiatric examination of young people undergoing identity crises always reveals underlying depressions, no matter what other pathological syndromes may also be present.

The great majority of students who drop out, whether from high school or from doctoral programs, are in the main beset by crippling work inhibitions. Dropping out is a symptom of psychopathology; it is rarely a matter of well-reasoned choice, though students may rationalize their situation by resorting to the current clichés—the irrelevancy of courses, the need to escape the rat race, and so forth. Actually, they cannot maintain stable work adaptations, and with such breakdowns they almost always experience reactive depressions. On the surface, many among them may appear very cheerful, even euphoric; as a rule, they are unaware of feeling depressed. Thus school dropouts constitute a discrete population suffering from masked depression.

A similar type of depression occurs among drug abusers and addicts. Most drug users are severely work-inhibited. Heroin addicts among the disadvantaged are the most work-inhibited people one sees clinically except for chaotic and disorganized schizophrenics.[1] Practically all heroin addicts are chronically depressed, though they hide their depression behind a patterned, superficial amiability that characterizes interpersonal relationships within the drug subculture. The high suicide rate from overdosage and the masochistically determined fatal accidents attest to the depth of masked depression among the addicted.

The characteristic hypomanic reactions noted among am-

1. S. Foster and I studied the school and work histories of fifty consecutive admissions to the heroin detoxification program at Metropolitan Hospital, New York City. Some patients could not work at all; others could not maintain any continuity in work function. All patients revealed histories of a marked drop in school or other work performance from six months to two years prior to their addiction.

phetamine addicts mask underlying depressions that emerge as soon as amphetamine is withdrawn. Their depressions are associated with work and sexual inhibitions. The drug is taken to break through inhibitions and to counteract depression.

In general, chronic alcoholics are chronically depressed. Depression is a crucial variable distinguishing alcoholics from heavy drinkers. Alcoholics cannot maintain stable work performance and drink to mask and narcotize depressive affect, whereas mere heavy drinkers use alcohol to facilitate successful functioning. Alcoholic binges are always the equivalents of depressive episodes. They represent acute masked depressions acted out in a masochistic storm, usually following a performance or situation perceived as meaningful and successful (3).

Compulsive overeating is closely related to addiction in that intake has a quieting effect on anxiety. Most obesity is, of course, psychologically determined. Psychodynamically, two clusters can be delineated: first, substitute gratification is sought through eating because of major frustrations in work or sexuality; second, a press toward obesity is a masochistic means of concealing or destroying physical attractiveness and health. The myth that obesity and cheerful good nature go hand in hand has long since been exploded. Even beyond that, an obese condition usually masks an underlying depression. Individuals whose life patterns change markedly, as in marriage or in starting a family, not infrequently become rapidly overweight, a development that points to a gathering depression. In some cases the obesity is short-lived; in others it becomes a chronic defense masking a chronic depression. Often when such individuals lose weight as a result of constructive effort, the depression emerges.

In summary, drug abuse or food abuse should be regarded as masking a depression. Therapeutically, such a diagnosis leads the clinician to search out what it is that the patient is experiencing as a significant loss so that the underpinnings of the depression can be tracked down.

Depression and Achievement

Few individuals develop their maximum potentials or use their talents consistently. Too often, work inhibitions interfere. Yet most people have a sense of their own capabilities, even if the awareness is subliminal. Such self-awareness may be expressed in dreams, in aspirational daydreams, and sometimes in terms that are gandiose when compared to accomplishments. When aspiration becomes operational, it is usually referred to as ambition. People who are openly ambitious not infrequently provoke suspicion and hostility in those who fear upward striving in themselves and others. In the sense that ambition consists of choosing the work one prefers and striving to develop in it and achieve constructive, realistic goals, it is a normal, desirable attribute. The absence of it is, in fact, pathological.

As among children, a significant decline in an adult's work level is a sign of trouble. In most instances a marked drop is symptomatic of depression, despite the absence of other clinical manifestations. The depression may be masked by psychosomatic complaints or rationalized as boredom with a job or preoccupation with finding new employment, perhaps in another field. A change to another field is sometimes attempted as a way of breaking through an impasse created by neurotic inhibition. Work difficulties are commonly ascribed to fatigue from overwork, but unless the fatigue can be accounted for by definite organic illness or actual overwork, it should be viewed as an indicator of masked depression. In the early years of psychiatry, depressions that were masked by fatigue were referred to as neurasthenia.

As I have noted, few people function consistently on a level of effectiveness congruent with their potential. A graph depicting work effectiveness over a given time period for the most patients shows rises and falls; the troughs reflect inhibition and at least some depression. When the curves are shallow, it is likely that work competency has not been seriously compromised. Such periods are generally viewed as "off days." Yet they represent minor depressions, and when they occur frequently or in depth, the diagnosis points to a full depression.

In middle age there are at least two types of depression that relate to work disorders. The first occurs during the late thirties or early forties and is associated with a growing awareness that youth is passing and ambitions may not be realized. The rationalizations such patients could maintain during their twenties and early thirties now begin to break down, and other psychological adjustments must be made. Some attempt to break through work blocks before resigning themselves to defeat and chronic depression. They may return to school, change a job for a better one, or take some other constructive step half-contemplated for years.

The anxiety that such self-improvement precipitates may set off a hypomanic reaction. If the individual is struggling with masochistic impulses to take flight and sabotage his efforts, the picture may be that of an agitated depression. In these cases the psychodynamics linked to long-standing work problems are unmasked in a crisis where time has become the precipitating dimension.

The second type affects women mainly—the involutional or menopausal depression, so called because the syndrome is associated with the cessation of menses, though I do not view such depression as endogenous. It occurs among those whose inner resources have not been used effectively and/or where there has been a neurotic reliance on youthful sexuality and a childbearing potential for a sense of self-esteem. Such women are frequently overly concerned about their physical appearance, and they become frightened and depressed by the changes that develop with age. During their younger years, they may have occupied themselves with child-rearing and running a household, but when their last child marries or goes off to college, they often feel they no longer have a raison d'être. They then become bored and restless, and feel that life has become empty of meaning. Some may begin to make excessive demands on husband and children for attention and companionship, thus creating a clutch of secondary problems.

In general, such patients reveal a history of pathologic dependency on others for initiating, structuring, and sustaining basic gratifications. While electrotherapy may temporarily alleviate the more obvious depressive symptoms, a favorable prognosis ultimately depends on their ability to relate to their social world in a broader way.

Creativity in Masked Depression

All normal children are creative. Observe them in imaginative play; look at their artwork. The many biosocial variables that go into the later development of a great creative painter, musician, or writer are still unsettled matters and beyond the scope of this chapter. Far more accessible to psychiatric observation and understanding are the psychological impediments to the actualization of creative potentials.

These problems are seen daily among patients. They form three major categories. The first consists of those who fail to develop their potentiality and wind up with enfeebled curiosity and enthusiasm. The second includes those who develop their creativity but cannot work effectively because of neurotic inhibitions—writers with a "block," painters who do not produce, singers who "lose" their voices, and so forth. A third group consists of those who can be creative and often are, but only privately; they cannot reveal their work to others, except perhaps to a trusted few. The fear of public performance provides a potential for depression, a potential that can easily materialize.

Secret artists may become depressed when they observe others doing what they can do but are afraid to expose because of unrealistic fears. They sometimes defend themselves against depression by avoiding situations in which others reveal their creativity. Avoidance maneuvers only serve to constrict even further a creative life style and strengthen depressive tendencies.

Pleasure Inhibition and Depression

The inability to partake in fun and enjoy oneself free of anxiety about doing so is not uncommon. Individuals who experience guilt and anxiety about leisure and pleasure may avoid taking holidays, or become anxious before or during a vacation. In the main, they avoid having free time by immersing themselves in compulsive work. Social activities may be considered a waste of time, and weekends away from work may be anticipated with dread. Such individuals may deride those who enjoy parties, dancing, games, and vacations by calling them "childish"; mirthful, witty people who elicit laughter from others are "crazy."

The so-called killjoys are gloomily aware that they cannot have a good time, and they have a feeling of inferiority about their inhibitions. When possible, they try to avoid situations in which others are enjoying themselves, because they become depressed by their inability to participate. A sour approach to life masks an underlying chronic depression. Such a person may become overtly depressed on beautiful days because he associates them with pleasure. He tends to be much more comfortable on rainy or foggy days.

Depression and Sexuality

Sexually directed object relations begin with the development of the Oedipal phase, in the second and third years of life. Money, Hampson, and Hampson (7) demonstrated that gender identification is well established by the end of the second year. A very small number of deviants come to resist their biological gender identity; later in life some of them become candidates for transsexual surgery.

In my clinical experience, all such patients have been schizophrenic. Personal histories reveal profound anxiety and even conscious depression all through childhood, though their schizophrenic behavior creates a picture of oddness of personality rather than of depression. In adulthood the depression deepens, but becomes heavily masked by preoccupation with gender change. Those who undertake transsexual surgery arrive at the magical belief that a sexual crossover will solve all their problems. After surgery, a significant number of transsexuals become overtly and intensely depressed; some, in disillusionment and regret, have committed suicide.

In a much larger category are those who have problems about establishing gender confidence. If they are men, psychiatrists describe them as having doubts about their masculinity; if women, they are said to have problems about accepting their femininity. These patients suffer from a sense of gender inferiority. They often feel that their peers do not accept them, a situation that is especially painful during adolescence, but is by no means confined to that period.

A history of poor preadolescent relationships with children of their own sex is the rule rather than the exception among men and women who become homosexual. This early social disability is always recalled as having been exceedingly depressing. During childhood, defensive masking may include omnivorous reading and indulgence in rich fantasies.

The prehomosexual picture is much more clear-cut for boys than for girls; the sexual outcome for girls is less predictable. In both sexes, however, when there is impairment in gender identification there are feelings of inferiority and a sense of awkwardness and discomfort with peers of the same sex. When prehomosexual boys are compelled to participate in certain peer-group activities—for example, participation in gym classes or going to summer camp—they become very anxious and depressed.

Doubts about acceptability to others or feelings of inferiority about any personal characteristics are the ideational forerunners of depression, but a sense of gender inferiority is an especially sensitive trigger point for depression. Attempts to compensate for feelings of gender inferiority may consist of efforts to be superior to others and in general to gain admiration in one way or another. But even when outstanding successes are achieved, feelings of inadequacy, self-hatred, and self-contempt remain.

Sexuality is so fundamental to human existence that any serious impairment of normal heterosexual functioning is a basis for a depressive reaction. When most reasonably normal adolescents begin to date, pet, and perhaps attempt sexual intercourse, homosexual youths and sexually frightened heterosexuals start to withdraw into themselves or seek out others like themselves with whom they feel a kinship. Thus their sense of difference increases as they mature, further consolidating a self-image of unacceptability that keeps exacerbating their underlying depression. The excitement of homosexual acting out may cover a depression and bring at least short-term relief.

Homosexuals, in the main, think of themselves and their life style as "gay," though the gaiety more often than not is the mask of depression. One cannot, of course, assert that each and every homosexual is chronically depressed; however, when homosexuals become patients, depression is invariably an aspect of their psychiatric status. Observations of many nonpatient homosexuals have revealed that a chronic underlying depression is usually concealed beneath the superstructure of the gay facade.

The inability to form a meaningful, committed heterosexual relationship first becomes apparent in adolescence, though teenage romances are usually experimental and impermanent. Those adolescents who continue into their twenties and thirties without having established a significant love relationship are well aware of what they are missing, and they become depressed about it. Many attempt to make up in quantity for what they cannot experience in quality, and lovers appear and disappear as through a revolving door. The continuing change and adventure of discovery provide evanescent excitement, which may mask the depression that accompanies the loss of each relationship.

Some individuals are able to establish a love relationship

but have fears about marriage. In many such cases, the failure to marry is well rationalized by one or another philosophical argument. If the beliefs are held with deep conviction, there may be no depression about remaining unmarried; however, acute depression follows the loss of a beloved who does wish to and can marry. If resistance to marriage (2) persists into the fourth and fifth decades of life, the inhibitory constellation constitutes an ongoing basis for depression not only because long-term mating has not occurred, but because, to the large majority, the single state is tantamount to renouncing the experience of having children.

Depression occurs with great frequency in the postpartum period. The overt, severe reaction that sometimes manifests itself between the third and tenth days after giving birth is, however, uncommon. Hamilton (6) found that severe reactions occurred in only one birth per thousand. The psychiatric syndrome is usually that of a depression, and physicians are very familiar with the condition.

A much less familiar, less dramatic, subtler syndrome, common to men as well as to women, is the postpartum masked depression. A depressive response to parenthood may be characterized by insidious symptoms that on the surface seem unrelated to the birth of a child. One or both parents may begin to create the conditions of a deleterious change in their relationship. They may become increasingly detached and distant from each other, or give vent to outbursts of unprovoked hostility and unexplained irritability.

Frequently there is a change in sexual behavior. Frigidity, complete or partial, may appear in women who previously were orgastic; potency difficulties may appear in men who had rarely been impotent, if ever. Perhaps the least recognized symptom of a postpartum masked depression is the initiation of extramarital affairs by persons who were previously monogamous. Such liaisons may be fleeting, though in some cases a new lover provides a romantic rationalization for terminating a marriage that has now become threatening.

Sometimes symptoms are manifested in a change in the relationship to one or more of the other children. A parent who has been close and affectionate may become withdrawn with the birth of another child. Sometimes a parent will respond with detachment from the newborn, but conceal it under the rationalization that the baby is "still a vegetable." If the depression is shallow and quickly dissipates, the parent soon begins to feel interest and affection, "now that the baby is more interesting."

These and other reactions may appear at any time after the birth of a child, and sometimes may last for years. When gathering a psychiatric history on a patient who is a parent, careful investigation of the periods following the birth of children usually yield significant data.

Work, the pursuit and experience of pleasure, sexuality, marriage, parenthood—these are the major areas of human functioning. If the clinician finds major defects in one or more of these areas, even though the more obvious manifestations of depression may not be apparent, the presence of a masked depression is strongly indicated.

References

1. Bieber, I. Pathological Boredom and Inertia. *Amer. J. Psychother.* 5:215, 1951.
2. Bieber, T. B., and Bieber, I. Resistance to Marriage. In *The Marriage Relationship*, ed. S. Rosenbaum and I. Alger, New York: Basic Books, 1968.
3. Bieber, I. Sadism and Masochism. In *Handbook of Psychiatry*, ed. S. Arieti, vol. 3. New York: Basic Books, 1966.
4. Bieber, I. Disorders of the Work Function. In *Science and Psychoanalysis*, ed. J. Masserman, vol. 16. New York: Grune & Stratton, 1970.
5. Freud, S. Some Character Types Met With in Psychoanalytic Work. In *The Standard Edition of the Complete Psychological Works of Sigmund Freud*, ed. J. Strachey, vol. 14. London: Hogarth Press, 1957.

6. Hamilton, J. A. *Postpartum Psychiatric Problems.* St. Louis: C. V. Mosby, 1962.
7. Money, J.; Hampson, Joan G.; and Hampson, J. L. Imprinting and the Establishment of Gender Role. *A.M.A. Arch. Neurol. Psychiat.* 77:333, 1957.

7

Masked Depression and Suicide

ROBERT E. LITMAN
and CARL I. WOLD

Most previous descriptions of masked depression (4, 5) have been based on psychiatric consultations, and the reports have been addressed mainly to physicians. Here we shall report observations on depression, overt and masked, from the viewpoint of the Suicide Prevention Center, a crisis intervention service with special emphasis on emergency telephone counseling. Most SPC telephone counselors are volunteer workers with little medical experience and varying degrees of mental health training. After a brief but intensive training course in the principles and practice of crisis intervention for suicide prevention, they require only occasional psychiatric consultation and supervision for special problems. How do the "multivariant masks of depression" appear in this rather different, nonpsychiatric setting?

Discussions and comparisons of the issues involved in depression and suicide are often somewhat unclear because both depression and suicide represent complex, multifaceted collections of behaviors. We shall try to clarify the following points: What do we mean by suicide? Can suicide be prevented? What do we mean by depression? What is the relationship between suicide and depression? What do we mean by masked depression? How does masked depression affect suicide and suicide prevention?

Suicide and Suicide Prevention

Why do people commit suicide? There are dozens of well-documented motives (3). For the great majority of present-day American suicides, however, there is a prevailing pattern that agrees with common sense. Suicidal individuals feel painful, miserable, despairing. They have lost hope of feeling any better in the future, through either their own efforts or the efforts of other people. To the extent that death is the goal of the suicidal actions, it is sought because it offers surcease, escape, and relief. Most presuicidal persons reveal their perturbation and distress, though some potential suicides conceal or mask their feelings.

The possibility of suicide prevention through crisis intervention counseling is based on five principles: (a) Most individuals approach suicide with great ambivalence; (b) the state of high suicidal risk is time-limited and has many aspects of a psychological crisis; (c) while they are in a suicidal crisis, people tend to communicate their feelings through words, acts, and changes in behavior; (d) important factors intensifying suicidal states are loneliness, social isolation, and lack of communication; (e) if the suicidal, isolated individual can be recognized and identified, then the crisis intervention counselor may help to relieve the loneliness and social isolation, and callers may redevelop their normal nonsuicidal, ongoing behaviors. Essentially, then, a model for suicide prevention through crisis intervention has two components. First, there must be recognition of the high suicide risk person in his situation. Second, there must be an action response that results in some sort of change in the person and his situation to reduce the suicide risk.

A standard current classification of suicidal behaviors divides such behaviors into committed suicides, suicide attempts, suicidal communications in words, and suicidal communications through action without words. We estimate that each year there are currently in the United States 25,000 committed suicides, 250,000 suicide attempts serious enough to need medical attention, and about 250,000 recognizable suicidal communications serious enough to raise anxiety in persons who receive the communications. How many cases of nonverbal suicidal behavior are there? Most commonly unverbalized suicidal behavior communications take the form of depression and masked depression, and we are unable at this time to estimate their incidence in the general population.

Individuals who are recognizable potential suicides are identified in the following contexts: (a) after they make suicide attempts and are seen by physicians; (b) when their depressive behaviors are correctly diagnosed and fully considered by physicians and others; (c) when verbal communications (threats) are received and heeded by relatives, friends, business associates, clergymen, or others; (d) when the person calls the Suicide Prevention Center or someone else calls about him.

The chief function of the Suicide Prevention Center is to serve as a recognition station or screening service for the identification and evaluation of suicidal persons. People identified as suicidal at the Suicide Prevention Center vary greatly in the degree of predicted suicide risk. On the average, they commit suicide at a rate at least twenty times greater than that of the unselected population. Several studies have shown that the suicide rate for persons in touch with a suicide prevention service is about 1 percent on a follow-up of one to two years (6, 10). Various factors tend to be associated with a prediction of high suicide potential. One recent study lists the following factors: age; alcoholism; absence of irritation, rage, and violence in behavior; history of previous suicidal behavior and longer duration of current episode; male sex; unwillingness to accept immediate help; no previous inpatient psychiatric treatment; and depression-somatic type (8).

Anecdotal clinical experiences suggest that many

would-be suicides have been turned away from a fatal outcome through the intervention of friends, bystanders, and
various types of counselors. These suicides were delayed, but
whether they were prevented over the long run remains un-
proven. In the United States, suicide rates have remained
remarkably stable overall, despite the introduction of various
psychiatric and mental health approaches, including the crisis
intervention centers.

There is some suggestive evidence from England that
rather massive community intervention of a semireligious
"befriending" model sponsored by the Samaritans has had
some effect in lowering the suicide rate (1). Actually, there is a
great deal of suicide prevention built into the social system in
the United States in the form of the activities of medical personnel, social workers, religious counselors, self-help groups,
and various social clubs. In our experience, suicide prevention
through emergency intervention is difficult and time-
consuming. Improved methods for recognizing and treating
potentially suicidal individuals are much needed.

Suicide and Depression

Depression is a symptom complex that affects people of
various ages and personality types with a fairly wide range of
symptomatic behaviors. There seem to be several varieties of
depression. According to Lesse, "The term, depression, as
commonly used by laymen usually refers only to a mood
which in psychiatric circles is more specifically labeled as
sadness, dejection, despair, gloominess, or despondency" (5).
At the Suicide Prevention Center, depression has been defined by the patient's responses to four questions on a fifty-
item questionnaire, indicating somatic aspects (recently the
patient experienced somatic problems such as disturbed appetite, sleep disorder, or excessive fatigue), affective aspects
(recently the patient had feelings of hopelessness, helplessness, worthlessness, guilt, or shame), and social aspects (re-

cently the patient withdrew from personal contacts and/or constricted his social interest and activities). Each of these three items was rated "none or slight," "moderate," or "severe." The fourth question concerned the duration of depression, if present.

During the last ten years there have been a number of surveys of Suicide Prevention Center contacts. In 80 to 85 percent of patients, the affective aspects of depression are moderate or severe. Between 60 and 70 percent of the callers report somatic aspects of depression, and between 50 and 60 percent report social aspects of depression. Approximately 95 percent of the callers report some type of depression. From these data, we concluded that suicide and depression are intimately associated.

Another viewpoint on the relationship between suicide and depression is offered by retrospective studies of persons who committed suicide. When these studies were conducted by psychiatrists (9), about half of the suicides were diagnosed as "depressive reaction." In addition, about 25 percent were diagnosed as alcoholics, about 10 percent as schizophrenics, and the rest as suffering from unspecified psychiatric disorders. The suicides with histories of chronic psychiatric disorder, maladjustment, and suicidal tendencies (the alcoholics, schizophrenics, and others not specifically diagnosed) had strong components of depression. Retrospective studies by SPC staff members indicate that about half the people who committed suicide were suffering from acute depression. The other half manifested chronic disturbances in which the depression was more insidious and was frequently masked by other, more dramatic symptoms such as alcoholism, chronic physical illness, chronic hypochondriasis, and chronic social withdrawal. We conclude that there is a consistent relationship between suicide and depression. However, when individuals have been chronically perturbed, the depressive features may be masked by physical illness, alcoholism and drug abuse, hypochondriasis, schizophrenia, or severe social withdrawal and isolation.

Models for Depression

Both from a theoretical viewpoint and from a practical therapeutic viewpoint, depression is not a unitary entity. Thus it is understandable that in different contexts, quite different treatment approaches have been effective. For example, tranquilizing drugs that tend to harmonize or unite the divided self have often been more useful than antidepressants or energizers. Rather than a single core problem in depression, there seems to be a complex nexus of problems requiring a holistic and multitherapeutic approach.

A psychoanalytic model for depression was described by Sigmund Freud (2):

> If we turn to melancholia first, we find that the excessively strong superego which has obtained a hold upon consciousness rages against the ego with merciless violence. . . . What is now holding sway in the superego is, as it were, a pure culture of the death instinct and in fact, it often succeeds in driving the ego into death. . . . [p. 53].
>
> The fear of death in melancholia only admits of one explanation: that the ego gives itself up because it feels itself hated and persecuted by the superego, instead of loved. To the ego, therefore, living means the same as being loved—being loved by the superego. . . . It sees itself deserted by all protecting forces and lets itself die. Here, moreover, is once again the same situation as that which underlay the first great anxiety state of birth and the infantile anxiety of longing—the anxiety due to separation from the protecting mother [p. 58].

Our concept of depression is basically psychoanalytic (7). Helplessness and hopelessness are the most important elements. As a model we refer to the anaclitic depression of infants, both human and monkey, separated from their mothers. The infants are at first restless and irritable; they cry and seem to be seeking substitute mothers. In time this behavior is replaced by an immobilized, apathetic, withdrawn behavior that can eventually lead to death. By the bereaved, depressed behavior, the infant signals that unless help is given quickly, it will die. A communication of depression —especially when accompanied by a threat of suicide—is a powerful releaser of affective reactions from persons who receive the communication. The communication "I will die if you do not help me" and the response of help probably constitute one of the basic and fundamental human interactions.

Depression and Masked Depression

Masked depression occurs when the direct communication of anaclitic need is no longer adaptive. Either it is apparent that no one will respond to the appeal, or internalized attitudes now a part of the depressed individual's own self will not permit a direct communication or gratification of dependency needs. Any pattern of behavior which covers up or distracts attention from the helplessness and hopelessness may serve to mask depression.

Lesse (4) has directed attention to a specific syndrome of masked depression in women who present hypochondriacal and psychosomatic complaints to physicians. Possibly these patients feel more hopeful that help can be obtained through somatic complaints than through direct appeals.

At the Suicide Prevention Center almost all patients admit to some degree of depression. There are differences in emphasis, however. In some people there is a change in behavior noted by others (only partly masked) but denied by the subject, so that someone else has to call the center, and offers of help are often refused. Such people often admit to depressive illness in the form of somatic complaints, but they deny the feeling disorder. *Table 1* compares depression in 500 Suicide Prevention Center patients who were still living at follow-up after two years, with 52 SPC patients who committed suicide within two years. Note that affective depression is present in most clients and is not a predictor of suicide. Somatic depression, however, is a predictor of suicide. In combination, the absence of affective depression and presence of somatic depression is a high suicide risk predictor; this combination of items describes masked depression.

TABLE 1   Depression in SPC Suicides and Nonsuicides

Type of Depression	SPC Suicides (%)	SPC Nonsuicides (%)
Somatic	79%	65%
Affective	87	88
Social	52	49

Psychological autopsies (reconstructions of the deceased persons' life styles and character traits based on interviews with survivors) indicate that a majority of persons who committed suicide had previously communicated their suicidal intentions (9). In about 20 percent of committed suicides, the pre-existing state of potential suicide was not communicated, and therefore was not recognized or suspected. We feel that many cases of unrecognized potential suicide represent examples of masked depression. Depression is often unrecognized in adolescent males, in old people, in people in hospitals, and in people who have obscured their depression by bizarre actions or self-destructive behaviors. Often deaths are certified as equivocal or accidental because it seems that the self-destructive behavior per se has led to the person's death rather than the (masked) depression. Examples of self-destructive behavior are chronic abuse of drugs, extreme sexual masochism, and risk-taking automobile driving.

Masking of depression may be consistent, as in many superindependent, authoritative men, or it may be inconsistent. Sometimes depression is concealed from the physician but not from the family, or the reverse may be true. Sometimes only the Suicide Prevention Center counselor is told. Sometimes the masking occurs after a suicide attempt. Masking may be quite deliberate: "If I were to admit that, I would get depressed, so I never will admit it."

Masked Depression and Treatment

Concealment of depressed feelings works against the recognition of potential suicides, and masking of symptoms leads to premature termination of treatment contacts. Table 2 shows that depression decreases rapidly in SPC contacts who are called back routinely in one week. At call-back almost 90 percent say they feel better and about 50 percent are no longer significantly depressed. Surprisingly, however, the number who say they are significantly depressed decreases relatively little after the first week. At follow-up after two years, 39 percent were still depressed (see *Table 3*).

TABLE 2   Depression in SPC Contacts

Type of Depression		At First Call (%)	After One Week (%)
Somatic:	None	27%	60%
	Moderate	42	31
	Severe	31	9
Affective:	None	18	56
	Moderate	36	34
	Severe	46	10
Social:	None	37	72
	Moderate	38	22
	Severe	25	6

TABLE 3   Depression in SPC Contacts

Any Expression of Depression	At First Call (%)	After Two Years (%)
None	1%	61%
Moderate	62	29
Severe	37	10

In a follow-up study of Suicide Prevention Center patients after two years, Litman (6) reported that only 35 percent had described an acute stiuational distress, such as the recent death of a spouse or recent financial failure, as precipitating the suicidal state. Suicidal problems were chronic for 65 percent of the cases; they had had at least one previous suicidal episode before the current crisis that led to the contact with the center. At follow-up, moderate to high suicide risk ratings were more frequent among patients who had had no acute situational stress and were considered chronically suicidal. At the follow-up, these high suicide risk patients usually reported no improvement in their symptoms and their environment, or they had improved in one of these factors but not in the other. When the patient had been labeled an acute rather than a chronic suicidal problem, low suicide risk ratings were more frequent at follow-up. The implication was that acute cases responded well to crisis intervention, but patients who suffered from chronic suicidal problems stayed depressed, and were depressed at follow-up.

Wold (11) replicated the previous SPC follow-up study with a larger number of patients and expanded measures. It was found that 50 percent of patients experienced the onset of suicidal feelings longer than three months previous to their initial contact with the Suicide Prevention Center, 33 percent longer than one year earlier. A two-year follow-up of these patients revealed that about 50 percent remained suicidal three months or longer subsequent to their contact with us, and about a third remained suicidal for over one year. In addition, about a third of the patients followed reported that they had attempted suicide during the two-year period subsequent to their initial contact with the Suicide Prevention Center. Of those patients who were initially rated high suicide risks when they first contacted the center, 60 percent remained high suicide risks at follow-up two years later. Sixty-one percent of these patients were still depressed. On the other hand, 40 percent of those patients initially seen as high suicide risks were rated low risks on follow-up; few suffered severe symptoms and most were reintegrated with family and community resources.

We concluded that most of the more serious suicidal crises encountered at the SPC represented short-term emergencies superimposed on long-term careers of depression, sometimes recognized, sometimes masked. Most of the suicides in our follow-up studies occurred in persons who had chronic or recurrent depressive states associated with personal isolation and exhaustion of personal resources.

In response to the finding that the suicide danger period extended over many months and was greatest in persons with depressive states of long duration, the SPC began to maintain continuing relationships with persons rated as high suicide risks. Volunteer workers stay in touch with the subjects through personal interviews and telephone calls at a minimal frequency of once a week. We find that 100 percent of high-risk subjects are moderately or severely depressed at first contact with the center. Two weeks after the first contact only 50 percent say they are moderately or severely depressed, and thereafter this proportion remains about the same. Each week about half of the subjects report they are depressed, although the individuals who report depression are not always the same ones week after week. If the SPC relied exclusively on the client's statement that he is no longer depressed as the criterion for ending the helping relationship, many persons would be terminated prematurely.

Summary

Both in theory and in practice, there is a close relationship between suicide and the state of mind known by both lay people and psychiatrists as depression. When the relationship is not clear in an individual case, the concept of masked depression usually provides a reasonable explanation. In persons who are chronically perturbed, the depression is often masked by other, more dramatic symptoms, such as alcoholism, drug abuse, unstable personal relationships, antisocial acts, confusion, and social withdrawal and isolation. Sometimes people who suffer from chronic depressive states cover up the depression temporarily to provide an illusion of recovery.

At the Suicide Prevention Center, the presence of somatic aspects of depression combined with denial of the affective components of depression is a predictor of high suicide potential. Crisis intervention is a useful and valuable approach to individuals in an acute suicidal crisis; for more than half of the clients of the Suicide Prevention Center, however, depression and increased suicide potential are chronic problems. Possibly a program of ongoing relationship will provide some degree of protection against complete isolation and sudden unbearable depression.

References

1. Bagley, C. An Evaluation of Suicide Prevention Agencies. *Life-Threatening Behavior.* 1:4, 1971.
2. Freud, S. *The Ego and the Id.* In *The Standard Edition of the Complete Psychological Works of Sigmund Freud*, ed. J. Strachey. London: Hogarth Press, 1957.
3. Kubie, L. S. Multiple Determinants of Suicidal Efforts. *J. Nerv. Ment. Dis.* 138:1, 1964.
4. Lesse, S. Masked Depression: A Diagnostic and Therapeutic Problem. *Dis. Nerv. Syst.* 29:169, 1968.
5. Lesse, S. The Multivariant Masks of Depression. *Amer. J. Psychiat.* 124:11, 1968.
6. Litman, R. E. Suicide Prevention Center Patients: A Follow-up Study. *Bull. Suicidology* 6:12, 1970.
7. Litman, R. E. Sigmund Freud on Suicide. In *The Psychology of Suicide*, ed. E. S. Shneidman, N. L. Farberow, and R. E. Litman. New York: Science House, 1970.
8. Litman, R. E. Models for Predicting Suicidal Lethality. *In Proceedings of the Sixth International Congress on Suicide Prevention.* Los Angeles: International Association for Suicide Prevention, 1972.

9. Robins, E., et al. The Communication of Suicidal Intent: A Study of 134 Consecutive Cases of Successful (Completed) Suicide. *Amer. J. of Psychiat.* 115:8, 1959.
10. Wilkins, J. A Follow-Up Study of Those Who Called a Suicide Prevention Center. *Amer. J. Psychiat.* 127:2, 1970.
11. Wold, C. I. A Two-Year Follow-up of Suicide Prevention Center Patients. *Life-Threatening Behavior.* 3:171, 1973.

8

Apparent Remissions in Depressed Suicidal Patients: A Variant of Masked Depression

STANLEY LESSE

Apparent states of remission in depressed suicidal patients may be viewed properly as the most serious and at times the most complicated type of masked depression. This problem has received insufficient attention, particularly in regard to the manner in which it can be recognized and avoided. I am referring to patients who have histories of preoccupation with suicide or who have made suicide attempts and in whom the drive to self-destruction appears to have been ameliorated.

Frequency of Occurrence

These states of apparent remission in suicidal patients are not infrequent. In one study (25), more than 90 percent of such patients had an exacerbation ("reactivation phase") of suicidal drives after a period of apparent marked improvement. It was after hospitalization, when these patients were considered improved and discharged into their previous environments, that the suicidal drives reappeared. Shneidman and Farberow (26) reported that 75 percent of suicides had histories of suicidal gestures (threats or attempts). They pointed out that almost half of the persons who killed themselves after leaving a hospital did so within a period of ninety days.

Early in this century Bleuler discussed this problem and emphasized that this period of apparent remission was particularly dangerous because "the impulse to suicide is still present while the patient's energy is no longer very inhibited" (2). He was referring primarily to those patients who had severe depressions associated with a marked decrease in psychomotor activity. In some patients an increase in psychomotor activity may be falsely interpreted as a sign of real improvement, whereas in reality it may merely reflect the fact that the patient has mobilized himself for a suicide attempt. A similar phenomenon may be noted in depressed schizophrenic patients who may show increased psychomotor activity after hallucinatory voices have "advised" them to kill themselves. Fortunately, during the past fifteen years other observers have extended warnings similar to those first expressed by Bleuler (5, 12, 22).

While a hospital setting is advisable for many if not most suicidal patients, hospitalization alone does not automatically guarantee full protection against self-destructive acts. In a recent paper on suicide committed during hospitalization in a large psychiatric institution, Chapman (3) noted that 18 acts of self-destruction were reported among 23,006 admissions (78 per 100,000). Of these, eight occurred in the hospital proper. Ten, or more than one-half of the 18 suicides, took place while the patients were on authorized leave. In other words, these ten patients were judged to have demonstrated sufficient improvement to be permitted to leave the hospital for various periods of time.

None of the patients who killed themselves in the hospital had histories of suicide attempts prior to admission. This does not mean, however, that they did not have suicidal preoccupations before they were admitted to the hospital. Seven of the ten patients who killed themselves while on leave were actively suicidal at the time of admission, but were considered to have responded well to treatment. Four died while on three-day passes; four were on trial visits at home. None of the ten had ever attempted suicide while in the hospital. It is very likely that these patients had evidenced very subtle symptoms and signs of suicidal ideation and/or drives that were not perceived by the attending staff.

Clinical Observations

While exacerbations of suicidal drives commonly appear to be precipitous acts, they are no more acute than the original suicidal gestures. In reality they represent severely decompensated states, the full intensity of which has escaped effective clinical detection by the psychiatrist, the psychotherapist, his assistants, and the patient's family and friends. The reasons for these clinical diagnostic scotomata are manifold, as we shall see later in this chapter.

A meaningful appreciation of these factors demands a clear conceptual understanding of the psychodynamics and sociodynamics of suicide and a keen alertness to the subtle manifestations of various clinical entities. This includes an awareness of the multivariant faces of depression as outlined in earlier chapters. It also entails an appreciation of the earliest manifestations of the feelings of hopelessness and suicidal ideation which are the precursors of suicidal drives. The ability to differentiate between (a) a manipulative statement of intent to "kill myself" which poses no realistic danger and (b) a meaningful symptom or sign of a true incipient suicidal act is one of the most difficult differential diagnostic challenges.

Suicide attempts in general and suicide attempts by patients who have had apparent remissions from their initial suicidal states can be prevented in most instances, but only if the psychiatrist or nonmedical psychotherapist develops an understanding of the psychodynamic, psychosocial, and symbolic meanings of suicide. He must also have enough diagnostic acumen to recognize the nidus of future suicidal drives, and must learn to appreciate the subtle manifestations of decompensation in patients with histories of depression.

The problems that occur in the management of suicidal patients in apparent remission depend upon several factors: the therapist, the patient, the patient's milieu. On most occasions, aspects of all three factors are involved.

Factors Pertaining to the Therapist

Some psychiatrists and psychotherapists should not treat patients who have severe depressions, particularly patients who have suicidal ideas and suicidal drives. This may seem to be a very dogmatic and even brazen statement, but it is of fundamental importance in the management of severely depressed patients. Indeed, it raises the question of the proper selection of therapists for patients with various types of illnesses and from various milieus. Many therapists, for example, do not have great empathy or great understanding for schizophrenic patients; and not all therapists can treat patients from all socioeconomic and sociophilosophic milieus with equal effectiveness (18, 19).

In a recent paper, Stone recorded a survey of suicides that occurred in a teaching psychiatric institution while the patients were in active therapy (29). In most of these instances the suicide attempts could be attributed at least in part to the therapist's inability to manage severely depressed or suicidal patients. If a therapist has a depressive propensity in his own personality, a severely depressed patient, particularly one with suicidal ideas, is frightening and often overwhelming to him, and he becomes preoccupied with a crescendo reaction in his own depressive matrix. The hostility that is so prevalent in depressed patients, either covert or overt, poses a difficult problem for some psychotherapists and causes them to retreat from the patient at the very moment when he requires the greatest amount of ego support. In other instances, the therapist may develop a countertransference reaction and react with hostility in response to the patient's hostility. These reactions in themselves might precipitate a suicidal gesture.

Frequently the psychiatrist or psychotherapist who treats a suicidal patient is so relieved to record some degree of improvement that he may overestimate the true degree of improvement, a reaction paralleling that seen in some surgeons whose patients have survived massive or very delicate operations.

Similarly, psychotherapists who treat depressed patients with histories of prior suicidal gestures tend to forget that knowledge of the psychodynamics of a depression per se does not indicate the severity of the depression at any given moment. *The psychodynamic modus operandi may be the same in a mildly depressed patient as in a patient with intense suicidal drives* (14). A meticulous investigation of the patient's daily environmental adaptation, his symptoms, and his affective behavior is necessary before one can ascertain the intensity of a depression at any point in time. This is the keystone of suicide prevention.

Problems in the prevention of suicide may develop if the therapist does not comprehend the true meaning of preoccupations with or attempts at suicide. Suicidal behavior does not always have death as its goal (4). The suicidal gesture may be a means of verbal or nonverbal communication by the patient to a significant other person. It may be a cry for help, usually unconscious, by a patient who reacts as if he is not receiving the support, recognition, love, or understanding he feels he needs or is entitled to. The suicidal gesture may also be a communication of overwhelming feelings of guilt or guilt-linked rage (14). For example, in patients with the so-called ataki syndrome (30), death is rarely the aim of the suicidal gesture.

At times the psychiatrist or psychotherapist does not respond adequately. Litman (22) has pointed out that a patient's suicidal behavior may immobilize people close to him even though they have been forewarned. Hostile partners at times may will the death of potentially suicidal patients (24). Hostility on the part of a therapist toward a patient, particularly one with a long-standing, unyielding therapeutic problem, may blind the therapist to the urgency of the patient's psychic state.

Philosophical concepts held by some therapists may inhibit their ability to react to the emergency of an impending suicidal act (23). These philosophic concepts may be legalistic, such as that proposed by Szasz (28) to the effect that an individual must have the right to kill or injure himself. Other therapists have expressed the opinion that overconcern with regard to the possibility of suicide may interfere with effective therapy (1, 9). Still others have stated their indifference with regard to the patient's possible death. Litman has recorded that some authors have expressed the opinion that the therapist has no responsibility for a patient's death by suicide (22).

At times the therapist is unable to present an image that is sufficiently strong to provide the ego support for which the patient overtly or covertly appeals (8). I have already referred to this type of therapist as one who should not treat severely depressed or suicidal patients (14, 16). The treatment of severely depressed patients requires a type of "ego-transfusion" technique which some therapists are emotionally unprepared to administer.

We are most fortunate at this point in the history of psychiatric development to have multiple therapies that are effective for various types of depressed and suicidal patients. Yet the very availability of electroshock therapy, psychotropic drugs, and various types of psychotherapy may give the psychiatrist a false sense of security simply because he is "doing something" for the patient.

Electroshock therapy, while it is a very effective method of treating depressed patients with suicidal drives, occasionally may merely blunt or mask the suicidal impulses, particularly if the frequency or number of treatments is inadequate (20). As a result, the psychiatrist may prematurely lessen his careful vigil during the course of treatment. Also, as the organic mental syndrome secondary to electroshock therapy clears, residual self-destructive drives may mushroom rapidly and end in an attempt at suicide.

Psychotropic drugs also may result in a similar premature relaxing of clinical vigil (14). Some suicidal patients may demonstrate apparent remarkable remissions following the administration of tranquilizers or antidepressant drugs. At times this change may be purely a tenuous placebo reaction, with the suicidal drive being only superficially masked. Any relaxation of clinical precautions during the early phase of treatment of suicidal patients, no matter what technique is used, may result in a self-destructive act.

Undertreatment is the great danger in the management of any severely depressed patient. At times this undertreatment takes the form of delayed hospitalization. In other instances it is due to an insufficiency in the frequency or total number of electroshock treatments. In still other situations it is secondary to the use of homeopathic doses of antidepressant and tranquilizing drugs. Finally, suicide attempts have been precipitated by toxic side effects of psychotropic drugs.

Factors Pertaining to the Patient

There are many factors pertaining to the patient which should alert the observant psychiatrist to the danger of an exacerbation of suicidal drives. The patient may signal these symptoms and signs verbally or nonverbally. As I noted earlier, a balanced awareness of psychodynamic and psychosocial mechanisms and a sharp appreciation of the patient's daily behavior patterns as well as his symptom manifestations are necessary to diagnose an exacerbation of suicidal ideas and drives.

I have pointed out on many occasions (14, 21) that a patient is often overtly much less anxious and depressed after a suicide attempt than he was before it. In a macabre fashion, a suicide attempt that the patient survives serves as an excellent tranquilizer or antidepressant. Several psychodynamic explanations are possible. In some instances the attention given the would-be suicide by significant others may satisfy his hunger for recognition and support. These needs usually stem from early developmental patterns. In other cases the pain and danger the patient experiences may satisfy, in great measure, the guilt-linked retroflex rage that is so often a prominent factor in severely depressed persons.

One cannot emphasize too strongly that the therapist should not be deluded into believing that the pseudoremission that often occurs following a suicidal act is stable and clinically reliable. It is most important that the psychiatrist be fully aware that this type of remission does not represent a positive response to his therapeutic techniques, but usually is a transient, unstable placebo reaction.

Every person who has suicidal preoccupations or who has attempted suicide must be considered to have very tenuous ego capacities. This is especially true of schizoid or actively schizophrenic patients. Schizophrenic patients have a high potential for repeated attempts. They should be kept under close observation until there are very definite evidences, from symptomological and adaptational standpoints, of marked ego strengthening. I am of the firm opinion that actively psychotic schizophrenic patients with suicidal preoccupations should always be treated in a hospital setting. Further, during the initial period of hospitalization, direct round-the-clock observation is advisable until there are clear-cut evidences of amelioration of suicidal drives.

Patients with true histories of manic-depressive psychoses who rapidly change from a manic state to a state of depression must be watched very closely. Some may change from a manic state to a deeply depressed state dominated by suicidal drives within a very short period of time. This is another example in which the rate of change in affect and symptom manifestations plays an important clinical diagnostic role if one is to avoid the tragedy of a suicidal act.

A suicidal patient with an organic mental syndrome must be followed very closely, particularly if he has an obsessive-compulsive personality matrix. Some patients who demonstrate a strong need to dominate the environment prior to their illnesses, and who find themselves handicapped by fading memory or failing intellect, may react with a precipitous attempt at self-destruction.

Fluctuations in the intensity of an organic mental syndrome also deserve close observation. When patients with such a syndrome are in a state of marked confusion, they commonly experience a decrease in the intensity of depression and suicidal impulse. However, as they regain relative clarity and insight into the nature and magnitude of their problems, a suicidal gesture may be forthcoming. For these reasons, patients with organic mental syndromes who have suicidal preoccupations should be treated in a hospital setting. I would like to emphasize that the greatest problems pertaining to suicidal ideas and suicidal acts in patients with organic mental deficits are presented by patients in whom the organic mental deficit is not of severe proportions. One must be particularly cognizant of any history of intermittent endogenous depression in a patient with an organic mental deficit. In some instances the depressive phenomena are masked by hypochondriacal and psychosomatic disorders, as I have described in detail in other chapters. These patients are extremely intolerant of any limitation in intellectual functioning. Another group that does not tolerate even mild organic mental deficits includes individuals with obsessive-compulsive personality traits who have been very successful either vocationally or socially. Finally, there is still another general group, consisting almost entirely of men, who are intolerant of the decrease in sexual capacity which may be associated with mild organic mental deficits. Sexual limitations do not always accompany mild organic deficits, but when they do the patient's intolerance of the situation may be fraught with danger.

Depressed patients suffering from somatic illnesses often pose special problems. Much depends upon whether the physical ailment is realistically severe or severe only in the mind of the patient. If the patient has a chronic, markedly incapacitating process, such as may occur secondarily to malignancies, repeated myocardial infarctions, neurological deficits, and the like, the threat of further incapacity, persistent pain, or impending death may serve as a stimulus for accelerated suicidal preoccupations or another suicide attempt.

Some individuals with insight into their impending death may, as a last act of defiance, want to control their own fate. A suicidal act can be the crowning example of such control. These are individuals who have found it necessary to control themselves and their environments in a most rigid fashion.

When pain is a major factor, the patient's pain threshold should be evaluated carefully. Evidence of a low pain threshold may be a danger signal in one who has made previous suicidal gestures. This problem occurs usually in individuals whose physical illness is subacute or chronic, rather than acute.

One should be cognizant of the intensity of a depression that may occur in patients awaiting surgery. Depressed patients who anticipate that surgery may result in significant facial or body disfigurement, impairment of sexual image, or loss of sexual potency demand careful observation. To some women, for example, a radical mastectomy implies an unbearable loss of femininity. The loss of sexual potency following a prostatectomy or injury to the genitals may be overwhelmingly threatening to some men.

Women who have histories of depression, particularly those who have histories of suicidal ideas or acts, who have been advised to have a hysterectomy for the treatment of various types of pelvic pathology must be managed carefully. To some women the loss of the uterus represents an unbearable act of defeminization, even though they may not have any further desire for children. This "loss of image" has been so overwhelming to some women that impulsive suicidal acts have ensued, usually within a few months after the operation. Similarly, facial traumata, even of minor degree, in women with previous histories of severe depression accompanied by suicidal ideas or acts may be fraught with danger. Some of these patients may be unable to accept any change in their physical images.

A large body of literature has appeared during the past few years concerning the advisability of informing a patient as to the presence of a malignant disease or the threat of impending death. The physician must weigh these decisions most carefully. A patient with a history of severe depression, particularly one who has had suicidal thoughts or strong suicidal drives, usually should not be told. Other patients with strong ego capacities do best if they can continue to manage their affairs right up to the final moments of their lives. They must be selected carefully. Some psychiatrists and psychologists involved in the study of dying patients are overly fascinated with the concept of death, a preoccupation that may prove to be cruelly adverse for some hopeless patients. These problems most frequently occur among nonmedical psychotherapists who have had very little previous close contact with dying and death.

Alcohol is often a major problem for depressed patients. Chronic alcoholism may sometimes be viewed as an attempt to escape depression. Suicidal acts may occur when a chronic alcoholic sobers up after a bout of heavy drinking. In some debilitated drinkers, the continuous imbibing of alcohol in itself may be viewed as an attempt at suicide. Alcoholic excesses have also been associated with suicide attempts in a number of other ways, particularly in patients with prior histories of severe depressions. Precipitous suicide attempts have been made by male patients in whom an alcoholic debauch has resulted in sexual impotence. Finally, it is not a rarity for a patient with a history of severe depression to make a precipitous attempt at suicide after making a "public spectacle of himself," either vocationally or socially, under the influence of alcohol.

In any depressed patient the lowering of the ego boundaries which occurs with an excessive intake of alcohol may permit unbridled development of feelings of hopelessness, rejection, overwhelming retroflex rage, or a combination of these reactions. I have noted similar effects in patients who have taken lysergic acid diethylamine. In some patients who have taken LSD the massive repressive reactions were not noted until several weeks following the "trip." This delay between the taking of the drug and the final precipitous act is not due to a continued biochemical effect; rather it is secondary to a process of psychodynamic decompensation in which tenuous ego defense mechanisms progressively but inexorably decompensate.

Depressed patients who are habituated to amphetamines may also pose major problems, particularly if their drug supplies are curtailed. Patients with histories of previous attempts at suicide who are habituated to amphetamines should be hospitalized prior to any attempt to take them off the drug.

Barbiturate habituates pose a somewhat similar problem. Chronic insomniacs who have become dependent upon large dosages of barbiturates, particularly if they have histories of prior severe depressions accompanied by suicidal acts, are quite likely to suffer recurrent massive depressions and to repeat their attempts at suicide. Quite often an attempt is made following a sleepless night. Sometimes the suicidal act may actually be unintended; the patient, groggy from the barbiturates he has already taken, wakes up in the middle of the night and helps himself to some more. Barbiturate withdrawal in patients such as these must be managed very carefully, preferably in a hospital environment. Abrupt withdrawal may precipitate convulsions.

Patients who alternately take large amounts of amphetamines and barbiturates represent difficult therapeutic situations.

Depressed patients in whom homosexuality is a factor, either latent or overt, also pose massive treatment problems. Precipitous attempts at suicide have occurred following a homosexual act that has filled the patient with overwhelming guilt. Similarly, suicide attempts have been made by patients with latent homosexual drives when an overt homosexual act was considered imminent. Patients such as these usually have long histories of intermittent depressions, often accompanied by feelings of hopelessness and preoccupation with suicide. A number of those who have had homosexual panic attacks have had histories of Don Juanism; their compulsive chasing of women has been an attempt to deny the underlying homosexual drives.

I will mention only in passing the problem of suicide in patients with the "depression sine depression" (masked depression) syndrome, since this has been discussed in great detail in earlier chapters. In this syndrome the depression is masked by hypochondriacal complaints or psychosomatic disorders.

As I have previously noted, by the time patients with the masked depression syndrome were referred to me, more than 42 percent had suicidal ideas. Hochstetter found that 10 percent of his patients with this syndrome had strong suicidal drives (7). By the time these patients are seen by a psychiatrist, they have frequently already made plans for an active attempt at suicide. In Chapter 1, I pointed out that years usually pass between the onset of the syndrome and the time it is correctly diagnosed. Hypochondriacal or psychosomatic manifestations following the remission of a suicidal state may be considered residuals of the underlying depression.

Symptoms of Exacerbation of Suicidal Impulses

An exacerbation of suicidal impulses may be signaled in various ways. A shift in affect, particularly if sudden and persistent, should be considered suspect. A depressed patient may appear calmer and less depressed than usual if he has come to the decision to take his life, or if he has chosen the specific technique he will use to kill himself. A hallucinating schizophrenic patient may appear calmer if his voices have told him to commit suicide. On the other hand, many patients react with increased anxiety and depression as they contemplate a suicide attempt.

Patients who have endogenous depressions in which the level of psychomotor activity has been markedly depressed must be observed closely if a sudden increase in psychomotor activity occurs. While this may indicate improvement, it may also indicate that the patient has made a decision to commit suicide. In contrast to those patients who have endogenous depressions, patients who initially demonstrate an agitated type of depression and then evidence rapid decrease in psychomotor activity must be watched very carefully. While this change may represent improvement, in certain instances it may be a forewarning of further decompensation with accompanying suicidal ideas.

The retroflex rage mechanism is of prime importance in many patients who attempt suicide (14). An increase in rage mechanisms, as indicated by the patient's behavior or dream material, could be forewarning of an impending suicidal act.

Increasing defiance, particularly if accompanied by great bravado, may be a last expression of angry protest before a self-destructive act. Increasing discontent may also be a communication of the need for increased recognition and support; ironically, patients with this problem often alienate their physicians, their families, and members of the hospital staff by their persistent nagging. Thus they are rejected by the very people upon whom they feel dependent for life itself.

Acting out by a suicidal patient with a history of impulsive antisocial activity under stress should be suspected as a harbinger of a suicide attempt. A homocidal rage is often followed by a suicide attempt. Schizophrenic patients, in catatonic excitement, may carry out sudden destructive acts, then turn their destructive behavior against themselves.

A residual depressed affect or expression of hopelessness obviously indicates a nidus upon which a severe depressive syndrome may develop. Other symptoms, such as marked insomnia or anorexia with substantial weight loss, may indicate that depression has not lifted entirely.

An exacerbation of a depression with suicidal drives is often heralded by changes in dream patterns (6, 10, 22). Dreams may be very direct in their manifest content, or their meanings may be masked by complicated symbolism. In one of my patients, a recurrence of suicidal drives was heralded by a dream in which he was lying quietly at the bottom of a lake. He first became consciously aware of his suicidal preoccupation one week following his dream. In a more direct fashion, another patient dreamed of seeing himself lying in a coffin. In reporting this dream the following morning, he became sharply aware that he had had vague suicidal thoughts during the previous few days.

A marked increase in guilt-linked anger may also be heralded by a dream. In some instances this too may be a precursor of suicidal ideation.

Factors Related to the Patient's Milieu

From a broad standpoint, the patient's socioeconomic and sociophilosophic background determines in great measure the type of symptoms and symbolism that may indicate a mounting depressive crisis with impending suicide. Environmental frustrations or stresses that are likely to have massive impact upon a depressed patient in one culture may have relatively little significance in another. In Japan, for example, the loss of a job may signify much more than merely the necessity of finding another place of employment. Traditionally, one does not change jobs in Japan; lifelong loyalty is expected of both employee and employer. The loss of one's job thus carries with it drastic loss of face, which may be a psychic trauma of such unbearable magnitude that the victim feels he has no choice but suicide.

Among other environmental factors that may significantly affect the suicidal patient in an apparent state of remission is a routine hospital staff rotation or the departure of the patient's psychiatrist for a vacation. Such a change might lead to a rapid exacerbation of suicidal drives if the psychiatrist had become the significant other person in the patient's life.

When a patient is treated in a hospital, the psychotherapist and the hospital itself become partners in the therapeutic regime. This is particularly important in the treatment of patients with histories of prior suicidal behavior, for any act that the patient could interpret as rejecting or punitive could lead to a depressive crisis and a precipitous suicidal act.

Psychotherapists working in hospitals often are deluded by the security of their environment and unconsciously feel that they can focus upon psychodynamic mechanisms to the exclusion of a meticulous investigation of the patient's day-by-day psychopathologic and behavioral changes. This feeling can be exceedingly dangerous for patients who have prior histories of suicidal acts—indeed, for any severely depressed patient. As I have noted before, a *detailed understanding of a patient's psychodynamic mechanism does not indicate the severity of the depressive reaction at any given moment*, and particularly it does not indicate the intensity of a patient's self-destructive drives. This type of clinical blindness is one of the main reasons for suicidal acts when patients are on weekend home leaves. If the staff therapist knows his patient as well as he should, such an act can almost always be prevented.

As I have already noted, 90 percent of suicides have an exacerbation or reactivation of suicidal drives after a period of marked improvement, and almost half of the people who kill themselves after leaving a hospital do so within ninety days. One of the reasons for this relatively short period of time between hospital discharge and a reactivation of suicidal drives is the fact that many hospital psychiatrists and psychotherapists fail to differentiate between the stresses that the patient must face in the hospital and those he is likely to face outside the hospital. *No matter how well a patient does in the sanctum sanctorum that is the hospital environment, he must be considered an unknown quantity as soon as he steps outside the hospital door.*

All patients with prior histories of suicide attempts ideally should be seen twice a week, and at the very minimum once a week, for several months following discharge from the hospital. In addition, if members of the patient's family are cooperative and not hostile toward the patient, they should be asked to come once a month with the patient in conjoint session. This is advisable because patients who have made previous suicide attempts may deny any evidence of an exacerbation of depression during infrequent visits following discharge from the hospital.

Situational problems, such as financial debts or losses or rejection by a lover, friend, or relative, may also precipitate suicide attempts. Returning too quickly to vocational or social responsibilities of overwhelming magnitude may likewise lead to massive exacerbation of suicidal drives. The therapist must constantly monitor the amount of vocational and social stress to which the patient is exposed, and as much as possible help the patient to avoid excessive responsibilities. In other words, it is wise to have the patient accept external pressures gradually, for failures at this phase of therapy may overwhelm the patient's relatively fragile ego capacity.

Similarly, patients who are "punished" by being demoted after an absence from work due to illness may experience the demotion as an overwhelming rejection. This in itself has sometimes led to a massive exacerbation of depression with a resultant suicidal gesture. It is well to repeat that a therapist must not permit such patients to assume obligations that are beyond the ego capacities they have firmly demonstrated.

Since the advent of the antidepressant drugs, more patients with suicidal ideation can be treated on an ambulatory basis. These antidepressant drugs, in combination with specially designed psychotherapeutic techniques, have been demonstrated to be effective alternatives to ambulatory electroshock therapy (14).

However, modesty is the order of the day in dealing with this type of patient, for unfortunately the unpleasant reality is that no one psychiatric technique or combination of procedures has been shown to be more successful than any other in the prevention of recurrent suicidal acts (27).

When the psychiatrist or psychotherapist cannot adequately protect the patient from overwhelming environmental stresses, the therapist must be prepared to hospitalize the patient if no other effective means of beneficial environmental manipulation is possible. Hospitalization or rehospitalization must also be considered if such a patient evidences symptoms or signs of exacerbation of an underlying depression. Psychiatrists who do not have readily available emergency hospital facilities should not treat this type of patient.

A patient with suicidal ideas always represents an urgent medical problem. A patient with suicidal drives constitutes a medical emergency comparable in severity to any and all crisis situations in organic medicine. An awareness of the subtle and overt manifestations of apparent remissions in suicidal patients should be an integral part of the clinical acumen of all persons who deal with sick individuals, whether the observer is a psychiatric or nonpsychiatric physician, a psychologist, a nurse, or a social worker.

References

1. Basescu, S. The Threat of Suicide in Psychotherapy. *Amer. J. Psychother.* 19:99, 1965.
2. Bleuler, E. *Textbook of Psychiatry*, p. 492. New York: Macmillan, 1924.
3. Chapman, R. F. Suicide During Psychiatric Hospitalization. *Bull. Menninger Clin.* 29:35, 1965.
4. Farberow, N. L.; Shneidman, E. S.; and Litman, R. E. The Suicidal Patient and the Physician. *Mind* 1:69, 1965.
5. Friedman, P. Some Considerations in the Treatment of Suicidal Depressed Patients. *Amer. J. Psychother.* 16:379, 1962.
6. Gutheil, E. *The Handbook of Dream Analysis.* New York: Liverwright, 1951.

7. Hochstetter, W. Depressive Syndromes. *Proc. Virchow Med. Soc. N.Y.* 18:116, 1959.
8. Jensen, V. W., and Petty, T. A. Fantasy of Being Rescued in Suicide. *Psychoanal. Quart.* 27:327, 1958.
9. Kubie, L. S. Multiple Determinants of Suicidal Attempts. *J. Nerv. Ment. Dis.* 138:3, 1964.
10. Lesse, S. Experimental Studies in the Relationship Between Anxiety, Dreams, and Dream-like States. *Amer. J. Psychother.* 13:440, 1959.
11. Lesse, S. The Evaluation of Imipramine Hydrochloride in the Ambulatory Treatment of Depressed Patients. *J. Neuropsychiat.* 1:246, 1960.
12. Lesse, S. Combined Use of Tranylcypromine and Trifluoperzine in the Ambulatory Management of Patients with Agitated Depressions. *N.Y. J. Med.* 61:1898, 1961.
13. Lesse, S. Psychotherapy and the Danger of Suicide. *Amer. J. Psychother.* 15:181, 1961.
14. Lesse, S. Psychotherapy in Combination with Antidepressant Drugs. *Amer. J. Psychother.* 16:407, 1962.
15. Lesse, S. Placebo Reactions and Spontaneous Rhythms in Psychotherapy. *Arch. Gen. Psychiat.* 10:497, 1964.
16. Lesse, S. The Technique of Combined Psychotherapy–Antidepressant Therapy in the Treatment of Severely Depressed Patients. *Compr. Psychiat.* 7:224, 1966.
17. Lesse, S., and Mathers, J. Depression sine Depression (Masked Depression). *N.Y. State J. Med.* 68:535, 1968.
18. Lesse, S. The Influence of Socioeconomic and Sociotechnological Systems on Emotional Illness. *Amer. J. Psychother.* 22:569, 1968.
19. Lesse, S. Obsolescence in Psychotherapy: A Psychosocial View. *Amer. J. Psychother.* 23:381, 1969.
20. Lesse, S. Management of Suicidal Patients. In *Current Psychiatric Therapies*, ed. J. Masserman, vol. 8. New York: Grune & Stratton, 1968.
21. Lesse, S. Apparent Remissions in Depressed Suicidal Patients. *J. Nerv. Ment. Dis.* 144:291, 1967.
22. Litman, R. E. Immobilization Response to Suicidal Behavior. *Arch. Gen. Psychiat.* 81:360, 1959.
23. Litman, R. E. When Patients Suicide. *Amer. J. Psychother.* 19:570, 1965.

24. Meerloo, J. A. Suicide, Menticide and Psychic Homicide. *Arch. Gen. Psychiat.* 81:360, 1959.
25. Moss, L. M., and Hamilton, D. M. Psychotherapy in the Suicidal Patient. *Amer. J. Psychiat.* 112:814, 1956.
26. Shneidman, E. S., and Farberow, N. L. Clues to Suicide. In *Clues to Suicide,* ed. E. S. Shneidman and N. L. Farberow, pp. 5–12. New York: McGraw-Hill, 1957.
27. Stengel, E., and Cook, N. G. *Attempted Suicide: Its Social Significance and Effects.* Maudsley Monograph no. 4. London: Chapman & Hall, 1958.
28. Szasz, T. S. *Law, Liberty, and Psychiatry.* New York: Macmillan, 1963.
29. Stone, A. A. Suicide Precipitated by Psychotherapy. *Amer. J. Psychother.* 25:18, 1971.
30. Trautman, E. Suicidal Fit. *Arch. Gen. Psychiat.* 5:76, 1961.

PART 2

9

Masked Depression in Children and Adolescents

JAMES M. TOOLAN

While the subject of masked depression and depressive equivalents is of great importance for adult psychiatry, it is even more significant for child psychiatry. Clinicians have been slow to recognize that depression in adults can be disguised in various ways, but they are well versed in the usual fashion in which it is manifested.

The situation is quite different with regard to children and adolescents. It is only recently that the subject of depression in youngsters has been discussed at all (31), and even today some still contend that depression does not exist in children. Kanner's (15) *Child Psychiatry* and the first edition of the *American Handbook of Psychiatry* (3) do not even mention the topic. Beck (4), in an exhaustive monograph on depression, does not refer to depression in children and adolescents, while Klerman (19), in a recent review of clinical research on depression, does not cite a single paper on the topic.

Following a review of the literature on depression in children, Rie (24) states:

An examination of the implications for child psychopathology of the dynamics of adult depression, including the roles of aggression, orality, and self-esteem, generates serious doubt about the wisdom of applying the concept of depression to children. . . . There may be room to believe that the fully differentiated and generalized primary affect characterizing depression, namely despair or hopelessness, is one of which children—perhaps prior to the end of the latency years—are incapable.

Recently several authors have come to a different conclusion. I have argued (31) that "we have to cease thinking in terms of adult psychiatry and instead become accustomed to recognize the various manifestations by which depression may be represented in younger people." It is of great interest that prior to mid-adolescence (approximately fourteen years of age) we rarely encounter the clinical picture of depression as we know it in adults. Rather we see it disguised and masked by various depressive equivalents. Thus unless we learn to recognize masked depression in children and young adolescents, we will continue to believe erroneously that depression is not encountered in younger persons.

As early as 1946 Spitz and Wolf (28) described anaclitic depression—which would be better labeled infantile depression—after studying a group of institutionalized children. They observed some who were withdrawn and had symptoms such as insomnia, weeping, loss of weight, and retardation of development. In a few cases this state progressed to stupor and death. Spitz and Wolf attributed this condition to separation of child from mother during the child's sixth, seventh, and eighth months. Goldfarb (14) described intellectual and social retardation in a group of institutional children who were deprived of close ties with their mothers or with mother substitutes.

Bowlby (7) has described the effect of maternal deprivation in the young child, especially during hospitalization. He notes three stages that the child undergoes when separated from the mother: protest, despair, and detachment. Bowlby was alert to the fact that often the stage of detachment is considered by the hospital staff to be a sign that the child is beginning to adjust to his situation, whereas in reality he is profoundly disturbed. Bowlby prefers the term "mourning" to describe this condition; I consider "depression" more suitable.

Keeler (17), in describing the reaction of eleven children to the death of a parent, noted that though they were depressed, they often masked their true feelings, and suggested the assistance of psychological testing to help determine just what their true feelings were.

Agras (2) believes that an underlying depression is often responsible for so-called school phobias. He uses the term "depressive constellation" to denote a tendency toward depression in both mother and child, and states, "It is suggested that these children show a syndrome comprising depressive anxiety, mania, somatic complaints, phobia, and paranoid ideation. This syndrome is close phenomenologically to the depressive disorders of adults." Campbell (9) has also suggested that many children with school phobias are depressed, but he believes they are manifesting symptoms of a manic-depressive psychosis. Statten (29) has described homesickness in children as "a symptom complex usually associated with separation from home, which reflects an underlying depressive state to which a child is attempting to adjust."

Sperling (27) and I (31) have spoken of equivalents of depression in children. We have both emphasized that the manifestations of depression are quite different from those observed in adults, and that anorexia, ulcerative colitis, and insomnia may be such equivalents. We both note that the mothers of such children are often depressed. Ling (21) has described headache as a symptom of depression in ten out of twenty-five children with the presenting complaint of headache. He also noted a strong family history of depression in his cases.

The Latency-Age Child

The latency-age child displaces depressive feelings with behavioral disorders such as temper tantrums, disobedience, truancy, running away from home, accident-proneness, masochism (as indicated by the child who manages to get beaten up by other children), and self-destructive behavior (31). The youngster is convinced that he is bad, evil, unacceptable. Such feelings lead him into antisocial behavior, which in turn only further reinforces his belief that he is no good. The youngster will often feel inferior to other children—ugly perhaps, or stupid. All of these symptoms should be considered as evidence of depression.

Joe, a nine-year-old boy, is a good example. He was described as being disobedient at home and school, antagonistic to his parents, and frequently involved in fights with other children. Previously a good student, he now showed little interest in his schoolwork and had begun to play truant. Joe's parents had been divorced about two years before I first saw him, and he had been living with his mother. Both parents stated that Joe had changed markedly since the divorce. Previously, they said, he had been a happy, outgoing child with many interests, who got along well with everyone. Since the breakup of the home, they both felt he was angry with them, and was expressing his anger by his unacceptable behavior.

It was true that Joe was angry with his parents, and he expressed such feelings easily at the beginning of therapy. He resented both of his parents and believed that they had deserted him. As treatment progressed, other feelings emerged. Joe began to speak of being unloved by his parents, whereas previously, as an only child, he had felt he was the center of their universe. Even though they had carefully explained that the divorce was due to their inability to live together without constant discord, Joe suspected otherwise. He was convinced that his father wouldn't have left home if he had really loved

him. It was only when these feelings were expressed and resolved that Joe's behavior began to improve.

The Early Adolescent

In preadolescence and early adolescence we see a picture similar to that described for the latency-age group. Boys often find it very difficult to face and express their true feelings, especially if they regard them as evidence of weakness. Youngsters will often utilize denial as a mechanism for avoiding depressive feelings.

Consider, for example, Michael, a twelve-year-old boy whom I saw at the request of his mother. She complained that he was obese, a compulsive eater, enuretic, fecally incontinent, and troublesome at home, where he constantly picked on his two younger sisters. She added that he was very disturbed in his relationships with other children. He refused to participate in their activities, and he always pointed out their scholastic inadequacies (he was a superior student himself).

I found Michael to be a sullen, negativistic fat boy. He stoically maintained he had no problems and didn't wish to see me. At the mother's insistence, however, he continued in therapy. For weeks the sessions consisted of brief recitals of the superficial events of the week, always phrased in the most optimistic terms: "Everything is fine." Chess was our only avenue of contact. Very gradually he began to reveal himself. He really didn't have any friends; he would like to compete in sports but he wasn't good enough.

Each step forward would be followed by two steps backward as he reverted to denial of any difficulties. He realized he was overweight, but there was nothing to be done about it—he couldn't control his appetite. Maybe he wet his bed and soiled his pants, but not often, and less than before (totally untrue). Eventually he could discuss his great shame over such infantile behavior and admit how horrible he felt when everyone called him Stinky. As time passed, he began to mention that he had never been like the other fellows; he couldn't remember ever being happy. He often fantasied being dead, and everyone being sorry for the way they had treated him.

Then for the first time he began to talk of his parents: how close he was to his mother, how he could get anything he wanted from her. Slowly his attitude to his father emerged. The father, a successful dentist, was a cold, aloof, hostile person who seldom was at home, and on these occasions constantly berated his wife and son. He called Michael lazy, fat, incompetent, a baby. He would beat him, bribe him—all to no avail. Eventually the boy's hostile, angry feelings, so long repressed, came into view. He would like to kill his father but was terrified of him. Why couldn't he and his mother live by themselves?

As these feelings were explored, the youngster changed dramatically. He lost twenty-five pounds, stopped wetting and soiling, began to relate to his peers, and for the first time tried out for a team and made it, much to his amazement. That summer at camp (which incidentally accepted him back only at my urgent request) he surprised everyone by his friendly, outgoing behavior and received a citation as the most improved camper.

The Adolescent

In the depressed adolescent one often encounters a set of symptoms generally recognized as depressive equivalents: pervasive boredom, restlessness, a frantic seeking of new activities, a reluctance to be alone. Even though all adolescents exhibit some of these symptoms, the persistence of such traits indicates pathology. The feelings of emptiness, isolation, and alienation so often described by teenagers can be indicative of depression.

Many so-called hippies, by banding together, hope to

find support and relief from these distressing feelings, and attempt to escape further by the excessive use of drugs such as marihuana, mescaline, amphetamines, and LSD. Sexual promiscuity, especially on the part of girls, is often a thinly disguised attempt to avoid feelings of depression, loneliness, and helplessness. Illegitimate pregnancies are often sought either consciously or unconsciously for the same reason.

A young girl who became a patient of mine is only too typical. She was admitted to the hospital at her own request because she was afraid she might kill herself. An attractive youngster, she appeared older than her fifteen years. Her history revealed that she had been a behavior problem since the age of seven. She had had frequent fights with other children, played truant from school, was disobedient at home. She was a bright child but her academic record was very erratic. At fourteen she ran away from home to live in Greenwich Village. There she enjoyed a hippie existence for a short time, indulged in long talking sessions, mood sessions, and poetry readings. Constantly dissatisfied, she attempted to find satisfaction by promiscuous sexual activity. As time passed she became increasingly depressed. She tried marihuana, but it provided only temporary relief. Suicide appeared the only solution, but upon the advice of friends she decided to give psychotherapy a trial before making a final decision. And so she came to me.

During our interviews she became aware of a deep sense of loneliness, depressions, and despair. She realized that she had had occasional awareness of these feelings before, but until recently she had been able to ward them off by frenetic behavior. As therapy progressed, she was able to give up her pseudosophisticated facade and behave more like a normal fifteen-year-old.

The Tired Teenager

The bored teenager frequently complains of being tired.

He alternates between overwhelming fatigue and inexhaustible energy. Undoubtedly some of this fatigue is physiological, the result of the very rapid growth processes taking place at this time. We should always be suspicious, however, when a physically healthy youngster's fatigue appears to be out of proportion to the energy he expends and when it interferes with his normal activity. Careful note must also be taken when the adolescent complains of being excessively tired upon awakening in the morning after an adequate amount of sleep. Of course, this is a common symptom in adult patients suffering from depression. Hypochondriasis and bodily preoccupation must also frequently be considered evidence of depression.

I saw Simon, aged twelve, at the suggestion of his pediatrician. The pediatrician was concerned because the youngster was constantly complaining of various physical ailments, which after examination proved to be either grossly exaggerated or totally imaginary. A slender, frail child, Simon came willingly to the interview, eager of discussing his problems. He said that he had been worried about his health for the past two or three years. Initially he would become frightened whenever he had a minor physical illness, such as an upper respiratory infection. He was afraid he would become seriously ill and die. As time passed he began to worry over more trivial matters, such as a muscle cramp or slight feelings of fatigue. During the past month he had become convinced that he had leukemia. This fear had begun after a class in biology at school in which the teacher described the symptoms of leukemia. He said that since that time he had had trouble falling asleep and felt anxious most of the day.

Simon was an only child whose father had been killed in a plane crash shortly after his birth. His mother had never remarried and remained devoted to the memory of her dead husband. Simon grew up closely attached to his mother and preoccupied with the image of his dead father. He had no close friends, although he maintained a superficial acquaintance with one or two boys younger than himself. As therapy progressed, it became evident that this youngster had introjected the image of a dead father whom he both idolized and hated for "deserting" him. Strong incestous ties to the mother gave rise to guilt feelings. He realized during therapy that he had seldom been happy, that he had always expected to die young (obvious identification with the dead father). As treatment progressed, the somatic preoccupation was displaced by a frank depressive reaction, which could then be handled directly.

The Dropout

Many depressed youngsters complain of difficulty in concentration. In fact, this is one of the chief presenting complaints to the school physician and should always be taken seriously, or within a very short time an otherwise capable student may fail in school, to the amazement of parents and faculty alike. Confronted with such a problem, the conscientious student will often spend long hours on his studies with little benefit. He will see others achieving better grades with much less effort and will soon become convinced that he isn't capable of mastering his work. Such a conclusion can only diminish his already weakened self-esteem and lead to further depression.

Nicoli (23), after studying a series of college dropouts, concludes that "depression is by far the most frequent and the most significant causal factor in the decision to interrupt or terminate one's college experience." He believes the depression is due to an:

> awareness of a disparity between the ideal self as a uniquely gifted intellectual achiever and the real self as one of thousands of outstanding students struggling in a threateningly competitive environment. This awareness, gradual or abrupt, results in the clinical picture frequently observed in the dropout; feelings of lassitude, inadequacy, hopelessness, low self-esteem and inability to study.

The Delinquent

Denial and acting out are frequently encountered in adolescents. In such youngsters acting out may lead to serious delinquent behavior. Kaufman (16) has written that "a crucial determinant [in delinquency] is an unresolved depression, which is the result of the trauma which these children have experienced." He adds, "We consider the delinquent acts of taking and doing forbidden things or expressing resentment and hostility to the depriving world as the child's pathologic method of coping with his depressive nucleus."

Burks and Harrison (8) view the aggressive behavior of many delinquents as a method of avoiding feelings of depression. Kaufman (16) has also emphasized that the delinquent suffers from a severly impoverished self-image and a profound emptiness of ego comparable to the emptiness of the schizophrenic ego. A sixteen-year-old patient of mine is an example of such delinquent activity masking depression.

I saw Richard at the urgent request of his parents, who had become alarmed at evidence of increasingly delinquent behavior on his part. He had recently been suspended from school for striking a teacher. The family lived comfortably in a middle-class suburb of New York City. Richard, the elder of two children, had always been somewhat small for his age—a matter of deep concern to him. A poor athlete, he tended to shun all competitive sports. He was extremely shy and frightened in the presence of girls, whom he avoided even though he was obviously interested in them.

The parents noted that about six months previously he had lost all interest in his schoolwork and in his usual friends, and had begun to associate with a delinquent street gang from a distant neighborhood. At this time he evidenced a distinct personality change. All previous signs of anxiety disappeared and he appeared cocky and self-assured. His parents had recently become aware that he had engaged in several gang fights, during one of which he had been stabbed with a knife.

When I first saw him, Richard looked like a typical hoodlum: cigarette hanging out of the corner of his mouth, black leather jacket, tight-fitting black dungarees. He was glib and expressed vast disinterest in the whole procedure. He had no problems except his parents, who were prejudiced against his new friends. The only help he needed was to get them to leave him alone. He hated school and was happy that he had been suspended. He was pleased to talk about his gang, and bragged about its delinquent activities and his own prowess in fighting. I asked him if he ever became frightened during gang fights and was surprised when, after much hesitation, he replied, "Yes, I'm afraid I'll lose control and kill someone." He was losing his temper with increasing frequency, he said; he had not intended to strike the teacher, but the teacher had pushed him and he lost his head. I remarked that perhaps this was important, and also that it would obviously interfere with his plans to pursue the Navy career he had been planning for several years.

As therapy progressed, it was readily apparent that Richard was a frightened, anxious, chronically depressed boy. He recalled how unhappy he had been before he joined the gang, how inferior he had felt in comparison with other boys, how scared he had been in the presence of girls, how stupid he had appeared at school, how worried that he would never amount to anything.

After he joined the gang, and by means of vicarious identification with the other members' supposed strength, he had felt different. "For the first time in my life I felt alive. I was a different person. I no longer worried, wasn't afraid of anyone." He began to go out with girls and felt equal to the social challenge.

As therapy continued, a crucial period came when he became aware of the significance of the gang in relieving his previous depression. He wanted to quit the gang but was afraid of the consequences—that he might again become depressed. He finally did quit the gang, and he did become depressed again, but now his depression could be properly handled.

Recognizing the Symptoms of Masked Depression

Many adolescents and adults engage in sexual acting out as a method of relieving their depressive feelings. Such a person frenetically seeks contact with another human being by means of sexual intercourse, the only method of relating that he knows. Quite often, as in the case of the alcoholic, this activity only produces further depression and guilt, which once again he attempts to relieve by further sexual acting out.

Masked depressive reactions continue throughout adolescence and adulthood. In addition, however, by mid-adolescence one not infrequently encounters the clinical picture of depression as classically seen in adults. The depressed adolescent often presents a confused self-identity—a symptom not usually seen in adult depressives. He will describe himself as unworthy and unlovable; he will complain of feeling isolated and alienated. He often resents his parents while at the same time he may be overly dependent upon them. Separation from home and parents due to departure for college or military service will often lead to profound homesickness and depression. This separation from home and parents, though often eagerly desired, is all too often experienced as a loss of love.

If one reviews the histories of depressed adolescents, one discovers that many of them exhibited the signs and symptoms of masked depression prior to the onset of their depressive symptoms. This fact would appear to support the thesis that such symptoms are manifestations of depression in younger persons. It is of interest that the symptoms of masked depression usually disappear when the overt clinical picture of depression develops.

I view depression as an affect that can be present in any diagnostic category—adjustment reaction, neurosis, psychosis, or organic brain damage.

The recognition of depression in children and adolescents can be facilitated by the study of dreams and fantasy material.

Depressed children will often dream of dead persons beckoning them to join them in the other world. Often in their dreams they picture themselves as being attacked and injured. On other occasions their dreams will depict bodily emptiness or dissolution, and loss of either inner or outer parts of the body. Like Kaufman (16), I interpret dreams of the loss of body parts as indicating a loss of a significant relationship, rather than castration anxiety.

Depressed youngsters often relate fantasies of being unloved and unwanted. Such a young person finds it difficult to identify with members of his family, and fantasizes belonging to another family. Fantasies of running away are very common, and fantasies of being dead are far from uncommon. Associated with both of these fantasies is the thought that someone (usually the parents) will be sorry for having treated them so unkindly.

Psychological testing can be of great assistance in recognizing depressive reactions in children and adolescents. The psychodiagnostic picture tends, however, to differ from that shown by adult depressives. Anger is often prominently displayed and openly expressed while depressive feelings tend to be overshadowed, the reverse of the picture usually seen in adult depressives. On the Rorschach there is a diminution of the color response as well as detailing of dark, shadowy colors. In addition, the Rorschach protocol reveals many images of body emptiness as well as angry, aggressive, sadistic images. The Wechsler scale usually shows a higher performance than verbal score, also the reverse of that seen in adult depression. The patterning may at times be similar to that shown by psychopaths; perhaps this is related to the tendency toward acting out.

Therapy

The treatment of children and adolescents is so complex that an adequate discussion of it would require considerably more space than is available here. Nevertheless, a few comments of particular import to the therapy of depressed children and adolescents can and should be made.

Treatment must, of course, be influenced by the age of the patient, his circumstances, the clinical picture presented, the facilities available, and so on. Groups of infants suffering from infantile or anaclitic depression require changes in their living arrangements. They need the affectionate attention of one significant person, preferably the mother. As Spitz (28) has reminded us, time is of the essence. Many of these children will not recover if the condition continues longer than three months. More important than the treatment of the infants is the prevention of the reactions. Children should be separated from their mothers only when absolutely necessary. If an infant requires hospitalization, his mother should be allowed to visit daily, to spend several hours with him, and to feed and care for him. Every infant living in an institution should have one person assigned to give him special attention.

The group of latency-age, preadolescent, and early adolescent children who present behavior problems requires an approach suitable for acting-out youngsters in general. These children seldom recognize that they need therapy, and unfortunately, their parents and others may not do so either. Frequently school officials or other authorities will urge the child and parents to seek help. If the child is living at home it is imperative that the parents be included in the treatment program, as they must be helped to understand the child's feelings of depression, pain, loneliness, and helplessness, and even more important, to change themselves in order to give the child the type of relationship he needs.

Psychotherapy of such youngsters is often difficult. Not only do they seldom recognize the need for it, but their use of denial and projection as mechanisms of avoiding facing their painful feelings requires judicious therapeutic skill. They will invariably test the therapist to see whether he really cares for them. The therapist must never lose sight of the fact that though these youngsters appear to be in desperate need of a close relationship to another human being, they often become anxious and frightened when they achieve this closeness, as it makes them only too well aware of the losses they have experienced in their lives.

Great patience is required. Premature interpretation must be avoided lest the youngster discontinue treatment. The therapist must realize that considerable time may be required before the youngster is even able to talk about his painful feelings. Michael, the twelve-year-old fat boy, is a good example. Many weeks elapsed before he was able to get beyond a simple recital of the events of the week, and then only in a censored version. In working with youngsters one must bear in mind that many of them are not accustomed to discussing their feelings even with those closest to them.

If therapy is successful within this group, the therapist can expect to encounter overt depressive feelings, which obviously require a different technical approach and pose other therapeutic problems. Many therapists become bored and impatient in dealing with depressed patients; they want movement and progress, not a repetition of sad, hurt feelings. Other therapists may be frightened by the possible risk of suicide and recommend hospitalization prematurely.

Evaluation of risk of suicide is never easy. A very depressed adolescent, especially one who is seen for the first time after he has attempted suicide, really ought to be evaluated in a hospital setting. This can often be arranged in the pediatric service of a general hospital. Such a period of hospitalization not only allows for observation, but also interrupts the conflict that may be going on between the child and his parents.

Whether psychotherapy is conducted on an in- or outpatient basis, the patient's relationship to the therapist is his main support. He must be able to trust and rely on the therapist in order to have the strength to face and explore his painful feelings. The depressed adolescent will often appear almost insatiable in his demands upon the therapist. He will oscillate between trust and distrust for long periods of time before accepting the fact that the therapist will not desert him. Many depressed patients feel so unworthy that they find it almost impossible to believe that anyone can truly care for them.

In one respect, at least, the therapist's task is easier with the adolescent than with the younger child who is manifesting depression by behavioral symptoms, as the depressed adolescent recognizes that he is troubled and ordinarily is eager to obtain help. As a general rule, treatment of depression in adolescents requires intensive therapy. Simple techniques such as environmental manipulation, support, suggestion, and reassurance may appear to resolve the problem, but usually the gains are temporary at best.

At the present time various methods of group and family therapy are being attempted with adolescent patients. Though it is too early to evaluate thoroughly the results of these newer techniques, family therapy would appear to be of great value, as the basic feeling of loss of love that adolescent patients experience can often be fruitfully worked with in family groups.

The question of medication for depressed children and adolescents is difficult to answer. Most workers have reported negative results with antidepressants. Perhaps the younger patient metabolizes these compounds differently than the older depressed patient, in whom they frequently produce beneficial effects.

Frommer (13) reports favorably on the use of phenelzine with depressed children from nine to fifteen years of age. Connell (10) also mentions the use of this drug in treating suicidal depressions in children.

There are very few reports in the recent literature on the use of electroconvulsive therapy with depressed children and adolescents. Many clinics have discontinued electroshock treatments even with adult depressives except following an unsuccessful trial of antidepressant medication or when the risk of suicide is considered especially serious. Most child psychiatrists do not use ECT at the present time. I suggest that this procedure be used only as a last resort for adolescent patients who present a clinical picture of overt depression, when psychotherapy and medication have proved ineffective.

The recognition and proper management of depressive reactions in adolescence is of the utmost importance. The suicide rate of the fifteen-to-nineteen age group in the United States has doubled over the past ten years. Even more important is the deleterious effect of depression upon the functioning of the adolescent, especially in his schoolwork. Many youngsters troubled by difficulty in concentration do poorly academically and drop out of school, with harmful effects on the entire future course of their lives. We still know little about the effect of depression during the adolescent years upon future psychic functioning. While some patients might spontaneously overcome their feelings of depression, it is likely that many will continue as depressed adults. One can only wonder in what way depressive feelings during adolescence may influence the psychotic depressions of the involutional years.

Discussion

At this point one can conclude that adolescents from fourteen years on do show depressive reactions quite similar to those seen in adults. Younger children do not. The question, as I have said before, is whether children younger than fourteen do not become depressed or whether they manifest depression in a different fashion. There is still no agreement on this point, but it would appear on careful study that the latter is the case.

Such a situation should not be surprising. Child psychiatrists and especially child analysts argued for many years over the question of whether schizophrenia occurred in children. Many, especially those of an analytic persuasion, argued on theoretical grounds that it was impossible for children to become schizophrenic. It is now generally accepted that children can become schizophrenic and that the clinical picture is quite different from that seen in adults. It it noteworthy that at about **fourteen years of age the clinical picture in schizophrenia** begins to resemble that seen in adults. I propose that a similar situation occurs with depressive reactions.

Child psychiatrists must not lose sight of the fact that we are applying a diagnosis to a developing organism—the child—and must therefore expect that the clinical picture would vary with the psychic maturation of the subject. As Boulanger (6) has written:

> A psychoanalyst may very well be reluctant to perceive in a child the equivalent of an adult's melancholia, for he is besieged at once by all the points of theory which are unsettled and passionately disputed within the school: the organization and functions of the ego, superego, and object relationships, the origins of the Oedipus complex and the complexities of the instinctual development, the purpose of masochism, and the validity of the death instinct.

Many theories have been advanced to explain the genesis of depression in adults. Abraham (1) and Freud (12) theorized that depression resulted from aggression and hostility turned inward against the self through the mechanism of a harsh superego. The depressed person identifies with the ambivalently loved object that has been lost. One must be cautious, however, about applying to children a theory that may be valid for the middle-aged. Both Abraham and Freud stressed the oral introjection of depression. Klein (18) has emphasized this point of view in her work on the depressive position of childhood, which she views as a normal developmental stage for all infants.

Almost all psychoanalysts have postulated that depression follows the loss of a significant love object, whether the loss is experienced in reality or in fantasy. Bibring (5) has offered an intriguing theory: "Depression can be defined as the emotional expression of a state of helplessness and powerlessness of the ego, irrespective of what may have caused the breakdown of the mechanism which established his self-esteem." He adds that the basic mechanism is "the ego's shocking awareness of its helplessness in regard to its aspirations."

The issue of self-esteem has begun to assume a nodal position in all theories of depression. This has led Rie (24) to question "at which point in the child's life such an experience develops with sufficient intensity to constitute what has been called low self-esteem." Citing Erickson (11) and Loevinger (22), Rie concludes that "it may be no accident that this level of ego identity, or ability to conceptualize one's self, and the typical adult manifestations of depression are both generally agreed to occur at the earliest during adolescence." Rie goes further in stating that an affect of helplessness is essential for the development of depression. Quoting Schmale (26) and Lichtenberg (20), he concludes: "There may be reason to believe that the fully differentiated and generalized primary affect characterizing depression namely despair or helplessness, is one of which children perhaps prior to the end of the latency years are incapable."

Sandler and Joffe (25) have modified Bibring's (5) view of the concept of self-esteem as regards depressive reactions in children. They "stress rather the basic biological nature of the depressive reaction, related to pain (and its opposite, 'well-being'), rather than the psychologically more elaborate concept of 'self-esteem'." In my opinion this modification answers Rie's objections.

Sandler and Joffe (25) make the significant point that depression "can best be viewed as a basic psychobiological affective reaction which, like anxiety, becomes abnormal when it occurs in inappropriate circumstances, when it persists for an undue length of time, and when the child is unable to make a developmentally appropriate adaptation to it."

They modify the concept of the significance of the loss of the desired love object:

While what is lost may be an object, it may equally well be the loss of a previous state of the self. Indeed we would place emphasis on the latter rather than on the fact of the object-loss per se. When a love-object is lost, what is really lost, we believe, is the state of well-being implicit, both psychologically and biologically, in the relationship with the object. The young infant who suffers physical or psychological deprivation in the phase before object-representations have been adequately structured may show a depressive response to the loss of psychophysical well-being. Even an older child, who can distinguish adequately between self and object-representation, may react with depression to the birth of a sibling; a reaction which is not in our view an object-loss but rather a feeling of having been deprived of an ideal state, the vehicle of which was the sole possession of the mother. . . . If his response is characterized by a feeling of helplessness, and he shows a passive resignation in his behavior, we can consider him to be depressed.

Sandler and Joffe note that as the child grows older, the object loss becomes more important than the loss of the state of well-being embodied in the relationship to the object. In brief, they view depression "as a state of helpless resignation in the face of pain, together with an inhibition both of drive discharge and ego functions." Some children, they add, will make strenuous efforts to restore the missing state, others may react with angry protests and aggression, and some may regress to an earlier phase.

If one accepts the thesis that depression is a reaction to loss either of an object or of a state of well-being with a feeling of diminished self-esteem and hopelessness, we can better understand the vicissitudes of depressive reactions at various ages. It is true, of course, that not every child reacts to loss with a depressive reaction. But certainly we are aware that individuals vary considerably in their abilities to tolerate pain or discomfort of any sort, whether it be physical or mental.

The end result of any object loss will depend upon the developmental level at which it first makes its effect felt. In general, the younger the child, the more serious the consequences. In infants ego development may be profoundly disturbed. There may be a lack of ego development or even profound regression. The infant or young child may find it difficult or impossible to form adequate object relationships. This difficulty will naturally affect his whole future psychic development. It will seriously impair his ability to identify with the significant figures in his life. Disturbances in identification will of necessity affect the formation of the ego ideal and superego and consequently the future personality structure. The impairment of ego development will seriously hinder the intellectual potential of some infants and children.

When the loss arises during the latency and early adolescent years, the child will often react with anger and hostility toward the love object who he feels has deserted and betrayed him. By reacting with anger and aggression he can ward off the painful feelings of impotence and helplessness. Such hostile feelings can often lead to serious acting out and delinquent behavior. Unfortunately, such defensive operations seldom prove successful; they lead to serious conflict with parents and drive them further away at the time the child still needs their love and support. Ironically, the more neglected the child is, the more he needs his parents love and affection.

The child will often inhibit the expression of anger in the hope that his parents may once again love him if he is "good." He often turns the anger and hostility against himself: he must be evil or he wouldn't have been deserted. Such a negative self-image can lead only to negative acts, the frequent acting out so often seen in depressed children. Such behavior, of course, can only reinforce the child's image of himself as a bad person, which will lower his self-esteem even further and increase his depressive feelings.

The child and adolescent will utilize many defensive operations to ward off the pain of depressive feelings. In addition to regression, they will commonly resort to denial, repression, and projection. During adolescence, displacement onto somatic symptoms is often attempted. Occasionally we encounter youngsters who utilize a reversal of affect.

As the child approaches mid-adolescence, his ego, especially its aspect of reality testing, develops significantly. He finds it increasingly difficult to use denial as a defense. He begins to recognize the role of his parents in the object loss he has suffered and as a result his hostility toward them increases, but so too do his guilt feelings. The hostility previously directed toward the parents is now directed toward their introjections within the child. As I have described elsewhere (30), the superego does not reach maximum development until middle or late adolescence. The superego's development, plus the realization that reality will not change, reinforces the child's feelings of lowered self-esteem and helplessness and leads to the clinical picture of depression described for older adolescents.

We must not overlook another important factor in the formation of depression in adolescence. The reactivation of the Oedipus complex and its resolution at this period cause a definite sense of loss leading to depressive feelings. Thus feelings of loss from an earlier age will often be reinforced.

References

1. Abraham, K. Notes on the Psychoanalytic Investigation and Treatment of Manic-Depressive Insanity and Allied Conditions. In *Selected Papers*. London: Hogarth Press, 1927.
2. Agras, S. The Relationship of School Phobia to Childhood Depression. *Amer. J. Psychiat.* 116:533–36, 1959.
3. *American Handbook of Psychiatry*, ed. S. Arieti, vol. 2. New York: Basic Books, 1959.
4. Beck, A. T. *Depression*. New York: Hoeber, 1967.
5. Bibring, E. The Mechanism of Depression. In *Affective Disorders*, ed. P. Greenacre. New York: International Universities Press, 1953.
6. Boulanger, J. B. Depression in Childhood. *Canad. Psychiat. Assn. J.* 11:5309–5311, 1966.
7. Bowlby, J. Childhood Mourning and Its Implications for Psychiatry. *Amer. J. Psychiat.* 118:481–98, 1960.
8. Burks, H. L., and Harrison, S. L. Aggressive Behavior as a

Means of Avoiding Depression. *Amer. J. Orthopsychiat.* 32:416–22, 1962.

9. Campbell, J. D. Manic-Depressive Disease in Children. *J.A.M.A.* 158:154–57, 1955.

10. Connell, P. Suicidal Attempts in Childhood and Adolescence. In *Modern Perspectives in Child Psychiatry*, ed. J. G. Howells. Edinburgh: Oliver & Boyd, 1965.

11. Erickson, E. H. Growth and Crisis of the "Healthy Personality." In *Symposium on the Healthy Personality*, ed. M. J. E. Senn. New York: Josiah Macy, Jr., Foundation, 1950.

12. Freud, S. *Mourning and Melancholia*, London: Hogarth, 1917.

13. Frommer, E. A. Treatment of Childhood Depression with Antidepressant Drugs. *Brit. Med. J.* 1:729–32, 1967.

14. Goldfarb, W. Effects of Psychological Deprivation in Infancy and Subsequent Stimulation. *Amer. J. Psychiat.* 102:18–33, 1946.

15. Kanner, L. *Child Psychiatry.* Springfield, Ill.: Charles C. Thomas, 1960.

16. Kaufman, I., and Heims, L. The Body Image of the Juvenile Delinquent. *Amer. J. Orthopsychiat.* 28:146–59, 1958.

17. Keeler, W. R. Children's Reaction to the Death of a Parent. In *Depressions*, ed. P. Hoch and J. Zubin. New York: Grune & Stratton, 1954.

18. Klein, M. A Contribution to the Psychogenesis of Manic-Depressive States. In *Contributions to Psychoanalysis, 1921–1945*. London: Hogarth Press, 1948.

19. Klerman, G. L. Clinical Research in Depression. *Arch. Gen. Psychiat.* 24:305, 1971.

20. Lichtenberg, P. A Definition and Analysis of Depression. *A.M.A. Arch. Neurol. Psychiat.* 77:519, 1957.

21. Ling, W.; Oftedal, G.; and Weinberg, W. Depressive Illness in Childhood Presenting as a Severe Headache. *Amer. J. Dis. Child.* 120:122, 1970.

22. Loevinger, J. A Theory of Test Response. In *Invitational Conference on Testing Problems*. Princton: Educational Testing Service, 1959.

23. Nicoli, A. M. Harvard Dropouts: Some Psychiatric Findings. *Amer. J. Psychiat.* 124:105, 1967.

24. Rie, H. D. Depression in Childhood: A Survey of Some Pertinent Contributions. *J. Amer. Acad. Child Psychiat.* 5:653, 1967.

25. Sandler, J., and Joffe, W. G. Notes on Childhood Depression. *Int. J. Psychoanal.* 46:88, 1965.
26. Schmale, A. A Genetic View of Affects with Special Reference to the Genesis of Helplessness and Hopelessness. In *The Psychoanalytic Study of the Child* 19:287–310. New York: International Universities Press, 1964.
27. Sperling, M. Equivalents of Depression in Children. *J. Hillside Hosp.* 8:138–48, 1959.
28. Spitz, R., and Wolf, K. M. Anaclitic Depression: An Inquiry into the Genesis of Psychiatric Conditions in Early Childhood. In *The Psychoanalytic Study of the Child* 2:313–41. New York: International Universities Press, 1946.
29. Statten, T. Depressive Anxieties and Their Defences in Childhood. *Canad. Med. Ass. J.* 84:824, 1961.
30. Toolan, J. M. Changes in Personality Structure During Adolescence. In *Science and Psychoanalysis,* ed. J. H. Masserman. New York: Grune & Stratton, 1960.
31. Toolan, J. M. Depression in Children and Adolescents. *Amer. J. Orthopsychiat.* 32:404, 1962.

10

The Question of Depressive Equivalents in Childhood Schizophrenia

DONALD I. MEYERS

The term "depressive equivalent," although originating in descriptions of certain adults (8), has interested some who work with children (11), perhaps because depressive responses in children are less well defined than in adults, with more rapid shifting of moods, more defensive reactions, and more resort to acting out. As with many relatively new terms, the tendency has been to apply it too broadly, with insufficient concern for conceptual clarity.

The mechanisms by which a potentially depressive response is manifested by symptoms of other sorts are varied and not completely understood. They range from neurotic defensive operations involving a mature and intact ego, and including mechanisms such as denial, substitution of obsessive-compulsive reactions, hypochondriacal preoccupations, and somatization, to mechanisms that result from pathological skewing in the development of the ego and superego, as seen in the schizophrenic and in the psychopathic personality. In between are mechanisms that are developmental in character, such as the acting out of children and adolescents which represent the normal immaturity and fluidity of mental mechanisms at those stages of development.

165

The application of the term "depressive equivalent," it seems to me, becomes more questionable as one moves from the neurotic defensive substitutions through normal developmental variations in children and adolescents to pathological ego and superego syntheses. In the instance of pathological ego integration, what is often seen in response to an experience that one would expect to cause depression, such as loss of an important object, is not the substitution of an "equivalent" response, but an expression of the defective mechanisms for affective, object-related response with some compensatory, often bizarre and magical efforts to adapt in the face of these defects. On the other hand, the use of neurotic mechanisms, such as denial in a person with a normal ego, implies, at least in some instances, an unimpaired basic capacity for depressive response, the encroaching painful depressive affect being warded off or defended against by denial and substitution of other neurotic formations.

Failure to Recognize Depression

Our experience at the Henry Ittleson Center for Child Research has included some observations of the vicissitudes of the depressive response in schizophrenic children. Depression in children is not a rare phenomenon, as one might guess by looking in the literature. Certainly symptoms of depression, particularly feelings of sadness and slowing of psychomotor response, are seen frequently in children—usually in relation to loss or to feelings of hopelessness over difficulty in coping with or mastering life's situations. Perhaps the reason for their sparse mention in the literature is the old failure to acknowledge the existence of childhood emotional reaction patterns unless they conform to the same clinical criteria that are used in the diagnosis of the related adult patterns.

For example, it took a long time for many workers to acknowledge a schizophrenic reaction of childhood, partly because such reactions did not show all the features of the adult schizophrenic response. There was a tendency to adultomorphize the reaction of the child and to ignore maturational factors. Certainly if one looks for a syndrome of depression in childhood which has the stability of the adult syndrome, one will overlook many episodes of true depressive response in the child. We have had much less trouble with the dramatic depressive responses of infancy and early childhood which occur as part of the mourning process in response to gross object loss, as described by Spitz (12) and Bowlby (3). In my own experience and in the experience of many of my colleagues with nonpsychotic children and adolescents, uncomplicated depressive response of varying degrees is often seen. The picture with the schizophrenic child is different.

Follow-up Studies

Observations over the past fourteen years of a group of eighty-two children who had had extensive residential and day treatment for childhood schizophrenia during their early school years, who after discharge were followed by biannual interviews, and whose current ages range from fifteen to twenty-six years reveal a strikingly low incidence of depressive response. This absence of depression is even more impressive when one considers the degree of impairment in adaptation and the related failures and defeats with which these individuals are frequently faced in their attempts to master satisfying relationships with their environments.

A related and not surprising finding is that, although the overall incidence and degree of depressive symptomatology in this group are diminished, the appearance of depressive symptoms is greater in the older children and in the children with greater ego development and object relatedness.

Observations of diminished, limited or abortive depressive symptomatology in a group of twenty patients, from six to fourteen years old, *during* residential treatment at Ittleson

Center are even more dramatic because of the opportunity to observe the patients intensively over long periods of time. Because these children are in treatment, the intrapsychic processes that occur in response to such experiences as loss of important objects are more accessible to examination. Sadness, the grief of the mourning reaction, is usually shallow if it occurs at all. There is a blandness, an apathy, sometimes anger, without any depression of mood, or there is a variety of atypical or bizarre responses. The younger or more ego-deficient children, when not totally withdrawn and unresponsive, often show a mixture of fear, bewilderment, and puzzlement, or an upsurge of their obsessive seeking for sameness when confronted with loss, or, for that matter, any change in their experience. These deviant responses to separation are most dramatically apparent when the child is separated from the family on admission to the center for residential treatment, when a child-care worker leaves her employment at the center, and, less dramatically, when the child returns from a home visit. The "homesickness" that has been observed in non-psychotic boarding school children is diminished or absent in schizophrenic children.

Superego Defects

Another pertinent clinical observation is the prominent incidence of serious superego defects in the group of schizophrenic children we have observed. Bender (1) has described a subcategory of childhood schizophrenia which she labels "pseudopsychopathic schizophrenia." This category is composed of children who, because of their antisocial behavior and their aloofness from personal relationships, are often diagnosed as psychopathic. I do not believe this represents a misdiagnosis, just an incomplete one. This is not an apparent psychopathy, but a real one that is part of the psychotic picture, and includes the often-seen emptiness and "as if" quality in combination with a lack of understanding—an inability to empathize or have warm deep concern about another. As a schizophrenic child under treatment becomes less withdrawn, a manipulative, even deceitful self-seeking pattern often emerges. This is coupled with lack of regard or an inability to have regard for the feelings of others. Guilt reactions are absent, shallow, or only simulated. There is concern about being caught in some misdemeanor rather than deeply felt guilt.[1]

This superego defect in schizophrenic children has not been stressed by other workers. It is my contention that such defects are implicated in those schizophrenic children who show little or no response to loss. Elucidation of the disorders in attachment and the disturbances in the internalization process which may lead to such defects in the conscience mechanism are not within the scope of this report.[2]

Case History - Psychotic Response Instead of Depression

The following case report is presented as one example of a psychotic response to a situation that would most likely precipitate a depressive reaction in a nonpsychotic child—that is, a situation of threatened and real separation from an important parent surrogate.[3]

1. It should be emphasized that children who come from broken homes or who have had histories of early gross emotional deprivation or early gross disruption of relationships with important parental objects are not included in this group. Therefore, the early factors that are usually associated with the development of psychopathic personality (2, 4) are minimized. The superego defects seen in these children appear to relate to more subtle impairments in object relationships than are usually seen in the histories of psychopathic personality disorders.

2. A recent related finding is the high incidence of psychopathic behavior in the parents of schizophrenic children studied at Ittleson Center.

3. This case has been previously reported by Green (7).

Phyllis, age ten, flew into a tantrum when Cynthia, her favorite counselor, failed to arrive one morning. The tantrum included a furious self-destructive attack, consisting of punching and tearing at herself. Later, when she learned of Cynthia's plan to leave the center, she displayed similar self-destructiveness, followed by a catatonic reaction during which she sat rigid and immobile on her bed, refusing to talk. After hours of coaxing by staff members to get her to respond, Phyllis suddenly blurted out, "Don't touch my penis."

Her catatonic behavior subsided only when she was allowed to take Cynthia's coat to bed with her. And she utilized additional techniques to cope with this separation experience: she asked Cynthia to exchange arms and legs with her, and persistently tried to steal her jewelry and clothing. Phyllis also identified with the abandoning object by crying out, "I'm Cynthia! I'm leaving the center!"

After Cynthia's departure, Phyllis developed a marked attachment to a doll she had named Cynthia. For several months she carried this doll wherever she went. She handled it as if it were alive, giving it real food and providing it with fresh air. Phyllis refused to let it out of her sight lest it be attacked and broken by the other children. The doll obviously represented herself, the abandoned baby who must be taken care of, as well as the lost maternal object. Another example of Phyllis' clinging to symbolic and part object representations of the maternal figure was her fetishistic attachment to new shoes that Cynthia had bought for her. She endowed the shoes with magical power to protect her from the evil witch, symbolic of her bad mother. On one occasion when the shoes were not available, Phyllis flew into a self-destructive rage and then threatened to cut off the counselor's breasts and take them to bed.

As detailed by Green (7), such responses to loss typically involve marked anxiety, confusion in personal identity, and loss of body intactness. These distortions in identity and body imagery are manifested through expression of loss of real or fantasied body parts, body contents, feelings of emptiness and hollowness, and splitting of the self-image. One girl referred to herself as three different girls: Margo, Argo, and Ishkabibble (her real self, her disturbed self, and her image as a silly baby). The defensive maneuvers utilized to simultaneously repair these distortions of the body image and undo the separation from the significant person include clinging to the significant person, magical reunion with the person through oral, anal, or vaginal incorporation of part or all of the person's body, clinging to parts of the significant person via possessions (clothing, jewelry, etc.), and clinging to symbolic representations of the person (dolls, transitional objects, etc.).

The preservation and repair of the body image is magically effected by such omnipotent fantasies of extending and enlarging the body image as becoming pregnant and having many babies, having an illusory penis, and being "queen of the world" and possessing great wealth and territory. Such children are preoccupied with retention of body substance and the corresponding orifices, and they carefully monitor the processes of defecation and urination and are concerned about the loss of nasal secretion, blood, and so on. They are similarly preoccupied with the structure and function of vital body parts. Self-mutilation is sometimes used to provide painful self-stimulation as a source of sensory input and a means of delineating body limits.[4]

It should be clear that, although these reactions occur in response to real or threatened loss of important objects, a context most often associated with depression, the use of the term "depressive equivalent" would neither do justice to the complex meaning of such responses nor add to diagnostic clarity.

In summary, extensive observations show that depressive reaction is less frequent and less intense in schizophrenic

4. Discussion of the factors contributing to the development of the fragile body image and the self-other confusion seen in schizophrenic children is beyond the scope of this report. The reader is referred to other Ittleson Center publications (5, 6, 7, 9).

children than in children with unimpaired ego development. In some cases of intense response to loss, the response is often lacking in depressive affect and involves a psychotic disorganization, including intense anxiety and gross disturbances in self-awareness and body integrity. Such reactions are generally accompanied by primitive defensive operations aimed at reestablishing body integrity and self-awareness.

The use of the term "depressive equivalent" to encompass such complex reactions of a defective ego is inappropriate.

Defects in superego are noted in schizophrenic children and are believed to be related to the shallowness of the depressive response observed in many such children.

References

1. Bender, L.: Schizophrenia in Childhood: Its Recognition, Description, and Treatment. *Amer. J. Orthopsychiat.* 26:499, 1956.
2. Bowlby, J. *Maternal Care and Mental Health.* WHO Monograph no. 2. Geneva: World Health Organization, 1951.
3. Bowlby, J. Grief and Mourning in Infancy and Early Childhood. *Psychoanalytic Study of The Child*, 15:9,1960.
4. Goldfarb, W. Emotional and Intellectual Consequences of Psychologic Deprivation in Infancy: A Revaluation. In *Psychopathology of Childhood*, p. 105. New York: Grune & Stratton, 1955.
5. Goldfarb, W. The Mutual Impact of Mother and Child in Childhood Schizophrenia. *Amer. J. Orthopsychiat.* 3:738, 1962.
6. Goldfarb, W.; Levy, D.: and Meyers, D. The Verbal Encounter Between the Schizophrenic Child and His Mother. In *Developments in Psychoanalysis at Columbia University*, p. 89. New York: Hafner, 1966.
7. Green, A. The Effects of Object Loss on the Body Image of Schizophrenic Girls. *J. Amer. Acad. Child Psychiat.* 9:532, 1970.
8. Kennedy, F., and Wiesel, B. The Clinical Nature of "Manic-Depressive Equivalents" and Their Treatment. *Transactions of the American Neurological Association* 36:19, 1946.
9. Meyers, D., and Goldfarb, W. Studies of Perplexity in Mothers

of Schizophrenic Children. *Amer. J. Orthopsychiat*. 31:551, 1961.

10. Meyers, D., and Goldfarb, W. Psychiatric Appraisals of Parents and Siblings of Schizophrenic Children. *Amer. J. Psychiat*. 118:902, 1962.

11. Toolan, J. Depression in Children and Adolescents. *Amer. J. Orthopsychiat*. 32:404–415, 1962.

12. Spitz, R., and Wolf, K.M. Anaclitic Depression: An Inquiry into the Genesis of Psychiatric Conditions in Early Childhood. In *Psychoanalytic Study of the Child* 2:313–41. New York: International Universities Press, 1946.

The Psychotherapeutic Management of Children with Masked Depressions

HILDE L. MOSSE

Depression is a decompensation of emotional balance. Emotional energy always strives to achieve an inner harmony, to relieve tension, solve conflicts. The pleasure principle is the guiding force here. It plays an even more important role in children than in adults because their ego structure is still in the process of formation and in the early stages of narcissism. Exceptionally powerful internal and external forces or a combination of both, and not just a transitory state of sadness, must be at work to cause a true depression in a child. Children's basic tendency is toward happy anticipation of the future. Their outlook is optimistic because their perspective is still limited. That is why depressions are relatively rare in childhood and respond well to psychotherapy.

Childhood depressions have an excellent prognosis provided they are recognized and the child is protected from self-destructive acts. The idea that Freud postulated for depression in adults is certainly true for children: "The way in which it [melancholia] passes off after a certain time has elapsed without leaving traces of any gross change is a feature it shares with grief" (11). Chronic depressions are exceedingly rare in children (35). They are always preventable and are signs of emotional neglect.

Literature

It is remarkable how limited the literature on depressions in childhood is. Sometimes references to them are not even listed separately (32). Although a few definite cases of psychotic depressions occuring prior to puberty in patients with manic-depressive psychoses have been described (2, 36, 37, 38), childhood depressions are usually subsumed under the psychoneurotic disorders (3). One reason for this is that the classic and obvious symptoms of depression occur infrequently in childhood (3, 7, 13, 16, 29, 32, 40, 41). The vast majority of children who are truly depressed (not just temporarily sad) show a very diverse symptomatology; indeed, their depressions are usually masked (13, 17, 39). The depressions are therefore either not recognized at all or classified as minor aspects of other diagnostic categories.

The importance of these so-called masked depressions —some authors use the term "depressive equivalents" (3, 30, 41)—was highlighted by a recent statistical study of suicide attempts by children and adolescents. Months before their suicide attempts, almost half of them showed marked and definite behavioral changes that were not recognized as serious indications of depression by their parents or their teachers. "The 'masked symptoms' of depression (defiance, truancy, restlessness, boredom, anti-social acts), so common among children and adolescents, are prone to be overlooked both by layman and physician" (20).

It is unfortunate that in these as in too many other studies in child psychiatry, no clear distinction is made between children and adolescents. Physically and psychologically there is a qualitative and not just a quantitative difference between childhood and adolescence. This, of course, affects the character of the psychopathology that is evidenced, and is especially important where depressions are concerned. Depressions and suicide are frequent in adolescence (19). This tendency is so pronounced that sometimes we can tell that adolescence has started by the quality of the youngster's depressive reaction (5, 14). I have therefore restricted the age of the patients in this study to the period from infancy to twelve years, inclusive. I have omitted patients within this age range in whom I found from physical evidence that adolescence had already started.

Clinical Study

I found forty-nine children (forty boys, nine girls) suffering from severe depressions among the approximately seven hundred I have examined and managed psychotherapeutically since 1946, when the Lafargue Clinic in New York City was opened (50). The majority were in individual psychotherapy with me. Most of these children were ambulatory patients treated in mental hygiene clinics, schools, courts, and private practice. I have also included some patients examined in consultation in pediatric hospital wards. These included children who had chronic diseases such as tuberculosis. Only four (all boys) of the forty-nine children were referred with the chief complaint of depression. Only in these patients was the depression obvious to their parents and teachers, and only these children themselves indicated that they were sad. The other forty-five (thirty-six boys, nine girls) were referred for other reasons, and their depressions became apparent only during their psychiatric examinations. The depressions were hidden behind a great variety of symptoms and had to be unmasked by special clinical methods.

Even when a child was referred following the death of a parent, the reason usually was not that he or she seemed dangerously depressed, but that the child's behavior had become disturbed or disturbing at home and in school. Sometimes the surviving parent suspected a depression, worried about suicide, and requested psychiatric help because the very absence of signs of sadness was alarming.

The mother of ten-year-old John, who had recently lost his father, consulted me because she was afraid he might be thinking of committing suicide. He had suddenly started to call her at work several times during the day, complaining that nobody liked him in school, and that she and his older sister nagged him too much. He wanted her permission to go out alone and said he did not want to be bothered by anyone.

I found that John was struggling with deep feelings of depression and grief that he did not want to show. He had become absent-minded, could not concentrate, and was not interested in his schoolmates. At home he was under constant pressure from his mother and sister. He did not want to run away to kill himself, but needed solitude to overcome his grief. This was an attempt at self-cure. His very struggle against expressing his feelings of depression caused symptoms that we may call masks of depression.

Of course, the type of medical practice one has will determine the frequency with which masked depressions are seen (15). Overt depressions are more frequently seen by psychiatrists in mental hospitals, to which children are more likely to be referred after suicide attempts.

In my series of patients, three of the four children with overt depressions had made unsuccessful suicide attempts. One had run in front of a car, another had jumped off a fire escape, the third tried to hang himself. All attempts were known to their parents and teachers. One of the boys had made a second attempt to hang himself. I found that this was not a true suicide attempt at all, as the child previously had told his mother of his plans in order to obtain her sympathy and to frighten her. Actually he had played "cowboy," tied a rope around his neck, and hanged himself in direct imitation of his favorite comic book story and television show (both dealt with the same hero). When it started to hurt too much, he got down. By then he had a red mark on his neck, which his mother noticed.

Influence of Mass Media

The influence of violent stories carried in the mass media, especially in comic books and on television, on the patterning or causation of children's suicidal thoughts and attempts is generally not sufficiently appreciated (21, 26, 27, 42, 43). Five of the forty-five children with masked depressions (one girl, four boys) had made unsuccessful suicide attempts. One such attempt, made by a ten-year-old girl suffering from a school phobia—a symptom of masked depression (1)—occurred in response to a television show. The child told me, "I saw in a picture how a lady killed herself with a razor. She cut her arm here," pointing to her wrist, which was covered with several scars. "My mother yelled at me. I didn't think she loved me anymore. I cut myself with a razor. I probably wanted to show her how badly I felt."

Frequently neither the depression nor the suicide attempt is known to the adults close to the child. This was true for three of the four boys.

Battered Child Syndrome

Masked depressions play a major role in the battered child syndrome (10, 29, 48). Maltreated children, whether subject to threats or actual physical abuse, are always depressed. They usually have to cover up their feelings to avoid further abuse. I have studied an eight-year-old girl with second-degree burns over her back, buttocks, and thighs caused by being dipped into scalding water by her father and brother "to boil the devil out of her." This child had been in psychotherapy for almost a year before she was admitted to the hospital for her burns. No one at the community center where she was under treatment had recognized her depression or the mortal danger to which she had been exposed. She had been threatened and punished brutally for years prior to the scalding. In her doll play during her psychotherapeutic sessions, one recurrent theme was that a little girl had to flee from murderous attacks. This was unfortunately misinterpreted as an expression of unconscious processes and fantasies, and no real-life danger was suspected. The theme of running away, however, whether we find it in the child's play or in his dreams, should lead us to suspect a masked depression. We should then look for the cause in the child's life situation first, before searching for it in his unconscious.

A masked depression in a child should always lead us to suspect emotional or physical neglect or both. It may be the first indication that the child is being subjected to physical abuse. In all of these patients we must examine the parents carefully for signs of alcoholism, because of the enormously important role played by alcohol in both mothers and fathers of battered children (10, 42, 48).

Masks of Suicide

All kinds of seemingly accidental injuries may actually be deliberate or unconscious suicide attempts (9, 18). I have seen self-inflicted cuts, fractures, sprains, burns, and bullet wounds that were thought to be accidents. The child may not have fallen out of a window, he may have jumped; he may not have been struck accidentally by a car, but may have purposely run in front of it; he may not have accidentally shot himself or his playmate with an "innocent" toy gun or a real one, but may have attempted suicide or murder or both (42).

A child may hope to be destroyed by dangerous and violent behavior or by the retaliation he provokes when he attacks others. Dangerous risks taken may be concealed suicide attempts. A child may set fires or commit other dangerous violent acts with suicidal and homicidal intent as an expression of an unrecognized depression. We know that some homicides are "extended suicides" (Wertham), and that the psychopathological process of catathymic crisis with self-destructive homicidal acts as its main symptoms may occur in depressions (21, 44, 45, 47). This highlights the necessity of recognizing and treating masked depressions to prevent violent acts (42).

Children frequently threaten suicide when they are angry (4). It is most difficult to determine when these threats should be taken seriously and when they can be ignored. Only by careful clinical judgment can this distinction be made. None of the four boys with overt depressions had made such threats, but three boys and one girl in the series of forty-five patients with masked depressions had, and these threats should have been taken seriously. At least they should have led parents and teachers to suspect an underlying depression and to look for other signs of depression.

Suicidal thoughts should be taken especially seriously when the child does not feel free to talk about them and conceals them from his parents. Eleven children (nine boys and two girls) revealed their suicidal thoughts for the first time only during the psychiatric and the psychological examinations. One boy mentioned suicide for the first time in his TAT stories.

Difficulties in Performance

A great variety of complaints and symptoms, either alone or in combination, turned out to be masks of underlying depressions in the cases I studied: inability to concentrate, shyness, withdrawal, sulkiness, daydreaming, excessive fears (of death, accidents, wars, the dark, the devil, punishment by God), nightmares, "hallucinations" (of monsters, skeletons, witches, the devil at night), lack of participation in family life, failure to play with other children, thumb-sucking, preoccupation with television.

Typical symptoms of school phobia were common masking processes. Reading and other learning disorders were very frequent. They were often related to factors such as an inability to concentrate (which is a typical depressive symptom), feelings of inferiority, preoccupation with sad fantasies, and the slowing down of all reactions which often occurs as part of the depressive mood.

A learning disorder also may be a cause of a childhood depression, and if it is not corrected, it can perpetuate the depression. Sudden mood swings and excessive anger are typical complaints, as are violent or disruptive behavior, defiance, disobedience, restlessness, hyperactivity, the destruction of toys, stealing (especially from the mother), lying, fire setting, running away from home, and sudden and excessive jealousy of siblings toward whom the patient feels inferior.

In several case histories the parents described masturbatory activities that they had not noticed before in the children. As this sex activity is usually used as consolation when the child feels unhappy, it may also mask a more severe depression. Overeating, which is also a form of consolation, was a frequent symptom. Many other children had hypochondriacal complaints such as headaches, stomachaches, tiredness, dizziness, fainting. Hypochondriasis is, of course, a frequent masking symptom of underlying depressions (12, 15). Many of the children seemed to be easygoing and unperturbed, in marked contrast to the way they really felt. These children had deeply depressed feelings (17, 40).

Diagnostic Difficulties

In many patients with masked depression, the depression exists together with a variety of other major and minor symptoms, not necessarily in a causative relationship to all of them. It is not always possible to unravel this complicated psychopathologic mosaic during the initial diagnostic examination. To establish these connections (which exist on different levels) is one of the tasks of psychotherapy. This very process may often be the essence of successful psychotherapy. It is not always possible to disentangle these complex relationships in every detail, nor is it always necessary to do so. The lifting of the depression in itself always alleviates many other symptoms as well.

As childhood depressions are easily missed, the psychiatric examination must be especially sensitive to this emotional disorder. The child will usually reveal his depressed feelings and suicidal thoughts openly and spontaneously during the course of the examination if he feels that an honest and sincere attempt is being made to understand him, to find out how he really feels, and that at last someone is really listening to him without interrupting him constantly and telling him what to do, as has been his experience with most adults. The psychiatrist must be familiar with the masks of depressions. He must know the signs pointing to a depression in order not to miss a clue or hint offered by the child.

A ten-year-old boy with what seemed to be rather ordinary complaints of disruptive behavior at school and at home played in an unusual way with a string he wore around his neck, to which was attached the key to his apartment. He was a "latch-key kid." He used both hands to pull and twist it so tightly that his skin turned red and then white. I took this strangulation gesture to be a clue of an underlying depression, and asked him during the course of the examination whether he had ever thought of running away. This is the most frequent mask of depression in childhood. He said he had, and described several such episodes in great detail. His parents knew nothing about them. I then asked him about suicidal thoughts, and he readily admitted them. He described several attempts at suicide, which had gone unnoticed.

Unless a child spontaneously uses words like "sad" or "mad" (children often use them interchangeably because to be sad means to be mad, and vice versa), "lonely" or "tired" (meaning uninterested or sad), or even "depressed" (which is not usually part of a child's vocabulary), the examiner should avoid them. As a rule, children try to please adults, especially when they are afraid of them, and they are so suggestible that they may confirm anything that is asked and repeat words used by the therapist, words whose meaning they may not even understand and which may not describe the way they really feel. It is therefore better to ask about symptoms known to be depressive masks and to help the child express his depressed feelings in his play and in his own words.

Suicidal thoughts especially are often so intimate and private that the child may not want to share them, and may deny them unless the ground is prepared before they are brought up in the course of the examination. Of course, we must always keep in mind that children are afraid of not being taken seriously, and especially of being laughed at.

Use of Psychologic Tests

Sometimes the depression is so disguised or so deeply repressed into the child's unconscious that the psychiatric examination alone cannot reveal it. Here psychological tests are indispensable. I consider them an integral part of my own psychiatric examination anyhow, and include the Duess fables test, the Koch tree test, the Machover figure-drawing test, and the mosaic test as a matter of routine whenever I examine a child (25, 46, 51). All forty-nine children also had thorough psychological examinations by clinical psychologists which included intelligence and achievement tests and various projective techniques, including the Rorschach.

Among the numerous depressive hints given in drawings and paintings I want to mention only one. The drawing of a clown on the figure-drawing test may signal a masked depression, paralleling a child's clowning (40).

I have found the mosaic test particularly helpful in diagnosing masked depressions and even in determining the degree of danger of suicide. Frequently the child's story is so complicated, his thoughts and feelings so contradictory and confused, that a depression, occurring either as the primary underlying mechanism or as part of the general picture, may be easily overlooked. When I note from the mosaic test that a depression is present, the child will invariably confirm my suspicion and will then divulge depressive feelings and episodes not formerly revealed. I have seen no exception to this clinical observation.

The mosaic test may also be the only projective technique that in addition to the depression will shed light on the child's tendency toward *(a)* mood swings (red pieces close to black or blue ones; see *Figures 1* and 2), *(b)* explosive outbursts (jutting red pieces as tops of piercing forms; see Figure 1), and *(c)* violent solutions to profound inner conflicts (contrasting designs; see *Figure 2*), as in cases of catathymic crisis (21, 44, 45, 47). This test is also an excellent measure of progress in psychotherapy. The depressive design disappears as soon as the child has recovered from his depression (see *Figure 1*).

Once a depression has been unmasked, regardless of its psychopathologic classification (psychotic, neurotic, or reactive), one must always determine whether or not the child is suicidal (4, 31, 39). Even severe cases usually respond well to psychotherapy, and they can safely be treated on an ambula-

Figure 1

tory basis. The decision whether or not to hospitalize a child does not depend solely upon the depth of his depression; it depends equally upon the ability of his family, his school, and all other adults in his immediate environment to protect him and to respond quickly to an emergency. I had to recommend hospitalization for only one of the forty-nine children. All others responded to ambulatory management.

One must be alert to the possibility that concealed suicide attempts may occur at any time during psychotherapy. The mother of eight-year-old Christopher, for example, called off a session because the child was sick in bed with a stomachache and was vomiting. I was treating this adopted child for neurotic and depressive symptoms following his adoptive parents' separation. His father's behavior toward him and his mother had been brutal. He had also been traumatized by the recent death of a beloved grandfather.

Christopher told me, upon his return to therapy, that he had tried to kill himself by drinking the contents of a bottle he

Figure 2

found in his mother's medicine chest. It was this that caused his vomiting and stomachache. He had not told his mother because he was afraid she would get angry. He had apparently waited to see whether he would become dangerously sick. He planned to tell her about the attempt at that point, because she then would feel sorry for him and give him her complete sympathy and undivided attention, which he usually had to share with his baby sister.

His deeply ambivalent feelings toward his mother were dramatized by this suicide attempt. The avoidance of going to school, where he was in trouble, also played a role. He did not really want to join his grandfather in heaven (in which he believed). During the week of his suicide attempt he painted a somber self-portrait in a black Batman suit (see *Figure 3*). Some time later he made a cheerful mosaic of a sailboat under a

Figure 3

blue sky. The mosaic test indicated that he had recovered from his depression, but that his tendency toward explosive outbursts, and with it the danger of suicide attempts, had not yet subsided (see *Figure 1*).

This type of "suicide" attempt is not infrequent and is always potentially dangerous, because it can easily result in death. Unfortunately, children are often not properly protected from access to their parents' medications (14).

Non-Depressive Acting-Out

In this connection it is important to point out, as I previously described in the case of the boy who played at hanging, that acts labeled by frantic parents as suicide attempts may not represent suicidal behavior at all. Emergency calls for psychiatric help in such instances are much more frequent, in my experience, than referrals of truly suicidal children. The call usually comes from the child's school after the staff, in a state of excitement bordering on panic, already has notified the parents. The child is usually quite calm and readily tells the whole story as soon as he or she is alone in the office of the psychiatrist, away from the atmosphere of reproachful agitation.

For example, an eight-year-old boy was sent to me because he had made a sudden dash for the window of a fifth-floor classroom, actually jumped out, and hung from the sill by his fingers. The teacher fortunately remained calm and told him to climb back inside at once, and he did. He told me that he had been playing Superman with the friend sitting next to him. The friend was Superman. He played the bad man who had to flee by jumping off a cliff (the window). He assured me that he had jumped from this same window before when no one had seen him, had landed safely on a third-floor landing, and had climbed back into the school building. His story could be verified. There was no evidence whatsoever of a depression.

It is also possible that a child may invent such voices to excuse his bad behavior. I have seen a number of children who told me quite matter-of-factly that they behaved badly and were sent to a mental hospital because they listened to a bad spirit. Only after their parents took them to a "spirit lady," who drove the bad spirit out and replaced him with a good spirit, had they been able to behave well, because now they listened only to this good spirit. This type of superstition is much more widespread than we realize, and we must take it into consideration in our diagnoses.

Withdrawal and Fantasies

Children referred because they are "withdrawn" present special problems. This term has become very popular and has a vague definition. Teachers frequently refer children with this complaint, adding that the children must be "psychotic," meaning schizophrenic. In the overwhelming majority of cases, this withdrawal is a symptom of a masked depression. These children do not communicate because their depressed mood slows down all their reactions. In extreme cases they may even be mute. Psychogenic mutism on the basis of a reactive depression was a frequent symptom among children who witnessed and suffered extreme brutality at the hands of the Nazis during World War II.

This depressive withdrawal should be distinguished from the behavior of children who do not respond to social relationships but who have less severe psychopathologic reasons. Many children are so narcissistic that they are not interested in others; others are so timid and fearful of making mistakes and of saying the wrong things that they do not talk. Feelings of inferiority and inadequacy play a large role here. Many children for whom English is a second language, and who understand and speak it only poorly, react in this way.

A specific kind of withdrawal which is schizophrenic

must always be carefully ruled out in these cases. It is usually combined with a morbid suspiciousness and a preoccupation with bizarre fantasies. I have seen too many children wrongly diagnosed as suffering from childhood schizophrenia because a depressive or even a more ordinary type of withdrawal was misdiagnosed (28). The large numbers of children who live under enormous social pressures, primarily children of minority groups, are most likely to be thus misdiagnosed, with important social consequences. This is not to discount the possibility that a schizophrenic child may also be depressed.

Children who describe vivid auditory, visual, or tactile experiences, which may seem to be more than dramatic fantasies and resemble adult hallucinations, present a special diagnostic challenge (28, 49). A child who has lost someone he loved may report that he hears a voice call him by name, and this voice sounds like the beloved person. This occurrence may indicate a depression. It may even indicate danger of suicide if the child tells us that the dead person is calling out to him to come and join her or him. Some children are led to believe that the dead can return in person or as spirits. The frightening appearance of such spirits may be a hysterical symptom, but it may also indicate a depression.

Frightening hypnagogic hallucinations of monsters, ghosts, witches, devils, skeletons, painted faces, or even entire television scenes may reflect marked underlying anxiety or depression. They disappear as soon as the level of anxiety and depression is decreased.

Oral or other types of messages coming from God or the devil may be symptoms of schizophrenia. Detailed examination of the child, however, may reveal that these are not full-blown hallucinations as in schizophrenia, but basically benign symptoms of a masked depression. When asked to describe exactly where these voices come from, depressed children are apt to say, "It's in my mind," or "It sounds like it's in my head," or "It sounds like I'm talking to myself," or "It's like my conscience."

Guilt feelings and ambivalence are basic to many depressions, and a child's preoccupation with God and the devil and even with their voices may be part of the depressive symptomatology. It may even give a crucial clue to a masked depression. In analyzing the case histories of children suffering from hallucinations described in recent child psychiatric studies (34, 49), I find that many should have been diagnosed as masked depressions.

Adults who develop manic-depressive psychoses do not have prodromata in the form of masked depressions in childhood. Even a severe depression before the age of twelve does not indicate that the child will get a manic-depressive psychosis later on. Very few patients with verified manic-depressive psychosis before puberty have been reported in the literature (2, 36, 37, 38). Their symptoms seem to belong to the masked depressions. None of my forty-nine cases belonged in this category.

Homocidal Acting-Out

Nowhere is society's ability to provide constructive psychiatric social action tested more dramatically than in the management of children suffering from depressions, especially masked depressions. It fails this test far too often. The difficulties I encountered when I tried to organize a clinically sound and socially constructive psychotherapeutic plan for twelve-year-old Donald are highly instructive.

Donald was the only child in the series of forty-nine who was so dangerous to himself and others that I recommended immediate hospitalization. The recommendation could have been avoided if he had been referred for treatment four years earlier, at the age of eight, when his symptoms were first noticed. They were not so severe then and could easily have been treated. His parents had frequently asked for help, but had been referred to a school social worker only after three years of trouble. Even then the boy was never examined individually. The social worker saw only the parents.

The principal changed Donald from one class for disturbed children to another, but the teachers' complaints were the same: Donald had extreme mood swings and an uncontrollable temper, he got angry easily and stayed angry for a long time, and he had great difficulty in learning how to read. They noticed that he wore orthopedic shoes, which he hated. As positive personality traits they reported that he tried hard to please, had friends, frequently made original contributions in class, could show leadership, and was good in math and science. When he was eight years old he achieved an IQ score of 136 on the school's group intelligence test. Obviously his intelligence was superior.

When I examined him he was already under the jurisdiction of the court because he had barely missed killing a boy by slashing his neck with a knife. He told me truthfully what had happened, felt guilty and subdued, and frequently hung his head, fighting tears and at times blocking. He complained of dizzy spells, headaches, inability to fall asleep, of seeing frightening moving shadows when the lights were off.

He told me no one in his family liked him, that neither his fifteen-year-old sister nor his thirteen - and nine-year-old brothers wanted to play with him, and that his father beat him so severly that he bled (this illustrates how important it is to study all the facts surrounding the battered-child syndrome). He showed me a fresh scar on his forehead from such a beating. Both his mother and his father confirmed his story. They admitted that he was the family's scapegoat, isolated and disliked because of his unpredictable and "crazy" behavior.

Donald told me that he sometimes felt like killing, and that he could not control this urge. Sometimes he even felt like killing himself. He showed me a scar where he had cut himself. Once when he felt very sad he had run away and no one had realized it. His parents just assumed he had stayed out late, and punished him. Once all of his siblings had to restrain him to prevent him from running away. He asked me to send him to a reform school, hoping that this would prevent him from hurting people and help him stay out of trouble. It would also take him away from his home. He had asked his parents for years to be sent to a reform school.

On the mosaic test he made a star and an arrow (see *Figure 2*), suggesting depression, severe conflict, and a tendency to violent outbursts. The psychologist found great variability of intellectual functioning, ranging from defective to superior on the WISC (Wechsler Intelligence Scale for Children), and tenuous reality testing, lack of emotional control, regressive features, negativism, and a view of the environment as threatening on projective tests.

My diagnostic impression was that Donald's emotional disorder was so severe that it amounted to a psychosis, that he was dangerous to himself and others, and that he should be hospitalized immediately. Donald himself wanted this, and his parents agreed.

This type of patient does not fit into any one of the official diagnostic categories. I felt that a masked depression caused his violent acts, hypochondriacal symptoms (dizziness, headaches), insomnia, hypnagogic hallucinations, mood swings, episodes of running away, suicide attempt, temper tantrums, and reading disorder.

This last symptom was both a cause and a result of his depression. Technical factors (i.e., absence of instruction in phonics from kindergarten on, and constant reading of comic books) prevented him from learning how to read properly in the early grades (22, 23, 24, 43). This reading disorder was a major cause for his depression in the third grade, when it first becomes a real handicap. Catathymic thinking was part of his depression, but did not appear in the form of a catathymic crisis (44, 45, 47). There was considerable emotional deprivation at home. He was in severe conflict primarily with his father, who was a weekend alcoholic and beat his wife as well as Donald. In addition, inferiority feelings that were both intellectual (reading disorder) and physical (obesity, orthopedic handicap, nearsightedness) formed the basis for his symptoms.

The judge did not accept my recommendation, but ordered Donald returned home for another six weeks, until the court psychiatrist could examine him. It was necessary to suspend him from school during that time. The court psychiatrist agreed with my findings and Donald was put on the hospital waiting list. Even though it was Christmas, he begged the judge not to send him home. He was remanded to the children's shelter.

The hospital psychiatrist who eventually examined him also agreed with my findings and recommended psychotherapy in a hospital setting. However, he was overruled by the chief administrative psychiatrist, who, without having examined Donald, sent him home with the diagnosis "personality pattern disturbance," with no provision made for drug therapy or psychotherapy. This act was disastrous from the point of view of violence prevention. Donald had tried hard on his own to prevent himself from committing violent acts, but he got no help from adult officialdom.

The probation officer tried, on his own initiative, to find a place for Donald in a residential treatment center. I encouraged him to do this, but we were unsuccessful. When Donald returned to school, he cut a teacher and a girl with a knife (she required six stitches) and was remanded to a reform school for boys. This was clearly the wrong place for this severely mentally ill boy. Instead of being transferred to a hospital, he was soon sent to a jaillike reform school for seriously delinquent adolescents which had no facilities for psychotherapy. His chances for recovery are now minimal.

Truly curative and humane management of Donald

and such children requires hospitalization until the crisis and the inner turmoil have abated and a secure psychotherapeutic relationship has been established. Psychotherapy should then be continued, preferably by the same therapist, on the outside. Of course, the child's parents and other members of his family should receive casework treatment or psychotherapy as indicated during the same in- and outpatient period.

Understanding the Central Conflict

The lifting of a state of depression and even the prevention of suicide in this age group may not require prolonged psychotherapy. The child may leave with a feeling of immense relief, with renewed hope, and in a cheerful mood even after a single psychotherapeutic session. Of course, this does not mean that this should be the end of the psychotherapeutic management of the child. But at times it is possible to understand the key conflict underlying the depression in only one session, to bring it out into the open, and to begin dealing with it.

This occurred in the case of nine-year-old Douglas, who had been in psychotherapy with me for an anxiety neurosis the year before. He seemed to have recovered, but suddenly asked his mother if he could see me again. She herself had noticed a change in his behavior. He seemed sullen and preoccupied, could not fall asleep, and was inattentive in school. He had been an excellent student.

When he entered my office he said anxiously, "Every time I hear about blood, my knees hurt, they feel weak." His remark indicated an unconscious fear of being crippled. More specifically, it represented castration anxiety. I knew that his mother had recently started to work as a nurse in a hospital delivery room. Spontaneously and in response to my questions Douglas revealed that he was preoccupied with the way babies are born. The bits of information he had picked up from his mother had confused him; the description of blood in the delivery room had frightened him. He had the common navel theory of birth, and thought that the doctor cuts the baby out of the stomach.

Factual explanation relieved the anxiety somewhat, but Douglas remained overtly depressed. I knew from my analysis of young boys that they may be surprisingly ignorant of the fact that only women can have babies. I asked Douglas what he thought. He said that he was not sure whether men could also have babies. When I told him that they could not, he gave a deep sigh of relief and the depression was gone. Of course, the female identification underlying this depressive episode required further psychoanalytic therapy.

Recognition and management of masked depressions require a knowledge of the origin of conscious and unconscious guilt feelings, as they often play key roles in the psychodynamics. Sexual and/or violent fantasies and activities are the most potent sources of such guilt feelings.

It is often not sufficiently appreciated how important religious dogma may be in causing confusion and psychopathology in children, especially masked depressions. For example, five-year-old Vivian was referred to me because of her extreme variations in mood, inability to concentrate, difficulties about separation from her mother, enuresis during the day when anxious, thumb-sucking, temper tantrums, destructiveness, and nightmares. I felt these symptoms were masks of an underlying depression.

During psychotherapy she showed anger and rage. She was also obsessed about getting dirt on her clothes. She would wipe them off, simultaneously repeating over and over, "I rubbed it off and it came off—that's magic!" The reason for this became clear only after several months of psychotherapy, when she told me with sadness and anger, "My mother has a sin on her soul and it'll *never* come off. My little baby sister, she doesn't have it. My daddy and my big sister have it. I have it, I have everything. I go to church. My little sister will only get it when she grows up, when she gets as big as me."

She clearly felt doomed. Only after her parents explained the doctrine of original sin to her on her own childish level of understanding, with a benign interpretation, did her depressive anger and anxious preoccupation disappear. Her jealousy of her little sister lessened, and she stopped struggling against growing up.

Sometimes the very act of talking about depressed feelings and thoughts may give enormous relief and help lift a depression. Depressed children are usually lonely children. They have no one to talk to seriously about their most intimate concerns. Giving names to mysterious emotions has a healing effect in all psychotherapy. This is certainly true for depressions. It is especially helpful for children who have to be treated in essentially depressive surroundings on chronic pediatric wards, because they suffer from chronic diseases such as tuberculosis. I have found that masked depressions lie behind almost all of the behavior disturbances so distressing to the nurses in their management of such wards.

It is important not to overlook the masked or overt depressions that sometimes develop in patients when they are recovering from severe and prolonged infectious diseases. Placing them in convalescent homes may be the most effective psychotherapeutic plan. I was able to observe its success in many children when I had a general pediatric practice (30, 37).

I have seen a number of adolescents who still suffered from unrecognized chronic depressions following the death of one parent when the patients were much younger. This type of lingering grief is particularly dangerous because these youngsters seem to have a greater tendency to commit suicide than other depressed adolescents (6, 33).

I did not find it necessary to use antidepressive medication in any one of the forty-eight ambulatory children, but other medication was frequently indicated, especially for insomnia. Such medication should always be given within the framework of the psychotherapeutic plan. The basic goal of psychotherapy of childhood depressions must be to strengthen the child's ego so that he can overcome his depression and learn how to cope with conflicts, tensions, and painful events with his own inner resources. The emphasis should be on psychologic, and not on chemical, means. Only in this way can further depressive reactions be prevented. The use of medication for psychological difficulties in children has certain dangers in any case. Children and their parents have been conditioned from preschool age on by television advertising to feel the need for a pill (always for two pills, actually) whenever they experience tension, anger, anxiety, or frustration. This weakens their psychologic defenses, causes mass hypochondriasis, and prepares the ground from which drug addiction springs (42, 43).

The psychotherapeutic management was successful in all forty-eight ambulatory cases. They recovered from their depressions. All were started on individual psychotherapy, which was continued as long as indicated. Many children were eventually put in group therapy, in combination with individual sessions when a crisis made this necessary (8). Reading disorders were always also treated educationally, either by placing the child in special classes or by employing reading specialists, often in combination with speech therapy. All parents were included in the treatment plan. In the various mental hygiene clinics they were usually seen by social workers or referred to other psychiatrists. This cannot always be done in private practice, so I also frequently had to see the parents.

My psychiatric examination includes a separate interview with each parent, and I always conclude it by seeing both parents together and then the entire family. This technique can be modified and used flexibly in the course of the child's psychotherapy. Regular conferences with teachers and other school personnel are, of course, integral features of all child psychotherapy.

Some depressed children were so deprived physically that arrangements for medical examinations had to be made. At times welfare agencies, housing authorities, the courts, and so on had to be called upon to modify the tensions and deprivations surrounding the child. Some children came to the various clinics and schools hungry and had to be fed. Some came with clothes so torn that arrangements for immediate repairs had to be made.

Childhood depressions, whether masked or overt, are basically benign, provided attention is paid to the child's plight. No suicide need ever occur. When it does, it is always a sign of family and social neglect.

References

1. Agras, S. The Relationship of School Phobia to Childhood Depression. *Amer. J. Psychiat.* 116:6, 1959.
2. Anthony, J., and Scott, P. Manic-Depressive Psychosis in Childhood. *Child Psychol. Psychiat.* 1:1, 1960.
3. Anthony, J. Psychoneurotic, Psychophysiological, and Personality Disorders. In *Comprehensive Textbook of Psychiatry*, ed. A. M. Freedman and H. I. Kaplan. Baltimore: Williams & Wilkins, 1967.
4. Ackerley, W. Latency-Age Children Who Threaten or Attempt to Kill Themselves. *J. Amer. Acad. Child Psychiat.* 6:242, 1967.
5. Balser, B. H., and Masterson, J. F. Suicide in Adolescents. *Amer. J. Psychiat.* 116:5, 1959.
6. Beck, A. T.; Sethi, B. B.; and Tuthill, R. W. Childhood Bereavement and Adult Depression. *Arch. Gen. Psychiat.* 9:3, 1963.
7. Burks, H. L., and Harrison, S. I. Aggressive Behavior as a

Means of Avoiding Depression. *Amer. J. Orthopsychiat.* 32:3, 1962.

8. Daniels, C. R. Play Group Therapy with Children. *Acta Psychother.* 12:45, 1964.

9. Finch, S. M. *Fundamentals of Child Psychiatry.* New York: W. W. Norton, 1960.

10. Fontana, V. J. *The Maltreated Child: The Maltreatment Syndrome in Children.* Springfield, Ill.: Charles C. Thomas, 1964.

11. Freud, S. Mourning and Melancholia. In *Collected Papers,* vol. 4. London: Hogarth Press, 1946.

12. Gillespie, R. D. *Hypochondria.* London: Kegan Paul, 1929.

13. Glaser, K. Masked Depression in Children and Adolescents. *Amer. J. Psychother.* 21:3, 1967.

14. Jacobziner, H. Attempted Suicide in Children. *J. Ped.* 56:519, 1960.

15. Lesse, S. Hypochondriasis and Psychosomatic Disorders Masking Depression. *Amer. J. Psychother.* 21:3, 1967.

16. Lesse, S. The Multivariant Masks of Depression. *Amer. J. Psychiat.* 124:11, 1968 (supplement).

17. Lempp, R. Die Depression im Kindes und Jugendalter (Depression in Childhood and Adolescence). *Der Landarzt* 41:3, 1965.

18. Lippman, H. S. *Treatment of the Child in Emotional Conflict.* New York: Blakiston, McGraw-Hill, 1956.

19. Lutz, J. *Kinderpsychiatrie.* Zurich: Rothapfel, 1961.

20. Mattson, A.; Seese, L. R.; and Hawkins, J. W. Suicidal Behavior as a Child Psychiatric Emergency. *Arch. Gen. Psychiat.* 20:100, 1969.

21. Mosse, H. L. Individual and Collective Violence. *J. Psychoanal. in Groups* 2:3, 1969.

22. Mosse, H. L. Observations of a Fulbright Lecturer. In *Pathways in Child Guidance,* vol. 7. New York: Bureau of Child Guidance, Board of Education of the City of New York, February 1966.

23. Mosse, H. L., and Daniels, C. R. Linear Dyslexia. *Amer. J. Psychother.* 13:4, 1959.

24. Mosse, H. L. Reading Disorders in the United States. *Reading Teacher,* November 1962.

25. Mosse, H. L. The Duess Test. *Amer. J. Psychother.* 8:2, 1954.
26. Mosse, H. L. The Influence of Mass Media on the Mental Health of Children. *Acta Paedopsychiatrica* 30:3, 1963.
27. Mosse, H. L. The Influence of Mass Media on the Sex Problems of Teenagers. *J. Sex Research* 2:1, 1966.
28. Mosse, H. L. The Misuse of the Diagnosis Childhood Schizophrenia. *Amer. J. Psychiat.* 114:9, 1958.
29. Poznanski, E., and Zrull, J. P. Childhood Depression. *Arch. Gen. Psychiat.* 23:8, 1970.
30. Prugh, D. G. Children's Reaction to Illness, Hospitalization, and Surgery. In *Comprehensive Textbook of Psychiatry*, ed. A. M. Freedman and H. I. Kaplan. Baltimore: Williams & Wilkins, 1967.
31. Resnik, H. L. P. Suicide Attempt by a 10-Year-Old After Quadruple Amputations. *J.A.M.A.* 212:7, 1970.
32. Rie, H. E. Depression in Childhood. *J. Amer. Child Psychiat.* 5, 1966.
33. Root, N. N. A Neurosis in Adolescence. In *The Psychoanalytic Study of the Child*, ed. A. Freud, R. Eissler, H. Hartman, and E. Kris. New York: International Universities Press, 1957.
34. Sachs, L. J. Emotional Acrescentism. *J. Amer. Acad. Child Psychiat.* 1:4, 1962.
35. Shaw, C. R. *The Psychiatric Disorders of Childhood.* New York: Appleton-Century-Crofts, 1966.
36. Spiel, W. *Die Endogenen Psychosen des Kindes- und Jugendalters.* Basel: S. Karger, 1961.
37. Stutte, H. *Psychotische und Psychoseverdachtige Zustande im Kindesalter. Paed. Fortbildungskurse,* vol. 9, 2d ed. Basel: S. Karger, 1968.
38. Stutte, H. Endogen-Phasische Psychosen des Kindesalters. *Acta Paedopsychiatrica* 30:1, 1963.
39. Stutte, M. L., and Stutte, H. Selbstmord und Selbstmordversuch im Kindesalter (Suicide and Suicide Attempts in Childhood). *Die Agnes Karl-Schwester* 2:21, November 1967.
40. Symonds, M. The Depressions in Childhood and Adolescence. *Amer. J. Psychoanal.* 28:2, 1968.
41. Toolan, J. M. Depression in Children and Adolescents. In *Adolescence*, ed. G. Caplan and S. Lebovici. New York: Basic Books, 1969.

42. Wertham, F. *A Sign for Cain*. New York: Macmillan, 1966.
43. Wertham, F. *Seduction of the Innocent*. New York: Rinehart, 1954.
44. Wertham, F. *Dark Legend*. New York: Duell, Sloan & Pearce, 1941.
45. Wertham, F. The Catathymic Crisis: A Clinical Entity. *Arch. Neurol. and Psychiat.* 37:974, 1937.
46. Wertham, F. The Mosaic Test. In *Projective Psychology*, ed. L. Abt and L. Bellak. New York: Knopf, 1950.
47. Wertham, F. *The Show of Violence*. New York: Doubleday, 1949.
48. Wertham, F. Battered Children and Baffled Adults. *Bull. N.Y. Acad. Med.* 48:7, 1972.
49. Wilking, V. N., and Paoli, C. The Hallucinatory Experience: An Attempt at a Psychodynamic Classification and Reconsideration of Its Diagnostic Significance. *J. Amer. Acad. Child Psychiat.* 5:3, 1966.
50. Wright, R. Psychiatry Comes to Harlem. *Free World*, September 1946.
51. Zucker, L. The Clinical Significance of the Mosaic and Rorschach Methods. *Amer. J. Psychother.* 4:3, 1950.

12

Masked Depression: The Essence of the Borderline Syndrome in Adolescents

JAMES F. MASTERSON

> Sorrow may be fated, but to survive and grow is an achievement all its own.
>
> —R. Coles
> *Children of Crisis*

The abandonment depression of the borderline adolescent differs from the usual depression in a number of respects (24). First, it is not the single affect of depression but a complex of affects including suicidal depression, homicidal rage, panic, passivity, helplessness, emptiness and void. Second, the patient experiences feelings of loss of vital supplies often expressed in terms of starvation, of dying, or of a loss of oxygen, blood, or a body part. Third, the patient, unable to tolerate awareness of these feelings, and too immature to use a sophisticated defense such as repression, defends himself against them by clinging ego (9, 10), object-splitting (7, 13, 14, 15), denial, and other defense mechanisms. Consequently the clinical picture is most often not that of depression, but of the defenses against it.

To understand the origin of the abandonment depression it is necessary to understand not only the theory of the role of the symbiotic and separation-individuation stages in normal ego development (16, 17, 18, 19, 20, 21, 22, 23), but more importantly the effect on ego development of a faulty separation-individuation.

This chapter briefly reviews the theory and illustrates it through an account of the treatment of an acting-out adolescent girl. Those interested in more detail may consult other, related publications (24, 25, 26, 28).

Role of Separation-Individuation in Normal Ego Development

Symbiosis

The symbiotic relationship can be defined as one in which the functions of both partners are necessary to each. The child's image of himself and that of his mother is of one symbiotic unit. The mother acts as auxiliary ego for the child, performing for him many functions that his own ego will perform later. For example, she sets limits to both external and internal stimuli, determines ego boundaries, and helps to perceive reality, tolerate frustration, and control impulse (16).

Separation-Individuation

The emotional growth task of separation from this relationship begins at approximately the age of eighteen months, under the impetus of the biologically predetermined maturation of ego apparatuses—i.e., the child's own individuation, including his physical development. The child now undergoes an intrapsychic separation and begins to perceive his own image as being entirely separate and distinct from his mother's.

This achievement brings with it many dividends for the development and strengthening of the child's ego (27, 28, 29, 30, 31, 32). The child introjects the functions the mother had performed—reality perception, frustration tolerance, and impulse control, for example—thereby strengthening his ego structure. The capacity for object-constancy (8)—i.e., the capacity to evoke the mental image of a person who is absent—develops and an end is put to the defense mechanism of object-splitting. These latter occurrences will enable the child later in life to repair object loss by mourning.

Three forces, (a) the child's individuation process, (b) the mother's encouragement and support (supplies), and (c) the mastery of new ego functions, press the child on his developmental way through the stages of separation-individuation to autonomy. A process of communicative matching occurs between mother and child in which the mother responds with approval to the child's individuation cues. The mother, as the catalyst of the individuation process, must be able to read and respond to these cues if the child is to pass through the stages of separation-individuation to autonomy (19).

Role of Separation-Individuation in the Borderline Syndrome: A Developmental Arrest

This theory is derived from application of the work of Mahler (16, 17, 18, 19, 20, 21, 22, 23) and Bowlby (2, 3, 4, 5) to the study of the borderline adolescent and his mother. The mother of the patient with a borderline syndrome suffers from a borderline syndrome herself (1, 12, 24, 33, 34). Her pathologic needs impel her to withhold support and encouragement of the patient's separation and individuation, and instead to cling to the child to prevent separation, discouraging moves toward individuation.

Abandonment Depression

Therefore, between the ages of one and a half to three years a conflict develops in the child between the developmental push for individuation and autonomy and the withdrawal of the mother's emotional supplies, which this growth requires. He needs the supplies to grow; if he grows, the supplies are withdrawn. Thus arise his feelings of abandonment (24)—depression, rage, fear, passivity, helplessness, emptiness.

The awareness of these feelings is intolerable and they are handled by the defense mechanisms of ego and object-splitting, clinging and denial. Although separated from the mother, the child clings to her to defend himself further against their return to awareness. The splitting and denial are further reinforced by other defense mechanisms: acting out, reaction formation, obsessive-compulsive mechanisms, projection, isolation, withdrawal of affect.

Nevertheless, the abandonment feelings continue to exert their overwhelming but hidden force, which is observable, however, only through the tenacity and strength of the defense mechanisms used to keep them in check. These defenses block the patient from fully developing through the stage of separation-individuation to autonomy. He suffers from a developmental arrest. He is caught, so to speak, in midstream, en route between two stages of development; he has separated from the symbiotic stage but has not fully progressed through the separation-individuation stage to autonomy.

Narcissistic-Oral Fixation

In order to understand the disastrous consequences of these events for the development of the child's ego structure we must shift to another framework, Freud's psychosexual continuum, which has common meeting points with the one we have been discussing. Freud spoke of two phases, the autoerotic and the narcissistic, which precede the oral phase of development. Symbiosis is a narcissistic phase and separation-individuation is ushered in by orality. It is likely that the developmental arrest of the borderline personality occurs either in the narcissistic (11) or early oral phase. The earlier this arrest occurs, the more likely the patient's clinical picture will resemble the psychotic; the later it occurs, the more likely the clinical picture will resemble the neurotic. In either case, the developmental arrest produces severe defects in ego functioning. There is a persistence of the splitting defenses, a failure to achieve object constancy, and the development of a negative self-image.

This has disastrous consequences for the development of the ego structure: it remains "narcissistic orally fixated." Two key characteristics of this ego structure, so important to an understanding of the patient's reactions to separation, are the persistence of object-splitting and the failure to develop object-constancy.

Prepuberty: A Second Separation-Individuation Phase

The child's defenses enable him to function until prepuberty—approximately ages ten to twelve—when a second marked developmental maturation of the ego occurs. This growth spurt, manifested by a thrust toward activity combined with a turn toward reality, is similar in scope to the maturation of the ego which occurred in the separation-individuation phase (16). This maturation, together with the need for further separation from the mother, produces a recapitulation of the separation-individuation phase of development—i.e., a second separation-individuation phase.

Precipitating Factors

All adolescents go through a second separation-individuation phase in prepuberty owing to the maturational spurt of the ego. In some borderline patients this alone is able to precipitate a clinical syndrome; in others this internal event, combined with an actual external environmental separation, exposes the patient to the experience against which he has been defending himself since early childhood: separation from the symbiotic partner to whom he has been clinging. This in turn interrupts his defenses against his feelings of abandonment, and they return in full force. The environmental separation precipitates the intrapsychic feelings of abandonment.

These precipitating factors—either the second separation-individuation phase alone or in combination with an actual separation—reinforce the feelings of abandonment and produce a clinical syndrome via the need for an intensification of the defenses.

The clinical manifestations will depend upon the patient's unique style of defenses against his feelings of abandonment. Regardless of the type of defense, however, the two diagnostic hallmarks of the borderline syndrome are the abandonment depression and the narcissistic oral fixation.

In order to illustrate how these patients experience and deal with these abandonment feelings, it is most useful to choose an adolescent and follow the lead of Rinsley (28), who suggests that the adolescent's experience is similar to that of the infants, studied by Bowlby, who had to undergo a physical separation from their mother by hospitalization at the very developmental period with which we are concerned—i.e., in the first two years of life.

Bowlby describes these infants as passing through three stages: protest and wish for reunion, despair, and finally detachment if the mother is not restored. The adolescent is unable to contain the affect associated with the second stage, that of despair.

A physical or emotional separation so reinforces the feeling of abandonment that the patient's defense mechanisms intensify until the clinical condition results. These defenses against the depression interfere with the work of mourning, so essential to further ego development.

The clinical picture portrays the repetition in adolescence of an infantile drama—the abandonment depression grafted onto the separation-individuation process that effectively halted further ego development.

A Clinical Example

There are as many clinical types of borderline syndromes as there are defenses. The treatment of an acting-out adolescent girl is described below.

History of Present Illness

Nancy is a sixteen-year-old girl whose clinical episode began at the age of ten when (a) her family moved from Indiana to Oregon, (b) her father began spending even more time away from home than before, (c) she was rejected by two girl friends to whom she had been clinging, and (d) her dog died. She lost interest in school, slept poorly, and ate very little. She had previously been an avid and excellent swimmer, but now she gave up swimming even though there was a pool in her own yard. Long standing conflict with her mother got worse as Nancy fought the mother's efforts to teach her to sew and cook.

As her abandonment depression deepened, Nancy turned to acting out to relieve it. At the age of eleven she began to get into fights with her girl friends and was frequently sent home for being assaultive. Her mood improved for a short period during her thirteenth year, when she established one good relationship with a friend. When this girl rejected her, her previous behavior returned, and she described herself as feeling lonely and apart from her family and peers.

By the age of thirteen her acting out had escalated, and her mother discovered that Nancy had been changing into hippie clothes and smoking in school. The mother became enraged and accused Nancy of being an untrustworthy sneak. The parents took on the roles of policemen, which produced constant battles. The father secured the combination to Nancy's school locker and searched it for cigarettes and "unladylike" clothing; the mother embarrassed Nancy by confronting her in the playground with her friends and having the girl empty her purse to check for cigarettes.

Nancy refused to see a psychiatrist, but her mother did so weekly for about six months, seeking advice as to how to manage her daughter. During this period Nancy was frequently disciplined by being kept home after school hours for six to eight weeks at a time. Communication between the mother and Nancy came to a standstill. The mother spoke to her only to enforce rules. Nancy felt her parents were unreasonable and interested only in making her into what they wanted.

Nancy now began to smoke marihuana and to engage in promiscuous sexual relations. By the age of fourteen she had begun to experiment with LSD and DMT. When the family moved again, the parents found that Nancy was associating with "the grubbiest kids in town." During her first semester at the local high school she began to smoke marihuana openly. Her parents took her to a psychiatrist, who advised them to put her in a private school. She attended this school for a number of months before being asked to leave because she not only used drugs and smoked marihuana but encouraged the other students to rebel. By this time Nancy was frightened. She could not resist her urge to take DMT during recesses and was anxious about being caught. When she was expelled from the school she remained home for four months before arrangements were made for admission to a hospital.

Past History

Nancy was born six years after the parents' marriage, following one miscarriage. Pregnancy and labor were uneventful. Nancy was a feeding problem for the first six months. The mother became more anxious and upset with each change of formula. The pediatrician's reassurance calmed the mother, and Nancy finally responded.

Bowel training was not completed until the age of four, and Nancy had nocturnal enuresis until the age of ten. During her second year Nancy became hyperactive and irritable. She whined and demanded a great deal of attention.

As age three and separation approached, the conflict with the mother again escalated, and Nancy responded with temper tantrums, breath-holding, and opposition to all her mother's wishes.

Nancy started nursery school at the age of four without difficulty. Her behavior was always better at school than at home. When she was five her only sister was born. The baby developed a urinary infection and had to be hospitalized for two weeks. At the same time her father was again transferred and had to leave home for several months. Nancy, left alone with a maid, became even more rebellious and uncooperative.

The family then moved to Indiana. Nancy cried a great deal, quarreled with her mother, was restless and unable to sit still. However, her behavior in school remained good. She then began to "lie," which her mother found particularly offensive. The mother took Nancy to see a psychiatrist, who reported that Nancy was an anxious, lonely child who was copying her mother in an effort to get more attention from her too frequently absent father. He did not suggest treatment, but rather that the father spend more time with the family.

Nancy always found it difficult to make friends. When she was seven she had one close friend whom she has kept as a friend to the present time. She never seemed able to play children's games. In this she reflected her parents' social difficulties. They had found it very difficult to integrate themselves into the local community since their arrival the year before.

Treatment

The treatment is comprised of three phases: testing, working through, and separation. In the testing phase the therapist must deal principally with the patient's behavior. Control of the behavior precipitates the abandonment depression that initiates the second or working-through phase, whose task is to work through the mourning associated with separation from the mother. This then leads to the third phase, whose principal task is to work through the remaining separation anxiety with the therapist.

PHASE I: TESTING[1]

Nancy's initial acting-out behavior in the hospital consisted of not going to bed on time, smoking cigarettes, being seductive with male patients, and wearing inappropriate clothing. As she re-created the dynamics of her family relationships with her therapist and the nursing staff, attempts were made to weave a continuity between her behavior on the floor, her feelings, and the content of interviews.

Clothing was the major issue in the hospital, as it had been at home. She would wear a short skirt, be sent to her room by the nurse, and react with fury. Her intense anger and rage toward her mother were displaced onto the nurses. As her customary avenues of expression were eliminated, she became first irritable and anxious and then panicky. She cried, paced the floor, reexperienced LSD-like symptoms, and once in a panic clutched the walls in fear. She denied that she had any problems and blamed the hospital for all her troubles. When asked, however, she could recall feeling just as bad prior to hospitalization.

As her behavior became controlled, the projection on the hospital as the source of her problems soon gave way to rage at her mother. After an interview in which she expressed this anger, she made a suicide attempt by scratching her wrists. Nancy: "Mother doesn't care how tense I am. She doesn't care what my arms look like. I'm afraid of what I'm doing to myself to get back at her. I don't know if I'll ever be able to do enough to her." The more she talked about this anger, the more she

1. Rinsley terms this phase the resistance phase of residential treatment.

wanted to act out, and the less she could, the worse she felt.

In the third week of hospitalization she said, "You keep bringing me back to myself—by making me talk about it, making me bring back everything that I carefully tucked away with my grass. Now all I have left is sleep." Her depression continued to deepen. She felt apart and alone; she felt she was the "black sheep." "Mother criticized me, laughed at me for wetting the bed, for being fat, even for such a small thing as cooking New Year's breakfast without fresh apricots."

PHASE II: WORKING THROUGH DEPRESSION

By the seventh week of hospitalization her behavior was no longer a primary issue and the sessions began to move into the content of her abandonment depression. She was now tearful and frightened, and complained that her therapist made her feel worse. She began to have feelings of which she had heretofore had only short, bitter tastes, and had then quickly avoided by withdrawing or using drugs. She complained, "You're making me feel worse. I feel there's a piece of glass between me and other people. I can't pay attention in school, everything seems different, nothing looks real. When I felt like this at home my parents didn't know, and when I did something they would ask me how could I ruin my little sister's life."

Moving further into her depression, she dramatically relived the scene when, at the age of ten, she came home from school and was told by her mother that her dog had been put to sleep and that she shouldn't cry. Though she didn't then, she now wept pathetically.

The tie to her mother was clearly expressed in a dream of running away from someone for fear of being smothered. Her first associations were trying to escape from her problems in the hospital, but then she said, "My mother haunts me, I can't get her out of my mind. Yes, just like in the dream. Oh, my God, I think it was my mother who was chasing me in that dream."

She then became resistant and stopped talking, saying

that it was much too painful and that she could not take it any longer. Coincidentally, her behavior worsened. When her therapist restricted her for piercing her ear for an earring, her resistance broke down and the underlying homicidal rage burst forth: "You're just like her, I hate her. When she had the operation last summer I hoped she'd die and one day when she was three hours late because of the snow I prayed that she had run into a tree. My God, how I really hate that bitch!" After expressing these murderous fantasies she began to talk more in interviews, and once again the acting out stopped.

During the fourteenth week of therapy she began to verbalize her feelings that her parents had abandoned her, that they did not care for her. "When I talk about them I don't get as angry as I used to get, I get sad and upset. It's an awful feeling."

Her therapist's departure for Christmas vacation caused her to reexperience the feelings of abandonment when her father left—feelings of her own worthlessness and sense of evil. Her fear of loss of control was vividly expressed in two dreams. In one she was walking through the flames of a fire she had set in the center lounge; in another she was driving at breakneck speed on an expressway when her therapist stopped her and told her to go and sit in a school bus. When her fear of abandonment was interpreted, these fears were allayed and her behavior improved. This improvement was further reinforced by help from her therapist in controlling her behavior and reestablishing verbalization in the sessions as a means of dealing with these emotions.

In the trough of her depression she confronted her feelings of utter hopelessness and despair. "I never felt that they really cared for me. If they did they wouldn't have treated me the way they had. But I don't know if I'm worth caring about. If they don't love me, I don't care about myself, and then I do things to make them care for me even less." Important memories crystallized around the beginning of the clinical episode at the age of ten. During that year her father traveled more and the family moved to Oregon. She felt depressed, alone, apart, different. Two successive new girl friends rejected her abruptly, and this reinforced her belief that something was missing in her. She believed that her demands on others were inordinate; nothing could make her feel close. "I'll never make it sex-wise with anyone because I'll always feel they don't care enough for me. I think I'll be lonely all my life."

By the end of the seventeenth week her depression was lifting, her behavior was in control, and she was ready for and given more freedom and responsibility.

JOINT INTERVIEWS

By the twenty-seventh week she had worked through much of her depression and was ready for family sessions. She feared her parents' rejection and at first handled this anxiety by deciding to demand various things of them. In the first session she yelled at them, in the second they at her, and from the third on the discussions were more mutual and typical of the family dynamics. As her parents confronted her with all she had done, she grew more depressed and hopeless. She talked of other patients who failed, and planned to live in an apartment with an ex-patient who was on drugs. The anger toward her parents for their rejection was once again channeled to her therapist and the staff in the form of withdrawal and complaints about the rules. After this behavior was interpreted in the fourth family session, Nancy and her mother became furious with one another. Nancy's mother wanted to leave the room; Nancy wanted to continue to provoke her. Through the therapist's intervention they both verbalized this anger in the session.

After this session both parents made greater efforts to understand Nancy. They told her that they cared for her, recognized now that they had been unaware of her feelings, and acknowledged the possibility that they too had a part in all that had happened. Nancy, made anxious by their response, rejected them and grew more depressed as she talked. Thus she was confronting her separation anxiety. She realized that by accepting them she had to commit herself to becoming independent and to working out her problems with them as an adult; that is, she had to give up dependency. By rejecting them or setting up a situation wherein they could reject her, she would prove her fears true and provide license for herself to continue in the dependent state. In the eighth conference Nancy and her mother discussed how each had made the other feel, expressed their wishes for more understanding, and earnestly inquired of each other what could be done.

PHASE III: SEPARATION

As the weekly family conferences continued and Nancy spent longer and longer periods at home, two themes emerged: Nancy's regressive acting out as a defense against her fear of being on her own, and then the fear of being on her own itself. Nancy made very unrealistic demands on her mother, and her mother tried to fulfill her every need. The lack of success filled them both with anger and frustration.

When the therapist interpreted Nancy's demandingness as a defense against her separation anxiety, Nancy would stop demanding, and then her anxiety would come to the fore. With each move forward she experienced this separation anxiety and then regressed either by acting out or withdrawing to displace her angry, frightened feelings.

She and her mother then began to get along better. They did things to please each other and went to great lengths to avoid anger-provoking incidents. On weekends at home Nancy prepared most of the meals and volunteered to serve as babysitter. The more receptive the mother was, the more anxious Nancy became about separating and being on her own. One month before discharge the therapist had to leave because he was changing his residency, and she responded at first with denial, but then was able to ventilate her feelings of anger to the substitute therapist.

As her discharge approached she became irritable, depressed, and anxious, verbalizing her fear of being able to make it on her own and that she might need rehospitalization. Also she verbalized her ambivalence about her mother, her seeking of her mother's protectiveness and her simultaneous fear of it. Her separation anxiety was further reflected in somatic complaints of menstrual cramps, anorexia, head-aches, and a head cold. She began seriously to doubt her own capacity to cope, her doctor's competence, her parents' willingness to help. When the time came to leave, she made no attempt to avoid the staff and her peers, but was able to face them and make appropriate good-byes. Nancy was dis-charged to live at home, attend a tutoring school, and see her therapist twice a week.

Nancy was seen in outpatient treatment twice a week for a year after leaving the hospital. She graduated from high school, was accepted in college. She requested a termination of treatment so that she could try college on her own.

Although the borderline adolescent's problem is severe, and therefore his therapeutic requirement high, there is no reason for discouragement. If we have understood and prop-erly treated the patient's pathology, we will have made it possible for him once again to harness the enormous power of his own inherent growth potential to his own ego develop-ment.

References

1. Bateson, C. F.; Mishler, E. G.; and Waxler, N. E. *Family Proces-ses and Schizophrenia.* New York: Science House, 1968.
2. Bowlby, J. Grief and Mourning in Infancy and Early Child-hood. In *The Psychoanalytic Study of the Child* 15:9-52. New York: International Universities Press, 1960.
3. Bowlby, J. *Attachment and Loss,* vol. 1. New York: Basic Books, 1969.
4. Bowlby, J. The Nature of the Child's Tie to His Mother. *Int. J. Psychoanal.* 39:350, 1958.
5. Bowlby, J. Process of Mourning. *Int. J. Psychoanal.* 42:317, 1961.
6. Deutsch, H. *The Psychology of Woman,* 1:3–23. New York: Grune & Stratton, 1944.

7. Fairbairn, W. R. D. A Revised Psychopathology of the Psychoses and Psychoneuroses. In *Psychoanalytic Studies of the Personality* London: Tavistock, 1952.
8. Fraiberg, S. Libidinal Object Constancy and Mental Representation. In *Psychoanalytic Study of the Child* 24:9–47. New York: International Universities Press, 1969.
9. Freud, S. Fetishism. In *Collected Papers,* ed. J. Strachey, 5:198–204. London: Hogarth Press, 1952.
10. Freud, S. Splitting of the Ego in the Defensive Process. In *Collected Papers,* ed. J. Strachey, 5:372–75. London: Hogarth Press, 1952.
11. Freud, S. On Narcissism: An Introduction. In *Collected Papers,* ed. J. Riviere, 4:30–59. London: Hogarth Press, 1953.
12. Giovacchini, P. L. Effects of Adaptive and Disruptive Aspects of Early Object Relationships and Later Parental Functioning. In *Parenthood,* ed. Anthony and Benedek. Boston: Little, Brown, 1970.
13. Guntrip, H. *Personality Structure and Human Interaction* New York: International Universities Press, 1964.
14. Klein, M. *The Psycho-Analysis of Children,* London: Hogarth Press, 1932.
15. Klein, M. Notes on Some Schizoid Mechanisms. In *Developments in Psycho-Analysis,* ed. J. Riviere. London: Hogarth Press, 1946.
16. Mahler, M. S. *On Human Symbiosis and the Vicissitudes of Individuation,* New York: International Universities Press, 1968.
17. Mahler, M. S. Thoughts About Development and Individuation. In *The Psychoanalytic Study of the Child* 18:307–324. New York: International Universities Press, 1963.
18. Mahler, M. S. Autism and Symbiosis: Two Extreme Disturbances of Identity. *Int. J. Psychoanal.* 39:77, 1958.
19. Mahler, M. S. On the Significance of the Normal Separation-Individuation Phase. In *Drives, Affects, and Behavior,* ed. M. Schur, 2:161–69. New York: International Universities Press, 1965.
20. Mahler, M. S., and Furer, M. Certain Aspects of the Separation-Individuation Phase. *Psychoanal. Quart.* 32:1, 1963.

21. Mahler, M. S., and La Perriere, R. Mother-Child Interaction During Separation-Individuation. *Psychoanal. Quart.* 34:483, 1965.
22. Mahler, M. S., and McDevitt, J. Observations on Adaptation and Defense in Statu Nascendi. *Psychoanal. Quart.* 37:1, 1968.
23. Mahler, M. S.; Pine, F.; and Bergman, A. The Mother's Reaction to Her Toddler's Drive for Individuation. In *Parenthood*, ed. Anthony and Benedek. Boston: Little, Brown, 1970.
24. Masterson, J. F. *Treatment of the Borderline Adolescent: A Developmental Approach.* New York: Wiley, 1972.
25. Masterson, J. F. Intensive Psychotherapy of the Adolescent with a Borderline Syndrome. In *American Handbook of Psychiatry*, ed. G. Caplan (special edition on adolescence). New York: Basic Books, 1971.
26. Masterson, J. F. Treatment of the Adolescent with Borderline Syndrome (A Problem in Separation-Individuation). *Bull. Menninger Clinic* 35:5, 1971.
27. Rinsley, D. B. Economic Aspects of the Object Relations. *Int. J. Psychoanal.* 49:44, 1968.
28. Rinsley, D. B. Theory and Practice of Intensive Residential Treatment of Adolescents. *Psychiat. Quart.* 42:611, 1968.
29. Rinsley, D. B. Psychiatric Hospital Treatment with Special Reference to Children. *Arch. Gen. Psychiat.* 9:489, 1963.
30. Rinsley, D. B. The Adolescent in Residential Treatment: Some Critical Reflections. *Adolescence.* 2:83, 1967.
31. Rinsley, D. B. Intensive Psychiatric Hospital Treatment of Adolescents: An Object-Relations View. *Psychiat. Quart.* 39:405, 1965.
32. Rinsley, D. B., and Hall, D. D. Psychiatric Hospital Treatment of Adolescents: Parental Resistances as Expressed in Casework Metaphor. *Arch. Gen. Psychiat.* 7:286, 1962.
33. Spitz, R. A. *The First Year of Life: A Psychoanalytic Study of Normal and Deviant Development of Object-Relations.* New York: International Universities Press, 1965.
34. Zentner, E. B., and Aponte, H. J. The Amorphous Family Nexus. *Psychiat. Quart.* 44:91, 1970.

13

Delinquency and Criminal Behavior as Depressive Equivalents in Adolescents

JACOB CHWAST

The information explosion we have been witnessing is so obvious that one simply takes it for granted. When I scanned the recent literature on masked depression, I was nonetheless surprised to run across an item in a 1971 issue of *Psychiatry Digest* (11) which almost upstages our beginning attempts to explore scientifically the dimensions of this phenomenon. The item consisted of an advertisement by a pharmaceutical company. It may well be that the exigencies of the private enterprise system account for the speed of knowledge transmission in this case. Anyway, here is the point made in the blurb: "Because anxiety is so obvious, underlying depression is often overlooked. . . . All too often anxiety and depression coexist. Often, the highly visible symptoms of anxiety can mask underlying depression." The ad then went on to push the sale of a particular tranquilizer. And here, essentially, the pharmaceutical house and I part company, at least as far as delinquent and criminal patients are concerned. There may be occasional ex-

219

ceptions, but to my mind, psychopharmacology has little to offer to these patients and to their depressions.

In another place in the same publication, however, another point is made which concurs with one I had previously made myself in discussing depression among delinquents: I had commented that "there is little difference in the intensity of depression as manifested by white and Negro children" (2). Tonks, Paykel, and Klerman (14) conclude that their "findings suggest that when appropriate controls are utilized, depressions among American Negro patients do not show specific symptom characteristics different from their white counterparts."

First Study
Evaluation of 121 Delinquents

In my psychological work with delinquent children and adult offenders I had long been impressed by their muted affectivity. When the occasion arose, I therefore undertook a more systematic investigation of this phenomenon (2). Since it seemed evident that delinquency could be charted along a continuum as an expression of human activity, it seemed reasonable that depression could be conceived in the same way.

From this point of view, specific syndromes might be perceived as nodal points on a continuum rather than as discrete and discontinuous phenomena. Conceivably this could mean that underlying depression could be invisible and thus exist in masked form at one end of the continuum and gradually move along to the point at which it would be visible. And there is still another possibility, one that seems particularly applicable to delinquents and perhaps adult criminals as well: some of the depression could be partially hidden by other symptoms, but not entirely, so that some of it shows, so to speak. It is also possible that even though a portion of the depression is visible, a larger amount is submerged. Symptomatically, this would mean that delinquent acting out or drug use or alcoholism or a psychosomatic complaint might serve as a depressive equivalent at the same time that some depression might be outwardly manifest.

Whether an expression of depression is manifest or concealed depends on the effect it will produce upon the person to whom it is communicated. Masking thus serves as a buffer to communication when certain feelings cannot be presented to full view: either others do not want to see these feelings or fail to see them, or the ego does not allow itself to recognize them.

Whether a child shows depression first or anxiety first may depend upon the results produced upon significant others when either one or the other is manifested. If anxious behavior succeeds, then feelings of loss and depression may be withheld. If, on the other hand, depression succeeds, then anxiety may not be shown. Both may be expressed at different times by the same child since each could work under altered circumstances.

In the study referred to above (2), I reviewed the cases of 121 children who had been referred by police juvenile officers for psychological examination. The evaluations and recommendations that resulted from these examinations were then utilized for disposition and treatment. Included in the examination procedure was the usual array of psychological tests, as well as child and parent interviews when feasible.

Age, Sex, and Race

The group consisted of 81 boys and 40 girls, a ratio of just about 2 to 1. Three-fifths were white, one-third was black, and the remainder was of Puerto Rican descent. The average age was 13.2 years, with the girls about a year older than the boys. For the group, the IQ averaged 90.6, reading retardation was about three years, and the children were retarded about four years in arithmetic. Since they had been handled primarily by the police rather than by the courts, these children could be regarded as moderately rather than severely delinquent.

To assess the amount of depression, I constructed a five-step scale of intensity: none, little, somewhat, substantial, and predominant. I tried to deal with the manifest material in the reports in rating the depressions. I was aware of the deficiencies in the approach because of the subjective nature of the judgments, the recourse to *post hoc* ratings, and the lack of adequate controls. These deficiencies would therefore necessarily make one question the reliability and validity of the data. Nevertheless, I continued the study and presumed to present the findings, and now I shall presume to present those of another study just completed.

But first a word about the research capability of the private practitioner who explores a problem of interest without the benefit of funds, tools, and sufficient time. It seems obvious to me that under these circumstances he is compelled to make do with what he has at hand. Consequently, he is not always able to perform the various technical procedures necessary to assure the acquisition of as many solid data as would be desirable, nor can he invoke the use of all of the scientific safeguards that he would wish for, but which even under ideal conditions are extremely difficult to obtain. This is especially true of the study of human behavior, which entails psychological and social variables. Here, then, is the dilemma in which I found myself.

In any event, let us return to the results of the first study of the 121 moderate delinquents. About one out of five showed *little* or *no* depression. Four out of five appeared at least somewhat depressed, and one out of two was *substantially* or predominantly depressed. About one in ten was severely depressed.

As for the boys, one out of four manifested little or no depression; three out of four were at least somewhat depressed; two out of five were at least substantially depressed; and one out of twenty was severely depressed.

Among the girls, only one out of six was not depressed or only slightly so. More than four out of five were at least somewhat depressed, three out of five were substantially depressed, and one out of five was severely depressed. These data would indicate that the delinquent girls in the sample were more depressed than the delinquent boys.

When the age factor was examined, it appeared that whereas one out of three children under thirteen years (the modal age of police reports for juveniles) was depressed little or not at all, about one out of six of those over thirteen was. From the other end of the telescope, while one in four children below thirteen years was substantially or predominantly depressed, more than half of those over thirteen, or about twice as many, were depressed at this level.

The ethnic factor was also considered, and here no discernible differences in the intensity of depression appeared.

On the basis of these data, I concluded "that delinquent adolescents tend to be more rather than less depressed . . . delinquent girls are more depressed than delinquent boys. . . the older the delinquent, the greater the degree of depression . . . and that ethnicity seems to be unrelated to the amount of depression displayed" (2).

Inasmuch as these children were seen at a time when they were caught up in the toils of the law, one could assume that the depression observed might well have been a result of that process. I did not think this was an overriding consideration, however, because with only one or two exceptions, all of the children were cooperative and put forth good effort in the examination procedures.

Overt and Covert Depressions

In the light of these findings, it seemed appropriate to question the common stereotypes of the delinquent, which picture him as being conscienceless, impulse-ridden, unable to tolerate frustration, hedonistic, and manipulatively exploitive of others. I asked, "Does not this picture of him painted in dark depressive hues come as a surprise?" And I answered, "There is no doubt that it does, if one accepts a monolithic perception of the delinquent's personality" (2). Since delinquency appears in many forms, one must study many samples of this universe in testing out various hypotheses, such as a relationship between depression and delinquency.

In discussing these findings, I suggested that while both overt and covert depressions are seen frequently among delinquents, the depression does not, generally speaking, fit into the usual diagnostic picture. It is most frequently observable in a prevailing dysphoric tone, which is probably the product of severe emotional and social deprivation.

Others have noted the presence of depression among delinquents and criminals. Harrower (10) described her group of 229 delinquents who had been referred to a court clinic as "interest-scarred, outlet-barred, and emotionally depressed."

Halleck (9) cites the case of a fourteen-year-old boy who had committed a serious delinquent act. Upon examination he was found to be timid and passive. His only companion was his dog, which had been killed a week earlier as he was standing nearby. After this "he was profoundly depressed and remained in this condition until he committed the crime." Fireman (7) observes that criminal activity is often preceded by severe depression. He believes that crime may serve as a way of warding off this undesirable affect.

Glover (8), referring to psychopaths, contends that manifest or covert depressive features are in operation before the outbreak of antisocial conduct. He suggests that this might be the result of "warping or hypertrophy rather than of stunting of unconscious conscience," and that depressive and self-injuring mechanisms commonly occur among psychopaths who are not exhibiting antisocial tendencies. He urges consideration of the possibility that some psychopaths may save themselves from a major psychotic depression or even a schizophrenic attack by their criminal abreactions. Woddis (15) notes the connection between some kind of depression and antisocial behavior. He indicates that criminal violence is found less often in mania than in depression.

Cormier et al (6), in a longitudinal study of delinquency from latency through adolescence to persistent adult criminality, describe two types: the primary delinquent and the secondary delinquent. Both types manifest persistent patterns of delinquency which are serious and result in prolonged criminality during childhood.

The primary delinquent functions on a more primitive level than the secondary. In many ways he has been abnormal from childhood. He is either restless, troublesome, and overactive or too passive. This boy is already not normal at the age of six. He is unable to participate with others inside or outside the family constellation. At school he runs into difficulty both intellectually and emotionally. Because of his primitive adherence to the pain-pleasure principle, the primary delinquent cannot control his impulses. His chief defense is aggression, and he responds to others with hostility or distrust, whether they treat him kindly or poorly. Cormier (6) observes that the primary delinquent cannot tolerate frustration, and he will destroy a friendship offered to him even though he truly greatly desires it. "This uncontrolled anger and its effects are manifestations of a deep concealed unresolved depression."

The secondary type of delinquent has progressed further than this, although he has never enjoyed a fully normal childhood. From the age of six to adolesence, he has adapted better to school and has been better able to conform and to avoid antisocial behavior. He is able to participate with others even though he may display anger, impulsiveness, or withdrawal. His defensive structure is better than that of the primary delinquent, although it does break down somewhat in adolescence. When he cannot control his delinquent behavior, the secondary delinquent suffers in consequence. "He can tolerate a certain degree of anxiety, tension, fear, and depression before acting out."

In comparing both groups, Cormier (6) notes that for primary delinquents, criminality is a protection against "painful insight and is a means of avoiding depression. The secondary delinquents are capable of feeling depression but they don't know how to deal with it."

Schmideberg (12) has also spoken of depression as the

dominant symptom in the ex-convict. Offenders, she has noted, usually feel hopeless. My own experience as a therapist with offender patients in the clinic at APTO (Association for the Psychiatric Treatment of Offenders) has underscored this observation.

One might conclude from all this that depression is often closely associated in some fashion with the onset and enactment of delinquent and criminal behavior. The specific way in which they are related varies from case to case. Generally, it would seem as if the masking effect of the external or criminal action is imperfect at best, if one looks closely. It is likely that some of the depression is handled externally as an equivalent and that the rest is visible as depression. This, I believe, is the basis for what becomes perceived as a dysphoric quality. Apparently the discharge of some of the underlying depression through hostile, aggressive activities does not suffice to offset delinquents' feelings of hopelessness and defeat. No matter how hard these children fight back, they are unable to win their battle for survival with an environment that represents so great a source of deprivation and frustration to them. As a result of these unsuccessful efforts, the delinquent is left feeling depressed to some degree.

One would surmise that because the more serious delinquent retaliates much more violently than other delinquent children, he feels even less hopeful and more depressed. There is no doubt that the feelings of deprivation of many of these children begin early in life within the family setting. A depriving social system reinforcing a depriving family delivers a double blow that too often appears virtually irreversible in its criminogenic potential.

A further application of the concept of the "malevolent transformation" seems helpful in elucidating the dynamics of anxiety, acting out, depression, and anger. According to Sullivan (13), the "malevolent transformation" occurs when a child has been chronically rebuffed by his parents. If other methods of coping with this rejection, such as regression or sublimation, are foreclosed to him, the child will exhibit his "bad" self when he seeks affection and tenderness. This "bad" side of himself is accompanied by feelings of disapproval, and so anxiety is induced. In the case of the delinquent (4), the anxiety may be momentarily subdued by anger, which allows him to hit back against the hostility he feels from his parents.

Might not the expression of the "bad" self, with all the attendant bad feelings, produce some depression as well as anxiety—the depression reflective of his feeling bad at failing his parents? If depression were the only result, obviously, the delinquent acting out would be practically absent. If, however, there is a mixture of depressed feelings and anxious feelings, would not the transformation of anxiety suffice to account for the acting out with the remaining depression still present and to some extent visible?

Depressive syndromes are rather infrequent among delinquents (2):

> What one encounters quite often is a quality of depressiveness induced by the emotional and intellectual impoverishment in their character structures; an impoverishment which is undoubtedly a reflection of the impoverishment they have encountered in the environment in which they have been raised. In part, delinquent acting out might be parsimoniously explicable as a means of filling a sense of emptiness the youngster might feel. If he did not fill it this way, might he not continue life as an empty shell? If the delinquent manifests little creativity and blunted affectivity, might he not simply reflect in his behavior the discord, violence, and antisociality he sees about him every day? With what else can he fill it? How else can he deal with his experiences in the absence of inner resources? He has so little to draw upon.

One sees many such children at the Educational Alliance, a settlement house located in the Lower East Side ghetto of New York City, where I serve as a consultant. Staff workers describe them as depressed, apathetic, and listless in their nonactive moments, which means most of the time.

> They seem to need excitement to feel alive, and hence acting out can seesaw with depression. There is Joe, a boy of sixteen

who had been arrested for stealing from the mail and had been involved in several gang fights. The son of an old man and a young woman, Joe has generally been a loner. The worker describes him as morose, nonverbal, and completely withdrawn." There is also Ronald, seventeen. He had been in a half-dozen fights and was also arrested for purse-snatching. He has been described as sullen, angry, and hostile. When depressed, he retires for a while and then comes out of it in physical ways. He looks for a fight and after it is relieved.

Second Study - Evaluation of 60 Children

My access to the Educational Alliance's groupwork staff, which is involved with various aspects of the youth program related to delinquency prevention, school dropouts, narcotics usage, and gang activity, encouraged me to embark upon my second study, and I asked the staff members to provide data on those groups in which delinquents were likely to be found. This investigation eventually yielded a population of sixty children, twenty-three of whom turned out to be delinquent, as operationally defined, and the others not. Since the agency serves about five hundred children in this age range, the sample is 12 percent of the total, but admittedly skewed in the antisocial direction.

As in the first study, circumstances precluded my mounting a carefully controlled and thoroughgoing research into the phenomenon in which I was interested, as I would have preferred, but I nevertheless persevered. I asked each of the five groupworkers who were closely in touch with the desired population to fill in a checklist on each child. This time, however, because I had not previously collected data on gradations in delinquent behavior, I asked the workers to report on this. I should mention that groupworkers often get to know their clients quite well, and so I felt some confidence that their observations would have some validity. In all honesty, however, I must concede that I was unable to check on the reliability or validity of what they reported, except that the results confirm the general findings of the first study.

I categorized delinquent behavior as mild (reported to the police but not arrested, or no more than one arrest), somewhat (arrested two or three times), and serious (arrested more than three times). Because only two cases were rated as somewhat delinquent, I merged these with the serious category on the premise that they were more than mild or adventitious. I also included in the checklist a three-point scale (none, occasional, and frequent) on the use of marihuana, alcohol, and drugs (narcotics, barbiturates, and the like). I was particularly interested in the significance of drugs as a factor in relation to depression among delinquents. As in the previous study, the degree of depression was rated as none, little, somewhat, substantial, or predominant.

Age, Sex and Race

The sample of sixty contained twenty-six boys (43 percent) and thirty-four girls (56 percent). The average age was 15.9 years; boys were a little older, on the average, being 16.3 years, and the girls were 15.5 years. Nineteen (31.7 percent) were white, thirty-two (53.3 percent) were black, five (8.3 percent) were of Puerto Rican descent, and three (5 percent) represented other ethnic groups.

Of the thirty-seven (61.7 percent) children who were not delinquent, fourteen were boys and twenty-three were girls. Of the twenty-three (38.3 percent) who were delinquent, twelve were boys and eleven were girls. In the delinquent group, fifteen were mildly delinquent and eight were seriously so (the two who were "somewhat" delinquent had been merged in this group, as I mentioned earlier).

Frequency of Depression

The findings reveal that almost three out of five (58.3 percent) of the children in the entire group of sixty were at least somewhat depressed, and about one-third were substantially or predominantly depressed.

When the nondelinquent is compared with the delinquent, it is strikingly clear that the latter is considerably more
depressed than the former. More than four out of five delinquents (82.8 percent) were somewhat depressed, in contrast to
the nondelinquents, of whom only two out of five (43.2 percent) evidenced the same degree of depression. It should be
noted that the figure for delinquents here is about identical
with that for delinquents in the first study.

Drug Factor

With respect to drug use, forty-five (75 percent) of the total
sample were free of drugs and fifteen (25 percent) were listed
as users (40 percent were seen as occasional users and 60
percent as frequent users). The drug-free total was at least
somewhat depressed (44.5 percent) and about one in seven
(15.5 percent) was substantially or more severely depressed.
This is in sharp contrast to the drug users, none of whom
escaped at least substantial depression. Two out of five drug
users were substantially depressed, and more than half were
predominantly so.

To ascertain the linkage of depression and delinquency
when the possible contribution of drugs is eliminated, the
non–drug users in the delinquent and nondelinquent samples
were compared. The sixteen delinquent non–drug users were
at least somewhat depressed (74.9 percent), and 31.1 percent
were substantially depressed, but none predominantly. Not
surprisingly, the twenty-nine non–drug users were the least
depressed of all groups. Only one-fourth (27.6 percent) were
somewhat or substantially depressed, compared with three-
fourths of the comparable delinquents. Significantly, also,
three-fourths of the nondelinquents manifested little or no
depression.

To ascertain in a limited way the linkage of depression
and drug use in concert with delinquency, the drug-using
nondelinquents were compared with the drug-using delin-

quents. All eight of the drug-using nondelinquents were at least somewhat depressed, and 87.5 percent were more than somewhat: 50 percent were substantially and 34.5 percent were predominantly depressed. The seven drug-using delinquents nonetheless showed the greatest degree of depression: about one-fourth (28.6 percent) were substantially depressed and about three-fourths (71.4 percent) predominantly depressed.

Despite the small sample size, the mild delinquents who did not use drugs were next compared to the serious delinquents who did not use drugs, in order to ascertain whether depression accompanies increasing antisociality without the added complication of drug use. In this case, 72.1 percent of the mild group were somewhat depressed and 27.3 percent were substantially so. Of the serious delinquents, 83.3 percent were at least somewhat depressed, 33.3 percent substantially depressed, and 16.7 percent predominantly depressed.

Again, even though the small sample size precludes more than the simplest of inferences, I scrutinized reports on children who used either alcohol or marihuana frequently, but no drugs. Three children were listed as frequent alcohol consumers. Two of these were mild delinquents, one was not delinquent. One (33.3 percent) manifested little depression and the two others (66.7 percent) were substantially depressed.

Eight children used marihuana frequently. Six were nondelinquent, one was mildly delinquent, and the last was seriously delinquent. Among these youngsters, two (25 percent) evidenced little depression; one (12.5 percent) was somewhat depressed; and five (67.5 percent) were substantially depressed.

On the basis of these data, considering the limitations of the sample and the method employed, the following conclusions seem indicated:

1. Delinquents in this population appear considerably more depressed than nondelinquents. This finding concurs with the finding of the initial study.

2. The more serious the delinquent, the more serious the depression.

3. Drug users as a whole manifest considerably more depression than non–drug users.

4. Drug-using delinquents are more depressed than non–drug using delinquents.

5. Nondelinquent non–drug users show relatively little depression.

6. Adolescents who frequently use alcohol appear more depressed than the average adolescent in this population.

7. Adolescents who frequently use marihuana appear more depressed than the average adolescent in this population.

The implications of these results for treatment seem to be obvious. The elimination of certain kinds of delinquency should be considerably furthered if the underlying depressive components were dealt with. Schmideberg (12) has commented that the objectives of psychotherapy with offenders is to replace their hopelessness with a sense of hope.

Depression and Criminality

In an interesting twist, Cormier (5) contends that depression may have a salutary effect in reversing the criminal process at a certain time in the criminal's life. He speaks of a saturation point in the offender's life, at which he begins to be aware of a sense of failure in his criminal career. "It is the time when a persistent offender, who because of his aggression was until then unable to be really depressed about himself and the world, begins to suffer about his criminality. The saturation point is the start of the process of abatement, which may take years." For the first time in his life, the offender allows himself to become aware of depressed feelings and utilizes them for reality testing. Depression will thus enable a persistent offender "to establish a true if painful contact with the real world."

As the criminal begins to reexamine his life, he appreciates that although his parents may have let him down, he was usually loved to some extent by his mother. "He faces the idea that no matter how he criticizes them, he himself was a bad son bringing sorrow to his family; guilt often becomes transiently exaggerated and the early parental figures seen as all good while he is bad—neither being true."

Cormier (5) notes that at the point of saturation the depression may attain the proportions of a psychotic state. He claims that for many offenders, the depression can lead at last to maturation. He holds that depression is worked through "with all the mechanisms in mourning, sadness, anger, guilt, and many others. They come out of it having gained, if only partially , a new ability to accept their loss and their lot." This makes it possible for the offender to form more meaningful object relations that offer protection against his deep impulses toward retaliation against society, and thus enables the offender to find his way back to membership in the normal community.

Cormier (5) concludes that this emotional crisis, as manifested by the depression, compels such criminals to "ask for help and accept it; it places them in a situation where, if they have enough strength and insight and are resourceful, they can climb out of their pit."

In the case of the delinquent, we may reasonably hope that the youngster need not reach a saturation point before treatment can be effective. Indeed, delinquency may yield much more rapidly than we think at times, given the right opportunities. A note inscribed on the back of one of the data sheets in the second study I completed at the Educational Alliance seems to make the point. The worker wrote:

I had trouble with this report because this youth was extremely depressed and hopeless last year; but this year he has become much more hopeful and I have seen some real changes in him, which I connect to (1) entry into and success in a training program which will lead to a good job, (2) finishing high school, (3) developing a sound relationship with his girl friend.

The reason this boy entered and succeeded in a job-training program, finished high school, and developed a sound relationship with his girl friend, it should be added, is that the worker acted as a bridge between the boy and the world outside. It is becoming increasingly apparent that work with delinquents, especially those from ghetto areas, requires the articulation of many services catering to a multiplicity of needs. Not only must the depressed delinquent be provided with a means of coping with his emotional problems, but probably even more important, he must be helped in dealing with his social, educational, vocational, and economic problems to boot. It is not the delinquent himself who must be changed, however; intractable agencies, institutions, and serving systems must also undergo searching reappraisals and radical revisions if they are to meet their mandates.

At the Educational Alliance (1) we have found that groupworkers are moving into new patterns of service in being more active on behalf of children so that bureaucratic machines do not heedlessly and needlessly disregard their pressing concerns. The simple process of adjusting a child to his environment is not enough any longer, if it ever was. Often the helping person must act as an advocate on behalf of the youngster so that he can negotiate with an otherwise unresponsive institution or system. There must be give and take on both sides if the delinquent is to be helped to receive and sustain the service that he so desperately needs, and which we so often desperately need to provide him.

References

1. Berkowitz, L.; Chwast, J.; and Shattuck, G. *Staying in School.* New York: Educational Alliance, 1971.

2. Chwast, J. Depressive Reactions as Manifested Among Adolescent Delinquents. *Amer. J. Psychother.* 21:575, 1967.
3. Chwast, J. The Social Function of Guilt. *Soc. Wk.* 9:58, 1964.
4. Chwast, J. The Malevolent Transformation. *J. Crim. Law Crim. Pol. Sc.* 54:42, 1963.
5. Cormier, B. M. A Criminological Classification of Criminal Processes. In *Crime, Law, and Corrections*, ed. R. Slovenko. Springfield, Ill.: Charles C. Thomas, 1966.
6. Cormier, B. M.; Washbrook, R. A.; Kennedy, M.; and Obert, A. A Study of Fifty Young Penitentiary Delinquents from Age 15 to 25. *Proceedings of the 4th Research Conference in Delinquency and Criminology.* Montreal, 1964.
7. Fireman, A. E. The Pre-Acute Crime Milieu. *Arch. of Crim. Psychodyn.* 4:269, 1961.
8. Glover, E. *The Roots of Crime.* New York: International Universities Press, 1960.
9. Halleck, S. L. *Psychiatry and the Dilemmas of Crime.* New York: Harper & Row with Hoeber Medical Books, 1967.
10. Harrower, M. Who Comes to Court? *Amer. J. Orthopsychiat.* 25:15, 1955.
11. *Psychiatry Digest* 32, March 1971.
12. Schmideberg, M. The Psychological Treatment of Adult Criminals. *Probation* 25:45, 1946.
13. Sullivan, H. S. *The Interpersonal Theory of Psychiatry.* New York: Norton, 1953.
14. Tonks, C. M.; Paykel, E. S.; and Klerman, G. L. Clinical Depressions Among Negroes. *Amer. J. Psychiat.* 127:329, 1970.
15. Woddis, G. M. Depression and Crime. *Brit. J. Delinq.* 8:85, 1957.

14

Masked Depression in the Elderly

ALVIN I. GOLDFARB

The term "masked depression" has recently become popular. Although the term serves no nosologic or diagnostic purpose, it has heuristic value, especially in the case of the elderly. It reminds physicians of what Dr. Frederic D. Zeman stated so well: "Illness in old age is characterized by chronicity, multiplicity, and duplicity." Perhaps it would be best, before discussing the details of masked depression, to attempt a brief definition of what is generally called depression.

The term usually refers to a subjective experience, accompanied by motor agitation or slowing and pessimistic, frightened, ruminative thinking. The latter may be variously elaborated and usually includes paranoid ideas. In addition there is usually decreased ability to attend, to concentrate, and to initiate action. A depression may evolve without any marked signs of vegetative disturbance.

There are persons who appear to have a hereditary susceptibility to depressive reaction, as suggested by depressions in several ancestors or contemporary relatives; a high proportion of them manifest anorexia or bulemia, constipation or diarrhea, and sleep disturbance characterized by rapid onset, dreamlessness, and early-morning waking. There is also rumination and, when the disorder is not uniformly intense, diurnal variation in mood, the mornings being worse than the evenings. The variation is more easily noticed at the onset of the disturbance and as it clears.

The depressive disorders in which autonomic system disturbance and a seeming shift to a new level of homeostasis is present are generally classified as endogenous. They tend to be cyclic; that is to say, more or less regularly recurrent. Also, they may alternate with episodes of elation and overactivity in which grandiosity, delusions, and even hallucinations related to self-importance may be prominent: hypomanic or manic states. In the states of elation there is verbal productivity, inattentiveness, distractability, inability to fall asleep, and disinclination to take time for personal hygiene, including eating, voiding, defecating, and bathing.

The dynamic evolution of depressive states is schematized in *Figure 1.*

In many depressive reactions the "search for aid" appears to be directed at psychically incorporated or fantasied figures. Possibly because the motivational aspects of these disorders is largely intrapersonal and obscure, many of these disorders are called psychotic. The appeal consists of action aimed at bringing about the appearance, or the conviction of reappearance, of a desired person by feeling, thinking, or behaving in the proper way, by performing the correct rites. Personal suffering is frequently believed to be the signal that will call forth the desired person and help. This belief leads to behavior classified as "pain-dependent pleasure mechanisms": pleasure is wooed by suffering; the individual behaves as though rewards will follow if suffering is of the right type or sufficiently intense. Such suffering may precede, accompany, or follow actual pleasurable events as "payment," as self-punitive and apologetic expiatory behavior for having experienced something forbidden or "bad" such as pleasure, or as self-punishment for having been self-assertive, because assertiveness is a seeming denial of the usefulness of and need for the desired parental figure.

This is as much as to say that depressive disorders that commonly come to psychiatric attention are elaborations of fear or anger associated with alterations of mood, thinking, and behavior. The disorders vary in accordance with the person's hopes, values, views of his social surroundings, habitual behavior or "way of life," and genetic factors.

What are recognized as the psychodynamics of depression are the special elaborations of emotion and affect which can be considered as intrapersonally integrative and socially motivated. They are intrapsychic maneuvers that are personally experienced as problem-solving and which are at the same time designed to attract help, attention, protective action, or care, or the promise of one or all of these.

The responsive behavior on the part of the person delegated by the search for aid is popularly called love, and the elaborations comprising the search for aid are usually dignified as searches for love or understanding. The elaboration is often but not always associated with subjective mood changes and behavioral attitudes of depression. In predisposed individuals the yearning nostalgic search may evoke and be accompanied by signs of shift in autonomic nervous system functioning which may contribute to the aggravation or the emergence of diabetes, hypertension, glaucoma, or colitis.

Chronic depression may be more a way of life than is generally recognized; certainly there are countless persons perennially, though unobtrusively and inoffensively, occupied in finding and holding others in relationships of this kind. Dislocation of the individual from accustomed techniques that previously proved effective in his compulsion to find and hold a "protector"—techniques that he believes promise success in finding and holding such a person—or the actual or threatened loss of a person regarded as protector, arouses fear and anger, and leads to modification or accentuation of the search for aid, so that it emerges more clearly.

At times it is easily recognizable as a depressive reaction; at other times, although the depressive nature is masked, from the motivational point of view it can be identified and recog-

Figure 1

MULTIPLE CAUSES (Early and late) → LOSS OF RESOURCES (Physical, mental, social, economic) → DECREASED MASTERY (Tension relief; gratification) → FEELINGS OF HELPLESSNESS (Decreased self-esteem, self-confidence, sense of purpose, failure, anticipation of failure, humiliation, shame) → FEAR → SEARCH FOR AID → RATIONAL (Search for skilled aid)

→ IRRATIONAL (Dependency striving—search for "parent substitute" or "significant other"; "regressive behavior," with or without search for skilled aid)

FEAR ← ANGER ← FEAR OF RETALIATION, GUILTY FEAR

1. Multiple causes or initiating factors which occur either early in life and are reinforced or modified with aging or occur late in life and are peculiar to old age; several of which may combine forces and some of which may be necessary but insufficient alone, result in

2. an absence or loss of resources for minimal, adequate functioning, so that

3. there is decreased mastery of problems, challenges, and adjustments posed by internal changes (biologically determined drives or acquired needs) and external changes and threats, with resulting

4. feelings of helplessness or actual powerlessness, and consequent

5. fear with accompanying or subsequent anger, with consequent

6. "rationally" or "irrationally" aimed and elaborated search for aid which becomes patterned in terms acceptable to the individual in terms of his personality organization based upon his past, his present, and his expectations; and contingent on his perception of what is acceptable to and likely to work in "his world" as well as by the social response it receives. In this search there are observable constellations of motivated personal action which range from apathy through pseudo-anhedonia, display of helplessness, somatization, hypochondriasis, depression, and paranoid states to the most open and manipulative behavior. In predisposed persons there may be a physiologic shift to a new and relatively inefficient homeostatic level with depressive states which are then revealed by altered appetite, bowel function, sleep, and other vegetative signs.

nized as a depressive equivalent. But both the disguised and the clinically discernible depressive reactions may be regarded as adaptive maneuvers that epitomize a previous, less clear and obvious way of life. Recognition of this new crystallization or modification of old ways is of special importance, lest distressing and environmentally disturbing patterns of thought, feeling, and action lead to self-harm (including suicide), exhaustion, or other physiologically dangerous states.

In these terms the importance of depression in the chronologically old cannot be overestimated. It is common, disabling, and painful. It constitutes a burden of suffering for the patient, his family, and often his friends or neighbors. Nevertheless, depression in old age often is not recognized. Complaints are ignored because the person is regarded as potentially unproductive, with short life expectancy, and not worth the expenditure of time, effort, and money. Complaints may be regarded as "normal" concomitants of aging. Disability may not be noted in this unemployed "leisure" class. Functional illness may be attributed to physical illness, to brain damage, or to social and economic conditions.

Such failure to identify, report, and deal with disorder may be shared by the patient, who holds these same "tolerant" cultural views and is highly responsive to his social environment. The disturbance is, so to speak, masked from the sufferer and those around him. This masking is favored by psychodynamic mechanisms that lead to a variety of complex behavioral patterns categorized as "denial"; by the culturally determined excessive tolerance of personal suffering in oneself and others; by ignorance or a lack of sophistication; by absence of funds, facilities, and personnel for proper care or treatment; and because the community is not ready to acknowledge the sociomedical nature of certain problems.

Obvious mental disorders in old age may therefore be termed medical or neurologic by the psychiatrist or the department of mental hygiene, social by the practitioner of internal medicine, and economic by social workers. The patient is left in limbo before and after being subjected to unnecessary laboratory and X-ray procedures, unhelpful periods of hospitalization for physical disease, or complex processes that attempt to solve socioeconomic or dispositional problems.

Nevertheless, many of these disorders eventually force recognition of their psychiatric nature. However, incorrect diagnosis of senility or cerebral arteriosclerosis may be self-fulfilling prophecies, because they lead to neglect or to actual brain damage. In addition, early recognition of depressive disorders may permit prevention of some of the suicides and accidents so common in old age. It might also decrease personal suffering, decrease disability with physical and mental impairment, decrease the severity of diabetes, glaucoma, and hypertension, spare families from onerous problems, and decrease community disturbance.

Common misconceptions that serve to mask depression from the sufferer and those around him include beliefs that decline in energy, listlessness, and easy fatigability are the rule in chronologic aging, and that anorexia, constipation, and insomnia (including early waking) are normal in old age. Because of these notions, cardinal signs and symptoms of serious depression are missed or ignored. The old need more sleep than other adults, not less. They may eat less but have good appetites when they are well. They do not lose weight or have notable changes of bowel habits "normally," but only when they are physically ill or depressed.

A depressed person may not be able to express his subjectively experienced mood, to the confusion of those who expect clear, subjective reports of mood change. Sadness or depressed feelings may be expressed as feelings of emptiness, envy, inability to feel pleasure or pain, or illness. This situation can be frustrating for therapists preoccupied with eliciting psychodynamic features.

"What bothers you?" asks the doctor.

"I guess I'm depressed," replies the patient.

"How does that feel?" (Or "What does that mean?" or "Tell me about it.")

"Well, it's always on my mind."

"What is?"

"That I'd like to feel all right."

"How is that different from how you feel now?"

"I used to feel all right."

"And how do you feel now?"

"Well, I'm worried about how I feel."

An old person may say to children, "You're going out to the movies? That's all right, I'll stay here alone. It doesn't matter. I won't feel good if you stay, I won't feel bad if you go. Nothing matters to me anymore. Go. Enjoy yourselves."

Empty ruminating on not feeling as one believes one previously felt and should feel, and envy of those who do not have this trouble and are therefore able to do other things than be preoccupied with the way they feel, appear to be ways of communicating that one is depressed. The patients may appear to be apathetic or pseudoanhedonic; they do not complain of subjective depression.

Other common personal patterns that mask depression are tendencies to complain about, find fault with, or provoke a spouse or child; the pleading of difficulty in caring for a spouse, sibling, or other person "who needs me" but makes excessive demands. Of great importance is the exaggeration of and emphasis upon the importance of somatic concomitants of emergency emotion, such as tachycardia, dyspnea, anorexia, constipation, sleep disturbance, decreased salivation, or mydriasis, and exaggeration of personal helplessness, including mental impairment, so that there is a picture of pseudodementia. These patterns may be categorized as displays of helplessness and somatization.

Illnesses or impairments that commonly mask depression are a preexisting mental disorder such as schizophrenia or compulsive neurosis; arthritis or neuromuscular disease, endocrine disorder, malignancy, nephritis, and any debilitating disorder that leads to repeated hospitalizations and is threatening to life. Exacerbation, aggravation, and exploitation of these illnesses or impairments occur in the "search for aid." A disabled person may be a depressed patient whose illness and impairment is aggravated and exaggerated by the mental disorder to which it is a contributory etiologic factor. Recently renewed attention has been drawn to the fact that the need for medical care and the use of hospitals tends to depress people, and that their depression in turn accelerates or intensifies physical decline.

Persons who use physical illness as a way of communicating distress or who have found illness to be a way of manipulating others, and, conversely, persons who regard health, "independence," or martyrdom as the most likely to attract favorable attention or bring assistance, tend to mold their behavior accordingly. Serious depressive disorders can be missed when somatic complaints are ignored or considered to be merely accentuations of "neurotic traits" or earlier foibles. A pseudoneurotic form of cyclic mood disorder, which escapes recognition as a psychosis in youth, frequently produces symptoms that are severe and socially disturbing in old age. Meticulous reporting by the patient of tachycardia, respiratory changes, or alterations in appetite and bowel movements, which are the concomitants of emergency emotions or the signs of changed autonomic system activity associated with depression, is one manner in which feelings of helplessness may frequently be expressed.

Exaggeration of and preoccupation with physical problems and exaggeration of personal helplessness are signs of depression. When mental impairment is exaggerated or exploited, a depression may masquerade as an organic mental syndrome, and neglect of the pseudodementia may lead to the very brain change it simulates.

Additional signals of depression in the elderly with organic mental syndromes are special types of paranoid reaction of the type described as the "illusion of doubles." For example, an aged woman who revered her long-dead father and remembered him as a protective person who was suddenly and cruelly taken away from her in childhood, when frightened by her own memory loss and the failing health of her husband, began to tell him he was a stranger. She wanted to know why he, a sick man, impersonated her healthy, helpful mate.

Another mentally impaired woman, frightened and depressed by her mental and physical failure, wanted her sister to remain with her by day as well as at night. She signaled her affective disorder by insisting that her working sister was an impostor. Her real sister, she said, would not have gone to work, but would have stayed home and cared for her.

An old and frightened man signaled his need for a strong and helpful mate by wandering about the streets looking for his wife. When told she was home in bed, he would reply, "That's not the wife I'm looking for."

Other old persons, on looking in the mirror, are disturbed and made angry by the image of a seemingly casual or even mockingly mimicking other person—an unhelpful and possibly dangerous stranger in their home. Such complaints and symptoms may be mistaken for "confusion" caused solely by brain damage, rather than recognized as part of a depressive elaboration in a person with decreased discriminatory capacity; it is a depressive elaboration related to the previous personality and to the stress of failing health and mentation.

As Hughlings Jackson once pointed out, when the sick man fails to recognize his nurse, this is indicative of brain damage; when he misidentifies her as his wife, it is indicative of his personality needs and expectations, and is part of an affective disorder.

It can be stated that at some time in the development or evolution of a depression the following behavior patterns may be found:

(1) Apathy—a seeming indifference, lack of interest, or lack of motivation for any action: inertia.

(2) Pseudoanhedonia—an expressed or displayed inability to experience pain or pleasure, which appears designed to call attention to misery while denying that it can be felt.

(3) Display of helplessness—expressed as nervousness and an "inability to cope," and accompanied by aggravation, exaggeration, and exploitation of existing impairments or illness.

(4) Somatic impairment—emphasis on aches and pains. These may be physiologic accompaniments of emergency emotion, such as tachycardia or respiratory distress, or the effects of hyperventilation or existing impairment or illness.

(5) Hypochondriasis—minor disorders or functionally determined symptoms are reacted to with fright and the conviction that disintegration and doom are imminent.

(6) Subjectively experienced or objectively notable depression of affect; a lowness of mood experienced as sadness, emptiness, feelings of futility or helplessness, or an appearance of being worried, anxious, preoccupied, withdrawn, irritable.

(7) Clearly depressive behavior and feeling, which may be accompanied by a shift in autonomic and homeostatic patterns.

(8) Hypomanic behavior.

(9) Manic behavior.

(10) Paranoid reactions, ranging from excessive irritability, anger, and faultfinding to delusions with ideas of reference and auditory, olfactory, and (rarely) visual hallucinations.

(11) Exploitive-manipulative activities—clinging, ingratiating, and demanding behavior that may alternate with

(12) Punitive, coercive, commanding, and domineering behavior.

These patterns or constellations of behavior may often be seen together or sequentially in a kaleidoscopically shifting way in all depressive disorders. This is true whether they seem to be genetically determined and recurrent or psychodynamically determined.

In the same person at different times, and in different persons in different cultures, one or another of these patterns may take precedence in a depressive reaction. The particular pattern that is emphasized appears to be a product of the individual's enculturation. Each person interprets, more or less correctly, what is most likely to succeed in gaining the desired response from parental surrogates or significant others in his social environment.

In the case of genetically determined depressive disorders, biochemical changes appear to come first and lead to decreased flexibility of functioning. They are causes of a decreased capacity for mastery and are part of the etiology of the total depressive response. They lead to the series of events which is finally experienced as a change in mood, to which the individual reacts with feelings of helplessness, fear, and anger. The helplessness and emergency emotions are then elaborated in motivated attempts to gain aid from others because of the devastating effect of the mood change and helplessness experienced.

In the case of psychodynamically determined depression, it is chiefly those psychological inhibitions acquired in childhood which have decreased the individual's ability to assert himself. The result is a need for assistance or the reassurance of its ready availability from parental surrogates throughout one's lifetime. When new physical, personal, or intrapersonal problems arise, especially the loss or threat of loss of parental surrogates, then the previously culturally acceptable search for or maintenance of relations with persons viewed as actually or potentially helpful may emerge in a new, less efficient, and more troublesome way. This way has been described in terms of the patterns that, alone or in combination, signal the presence of what is here called depression.

In some depressions a biochemical disorder is triggered by the emergency emotions that accompany or follow the feelings of humiliation, shame, or guilt which signal or represent a loss of self-esteem or self-confidence. This is part of the anticipation or experience of failure felt as helplessness. Here it is the life experience and the intrapsychic or psychodynamic events that lead to pathophysiology. These biochemical changes are like those that appear to have no psychodynamic precipitants and "come out of the blue" as recurrent episodes related to genetically determined factors and, once developed, diminish adaptive resources so as further to decrease the capacity for mastery.

In any individual, the behavior patterns that characterize the depression may change along with changes in the personal situation as the individual is more or less successful in decreasing fear, anger, and feelings of helplessness, or as biochemical changes occur. Many depressive reactions that begin with a display of feelings of helplessness, or with pseudoanhedonic complaints, progress to include somatization and then become clearly hypochondriacal. All this may occur before subjective depression is clearly experienced or displayed. Similarly, persons who have a propensity for recurrent mood disorder, especially of the cyclic type, may experience sleep disturbance, anorexia, constipation, decreased capacity to concentrate, and lack of initiative long before subjective depression is noted and before any of the behavior patterns described are elaborated.

Psychotherapy is the primary mode of treatment for the apathetic, pseudoanhedonic states and for outstanding displays of helplessness. There are many vehicles for its delivery. Helpful therapist-patient relationships can be developed by way of physiotherapy, recreational therapy, small social group meetings, special projects, sheltered workshops, and group or dyadic therapy. Sedatives and antidepressants can help to encourage, crystallize, and maintain the relationships established. The same is true for somatizing, hypochondriacal, and subjectively depressed persons who have few or no vegetative signs and little or no biochemical or pathophysiologic changes.

Where there are clearly pathophysiologic concomitants, antidepressant medications and electroconvulsant therapies are the primary modes of treatment, but psychotherapeutic relationships help to initiate the patient in them and to maintain him in the proper treatment regime. When there is manic and paranoid behavior, the primary modes of treatment are also pharmacological and physical. Physical and pharmacotherapeutic methods are required for many exploitive, manipulative persons, but their exposure to consensus by way of group therapy is often helpful and usually clearly indicated.

This is as much as to say that depressive reactions that are largely or entirely psychological in origin, and which are accompanied by no significant degree of biochemical change, are the ones most likely to be improved by psychotherapy, and are least helpfully influenced by medications. When biochemical changes are etiologic or become significantly involved, pharmacotherapy is required to decrease suffering and shorten the duration of the disorder. In the former, psychotherapy helps patients to take and benefit from the drugs. In the latter, drugs help the patient accept and benefit from the controlled life experience called psychotherapy.

In summary, it seems that depressive reactions that may otherwise escape attention can be recognized if one views aberrant behavior as an embarkation upon a personally wasteful, socially troublesome, and generally inefficient mode of appealing for and guaranteeing supportive relationships. The goals of such behavior presumably could have been more easily or pleasurably achieved by fulfillment of socially ascribed roles for which the individual is unprepared or which society has made it difficult for him to find, learn, or fulfill.

Effective treatment of depressive disorders becomes possible if therapists recognize the apparently universal propensity of patients to search for and make use of special relationships as equivalents of actual role fulfillment. These relationships produce the confidence, sense of security, pride, and pleasure that would otherwise be obtained by constructive problem-solving activity or by way of similar relationships in courtship, marriage, friendship, religion, or medical or legal care.

A relationship that serves to help the depressed, aged person toward increased self-confidence and self-esteem, and from which he derives pleasure and a sense of purpose, is helpful in itself and makes possible or increases the efficacy of other treatment modalities when they are needed.

PART 3

15

Psychotherapy in Combination with Antidepressant Drugs in the Treatment of Patients with Masked Depressions

STANLEY LESSE

From a technical standpoint the treatment of patients with masked depressions poses very esoteric problems. I am referring particularly to those patients in whom the depressions are masked by hypochondriacal complaints or psychosomatic disorders, since these represent the most common masking patterns seen among adult patients.

As I noted in Chapter 4, it is usually only after months or even years of repeated physical and laboratory examinations and after the failure of multiple medical and even surgical procedures, or following the rapid mushrooming of a severe undisguised depressive affect, that the psychiatrist is called upon as a consultant. Approximately three-fourths of these patients have been ill for more than one year, two-thirds for more than two years, and almost one-third for more than five years by the time they are seen in neuropsychiatric consultation.

In earlier chapters I have also noted that in most instances the underlying depression is of severe proportions by the time the patient is seen by a neuropsychiatrist and more than 40 percent of the patients manifest at least intermittent suicidal preoccupations. In these circumstances the patient may require urgent or even emergency treatment.

Despite the severity of the underlying depression, however, the majority of these patients will obsessively present themselves as having severe, chronic organic illnesses that have been "misdiagnosed" or "mistreated" by a parade of physicians, dentists, osteopaths, or chiropractors. Those few who admit to being depressed will forcefully and repeatedly protest that their depressive manifestations are fully justified by the fact that they have "suffered physically so painfully and so long."

As the result of many difficult experiences, I learned that these patients, in the main, will resent being referred to a psychiatrist and will run from therapy if the initial psychiatric evaluation is too overt and is undisguisedly aimed at digging out psychopathologic symptoms and signs or psychodynamic mechanisms.

I have had an advantage over most psychiatrists and psychotherapists in that some of my patients are referred to me in my role as an attending neurologist at the Neurological Institute of the Presbyterian Hospital of New York. Some of these referrals come from specialists in organic medicine or psychiatrists who wish to rule out a neurologic problem.

During the past decade and a half, in response to my clinical documentation of dramatic positive therapeutic results, a large number of my nonpsychiatric medical and dental colleagues have come to recognize the masked depression syndrome. When they refer a patient to me, they often represent me as solely a neurologist, since they too have become aware that these patients resent any suggestion that they may have "emotional problems." The patient comes to the initial examination hoping for or expecting an organic diagnosis that will be followed by organic treatment, either medical or surgical.

I described in Chapter 4 how one must be gently patient

in taking a most careful neuropsychiatric history, using the patient's suppliant cry for help and magical expectancies as tools in effecting a strong transference reaction. Any reference to the patient's obvious emotional distress must be made very gently and tenuously, and at all times must be related to the patient's real or imagined physical distresses, which are more commonly than not of mild proportions or iatrogenic in origin.

In patients with masked depressions it is essential to obtain a rapid amelioration of the underlying depressive affect if a significant, lasting therapeutic result is to be eventually obtained. Since the hypochondriacal complaints or psychosomatic disorders are directly related to the depressive core, these manifestations are ameliorated, either in part or completely, whenever any remission of the basic depressive core occurs as the result of therapy.

Treatment is much less complicated in those patients who are aware of a depressive reaction paralleling their "physical" complaints. Unfortunately, such individuals represent a very small proportion of the patients I have seen.

The treatment of choice in patients with masked depressions, when the underlying depressions are of severe proportions, is a combination of antidepressant drug therapy and appropriately designed psychoanalytically oriented psychotherapy.

In 1962, I presented the initial papers on the use of antidepressant drugs in combination with psychoanalytically oriented psychotherapy in the treatment of severely depressed patients on an ambulatory basis. These initial reports were based upon a five-year experience with 180 severely depressed patients (1, 2). By early 1971, I had employed this technique in the treatment of 402 severely depressed patients (3).

In general, the results obtained with this technique have been extremely satisfactory. In persons with overt depressions, excellent or good results, as defined by a remission of symptoms and the patient's ability to resume vocational and social responsibilities with a high degree of pride and pleasure, were obtained in over 80 percent of the patients treated

(4). These short-term results approached those obtained by electroshock therapy, in my experience, and have proven significantly more successful than antidepressant drugs alone.

I do not consider or use the psychopharmacologic therapies as an end in themselves. I consider them rather as adjuncts to psychotherapy: they enable the patient to attain a level of ego stability that permits him to cooperate more effectively in a psychotherapeutic relationship. While many patients may show definite evidence of improvement with antidepressant drugs alone, and are able to return to a satisfactory level of vocational and social functioning, others become worse, though they continue to take the medications. In great measure this can be accounted for by the fact that these patients return to the same habit patterns that had led to the original psychiatric illnesses. No drug, no matter how efficacious it may be, can give the patient insight into the mechanisms of his basic intrapsychic or psychosocial problems and teach him how to live in a more mature fashion and to function within his ego capacities.

In general, mildly depressed patients—those who are able to function actively, both vocationally and socially, and whose depressions are not accompanied by marked feelings of hopelessness or suicidal preoccupations—can and should be treated purely by psychotherapeutic techniques. However, as I have noted, the vast majority of patients with masked depressions are severely ill by the time they are referred for neuropsychiatric consultation.

Ambulatory management of severely depressed patients—those who are unable to function vocationally or socially and who may be plagued by feelings of hopelessness or constant or intermittent preoccupation with suicide—by psychoanalytic or psychoanalytically-oriented techniques alone is archaic, fraught with danger, and indeed cruel in the light of current psychiatric developments. These techniques needlessly expose the patient to the dangers of an impulsive suicidal act. They cannot guarantee rapid improvement, and therefore expose the patient to the prolonged agonies of his depression.

While the psychodynamic patterns behind a severe depression are, as a rule, easily discernible from the material gathered in the first interview, *a knowledge of the psychodynamic mechanisms per se does not indicate the severity of the depression at any given time.* A psychodynamic modus operandi may be the same in a patient in a mildly depressed state as in a patient with strong suicidal drives.

As I have previously noted, the vast majority of patients who appear with masked depressions will react negatively to any obvious psychotherapeutic approach attempted at the very outset, for this is alien to their expectations. Unless the expectations of the patient and the therapist seem to be congruous, therapy, particularly in its initial phases, is destined to be ineffective. At the start of psychiatric treatment, this type of patient will accept the use of drugs that are presented to him as being muscle relaxants that will alleviate his marked increase in muscle tension.

The use of the combined technique requires that the psychiatrist first of all be a physician who understands the biodynamics of the antidepressant drugs, their potential benefits, their limitations, and their toxic side effects. Second, he must be trained in intensive psychoanalytic and psychoanalytically oriented psychotherapeutic techniques, especially with the briefer forms of dynamically oriented psychotherapy. Lastly, the therapist should be thoroughly conversant with the assets and liabilities of electroshock therapy, for in the earlier phases of treatment, EST or hospitalization or both may be necessary for a small but significant number of patients.

Selection of Patients

As I have noted, the vast majority of patients with masked depressions require urgent or emergency treatment. Accordingly, this technique may be divided into (*a*) an initial phase, and (*b*) a phase utilizing psychoanalytically oriented psychotherapy.

During the initial phase the patients are seen at least two to three times a week. The overall treatment period usually lasts from two to six months. The vast majority of patients are from forty to sixty-five years of age, with the average age being somewhere between forty-three and fifty-three. As I have already described in previous chapters, masked depressions occur more than twice as frequently among women as among men. Among those patients who have atypical facial pain of psychogenic origin, the ratio of women to men was 9:1.

The patients I selected for treatment by this combined technique were unable to function vocationally, socially, or sexually. The underlying depression was accompanied by strong feelings of hopelessness in most of the patients. Almost half had intermittent suicidal preoccupations. All complained of insomnia, anorexia, loss of interest in themselves and their environment, inability to concentrate, and poor memory. The slightest task was an ordeal. Most of them expressed feelings of inadequacy and marked self-derogation. All felt they were a burden to others and felt very guilty about it.

In my experience gathered from long and bitter therapeutic trials, all of the patients were poor candidates for any of the psychotherapeutic techniques alone on an outpatient basis.

Not all patients were considered good candidates for the combined antidepressant-psychotherapeutic technique on an ambulatory basis. For example, there was a small number of regressed schizophrenic patients in whom the depressive reaction was masked by somatic delusions. These patients were not good subjects for this combined procedure, because they were poor candidates in general for drug therapy and/or psychotherapy on an ambulatory basis. Electroshock therapy remains the preferred treatment in these cases. Similarly, those patients who manifested severe depression, masked or overt, in the matrix of an organic mental syndrome were not treated by this technique on an outpatient basis. In my experience, it is necessary to hospitalize such patients, since any type of therapy on an outpatient basis involves great risk of an impulsive suicidal act.

Some severely depressed nonschizophrenic patients who have constant suicidal preoccupations are also too ill for treatment on an ambulatory basis with this combined technique. There is no one factor in every patient that determines this decision, which depends on one or more of the following factors:

(a) Recent history of a suicidal act.
(b) History of earlier suicidal ideas or acts.
(c) History of family suicides.
(d) Acting out as a prime expression of increased anxiety.
(e) The intensity of manifested guilt feelings.
(f) The intensity of overt or covert hostility.
(g) Prior history of poor results with drug therapy or psychotherapy.
(h) Hostility to any psychotherapeutic procedures.
(i) Absence of any responsible relative or friend.
(j) The presence of a debilitating physical disorder.

These factors and others must be reviewed very minutely. This meticulous pretherapeutic evaluation is a necessary precaution against a precipitous suicidal act during treatment.

I cannot emphasize too forcefully that each patient must have a thorough general and neurological examination before the combined technique is introduced. This admonition is particularly important since the vast majority of these patients are past forty years of age.

Drug Selection

From 1957 to early 1971, I used essentially only three antidepressant drugs. They were (a) iproniazid (Marsalid, discontinued in 1959), (b) imipramine hydrochloride (Tofranil), and (c) tranylcypromine (Parnate, SKF) in combination with trifluoperazine (Stelazine, SKF) and usually also with diazepam (Valium, Roche).

The selection of the proper antidepressant drug was of

prime importance, for in my experience, iproniazid and imipramine have not been statistically of significant benefit to patients with agitated depressions; they appear to be of value primarily in the treatment of patients with depressions associated with decreased psychomotor activity (5). In contrast, the tranylcypromine-trifluoperazine combination, particularly when used together with diazepam, is of definite benefit to agitated depressed patients, but not to patients with decreased psychomotor activity (6).

As I noted earlier, a rapid initial amelioration of the depressive core is necessary in this type of patient if any lasting benefit is to occur. There are several reasons for this. First, most such patients are very ill, and almost half of them have suicidal ideas. Second, almost all are convinced that their symptoms are entirely organic and are strongly averse to active psychiatric treatment. Third, most of these patients are chronically ill and additionally handicapped by massive iatrogenic overlays.

Initial Phase of Therapy

In the initial phase of combined therapy (the first one or two weeks of treatment), the psychotherapeutic aspect of the treatment process is mainly supportive in character. It is conducted in a face-to-face setting. The patients all demonstrate an extremely limited ego capacity. They are all dominated by the exquisitely terrifying psychic pain that is so uniquely a part of depressive syndromes.

They are almost all infantile in their helplessness and dependency. Most have lost all hope of recovery and cry out in a suppliant fashion. In addition, most of the patients give evidence of strong rage-linked guilt mechanisms. They plead for help, but most of them do not feel they deserve it.

In this initial phase of treatment all of the patients require a strong, almost psychic-transfusion type of therapy. The patients have childlike, magical expectations, and it is necessary for the therapist to be a strong, all-wise, all-forgiving, protective parental surrogate. These severely depressed patients require and receive direct and repeated reassurance that they will get well.

A strong positive transference is deliberately fostered. In this initial emergency phase of treatment the therapist should not be concerned lest this deliberate supportive "giving" technique be considered as evidence of infantile countertransference.

No active attempt is made at this stage to probe into the deeply repressed conflictual material, and no effort is made to indicate to the patients that their problems are either entirely or mainly psychogenic. Any action of this type would cause the patient to run from treatment.

To those patients in whom "somatic" complaints are manifestations of underlying depression, a pseudoscientific explanation is presented which suggests a relationship between emotional stress and their physical disorders. For example, in patients who have atypical facial pain of psychogenic origin, I present this general explanation: "The original damage is no longer present. However, there is a great deal of muscle tension and muscle spasm present." (In reality, in most of these patients there is increased tonus in the muscles of mastication due to bruxism and chronic hypertrophy as a result of chronic clenching of the jaws.) Almost without exception the patients will initially accept this explanation. I then proceed to give an example of the relationship of chronic muscle contraction to pain.

In general, all of the statements are biochemically and physiologically correct, although they may have at best loose application to these organically scotomatized patients. But they form the theoretic bridge between the organic and the psychologic.

"It is well known that muscles that are under tension for long periods of time become painful. For example, if you were to lift your arm and hold it straight out for fifteen to twenty minutes, the muscles of your arm would become extremely painful." Invariably the patients would nod their heads at this point. "The same thing occurs with regard to your facial muscles. The initial trauma, whatever it was, produced pain. The muscles supplied by the involved nerves defensively went into spasm. However, as I have just explained, muscles that remain in spasm for a long period of time become painful. Persistent pain is emotionally exhausting." The patients would nod or otherwise express agreement.

"When one is under emotional stress, muscle contraction is a very common manifestation of this emotional reaction. This in turn increases the muscle spasm in the face and forms a type of vicious cycle, with the muscle contraction producing pain, the pain producing increased emotional distress and fatigue, and the increased emotional stress and fatigue producing more muscle contraction. My aim is to break into this vicious cycle. I plan to do this by causing marked muscle relaxation, which very often can be accomplished within a few days to a week by the use of a combination of medications."

Admittedly this type of explanation seems extremely simplistic. But it is really quite sophisticated, and it can be modified to fit problems involving any and all organ systems. Most important, it should be noted that these very ill patients have magical expectancies that are utilized in the rapid development of a strong transference reaction.

The agitated depressed patients often "confess" to real or imaginary wrongs they have committed. If they do, they receive complete expiation of their "sins" at this phase of the process. Also, since with rare exceptions agitated depressed patients are hard-driving, meticulous, capable persons who have functioned at a high level prior to the onset of illness, they are given recognition for what they have tried to accomplish. They are told that, at least in part, their persistent discomfort is due to "exhaustion" resulting from their continued effort to "perform despite their discomforts."

This simple technique is strongly ego-supportive to this group and usually decreases, at least temporarily, the intensity of the guilt mechanism. Without exception these patients are intolerant of their inability to perform vocationally or socially.

The patient's family is usually consulted closely to obtain information concerning the patient's background and personality matrix. Among my patients, married women are almost invariably accompanied by their husbands, from whom a description of the basic personality matrix can be obtained. On occasion the husband, who is usually a passively dependent man, echoes the patient's conviction that the entire process is organic in nature. At times this dependent identification pattern is so strong as to be reminiscent of a *folie à deux* mechanism. Under no circumstances at this point do I attempt to dissuade these men from their convictions as to the organic basis for the wife's complaints.

It is extremely important to obtain a description of the quality and intensity of the patient's behavior patterns. When suicidal patterns are present, the family is clearly informed of the seriousness of the patient's illness and of the fact that if the patient does not begin to respond in from one to two weeks, or if she appears to be worse in any way, hospitalization will be recommended. I inform those relatives who can comprehend the seriousness of the underlying depression that if the drug therapy in combination with psychotherapy is not rapidly effective, at least in ameliorating the suicidal ideation and the overt depressive affect, electroshock therapy may be necessary. The omnipresent danger of suicide in any depressed patient is brought out forcefully and repeatedly to the family members.

The patient's family is urgently advised to observe the patient carefully during the initial phase of treatment, and both the patient and the family are urged to phone the therapist if they wish. Indeed, during the first weeks, specific times are scheduled in which reports on the patient's status are to be given by telephone during intervals between visits.

If there is any question as to the patient's ability to take care of his or her own medication, it is managed by a family member. At the very outset, the possible common side effects are described. The patients, and members of their families if necessary, are instructed very clearly, both verbally and in writing, on how the medications are to be administered, and what foods, drugs, and activities, if any, should be avoided or modified.

Initially the patient is instructed not to assume any responsibilities. This tends to relieve the strong guilt feelings that stem from his inability to function. This directive, coming as part of the medical regime, is of great help and is usually grasped eagerly by the patient.

During the first few weeks, particularly the first week, the patient's status is minutely probed by direct observation and by questioning the family when this is possible. The intensity of the depression, together with the degree of hopelessness and suicidal preoccupation, are kept in sharp focus. Changes in sleeping habits are scrutinized carefully. Observation of the degree of psychomotor activity is of particular importance, because a change in the direction of a more normal pattern is almost always the first sign of improvement.

A change in psychomotor activity sometimes occurs in the first twenty-four or forty-eight hours when tranylcypromine is used. Shortly after this is noted by the patients, they observe an improvement in the intensity of their "physical discomforts." If one questions the patients extremely closely at this point, usually one can record that an improvement in mood preceded or accompanied the improvement in the "physical symptoms." Most patients are seen on at least two occasions during the first week, in addition to telephone conversations.

An improvement in the patient's status permits a gradual expansion of the psychotherapeutic procedure. In most instances, a history of significant emotional distress can be recorded as having occurred prior to the onset of the "physical problem." With improvement in their chronic symptoms, the patients are increasingly willing to accept the presence of a significant depressive reaction. The therapist must be very patient in expanding the tie between physical and psychological processes. This requires a very sensitive appreciation of the patient's ego capacities at a given point in therapy.

When this combined technique is used on an ambulatory basis with severely depressed patients in whom suicidal ideation is very prominent, if the patients do not show a definite improvement during the first week, or if their conditions worsen, ambulatory electroshock therapy or hospitalization is considered. The therapist must be definite and firm in his decisions if either of these courses is considered necessary, because many decompensating depressed patients have committed suicide because of indecisiveness on the part of the psychiatrist or of their own families.

The time limit of approximately seven to ten days allowed for the first symptoms and signs of improvement was established for good reasons. As I noted earlier, if ambulatory depressed patients do not begin to respond to imipramine in one week, there is little likelihood of any significant change except by placebo effect (5). On the other hand, patients who respond to the tranylcypromine-trifluoperazine combination commonly will begin to do so from twenty-four to seventy-two hours after the onset of drug treatment. It is my experience, based on the observation of hundreds of patients, that if this drug combination does not produce a significant change in psychomotor activity and mood in from seven to fourteen days at the very longest, there is little use in continuing these medications.

As the patient improves, the active cooperation of the family is decreased and finally eliminated.

During this initial phase of the combined therapy technique the results depend in great measure upon the duration of illness. They also depend upon the amount of medical treatment, particularly the amount of drug therapy and the number of surgical procedures, to which the patient previously has been exposed.

The results also depend upon the organ system involved. Female patients who have symptoms referable to the face or head and neck, or to their mammary or genitourinary systems, pose more difficult problems than those who have problems related to other organ systems.

Considered as a group, more than 75 percent of those patients in whom the depression is masked by hypochondriacal complaints or psychosomatic disorders obtain excellent results if the illness is of less than one year's duration. By "excellent" I mean that their symptoms disappear, the level of psychomotor activity becomes appropriate, and they are able to function vocationally and socially with pride and pleasure. Approximately 50 percent of those patients who have been ill for less than two years and who do not have strong iatrogenic overlay secondary to surgical procedures obtain excellent or good results during the initial period of therapy.

When a patient has been ill for more than two years, particularly if he or she is plagued by marked iatrogenic complications resulting from prior drug or mechanical therapies, it is difficult to predict how successful the combined therapeutic technique will be. Overall, approximately one-third of such patients obtain excellent or good results from combined therapy. While one cannot be so certain of the results that will be obtained in more chronic patients, individual excellent responses have been obtained in some who have been ill for as long as fifteen to twenty years.

It is the duration of the illness rather than the age of the patient that is the prime determining prognostic factor. However, age does play a role in determining whether a given patient can accept an advancement to a more sophisticated type of psychoanalytically oriented psychotherapy in an attempt to develop an understanding of the basic psychodynamic and psychosocial mechanisms behind the underlying depression. A schizoid personality matrix also limits a patient's capacity to respond to an expanded therapeutic procedure. Finally, factors such as an extremely rigid, obsessive-compulsive personality matrix and evidences of early organic mental deficits will limit any expansion in the psychotherapeutic procedure. For these patients, the psychotherapeutic aspect of the combined technique continues to be supportive and directive in nature.

Drug therapy is continued for many months, and in no instance is it discontinued precipitously. Dosages vary, depending upon the response of the patient, the presence of side effects, the degree of stress to which the patient is exposed, and the ability of the patient to function in a meaningful fashion vocationally and socially.

Psychoanalytically Oriented Phase of Therapy

Following the initial decrease in the patient's "physical complaints," the severity of the depressive affect, the disappearance of feelings of hopelessness, and especially the amelioration of all suicidal preoccupations, the psychotherapeutic techniques are broadened in scope. The psychotherapeutic process at this point is designed to be strongly ego-supportive, for marked ego depletion is characteristic of all severely depressed patients, whether the depression is masked or clearly overt.

The improvement during the first few days to two weeks, due primarily to the pharmacodynamic effects of the antidepressant drugs and/or to placebo effects, is often remarkable. Within this very short period the patient may be transformed from an anergic or extremely agitated individual dominated by feelings of hopelessness and even suicidal preoccupations and drives into a person whose psychomotor activity is within the normal range and whose depressive affect is markedly or completely ameliorated.

The therapist must exert extreme caution at this point, for much of the improvement may be due to a purely transient placebo effect. Precipitous suicidal acts can occur in this phase if the therapist is inexperienced or negligent in maintaining close contact with the patient. The patient has little or no insight into the basic problem at this point. Thus far he or she has been helped primarily by a pharmacophysiologic process, and secondarily by the strong protective role of the therapist.

For a significant number of patients with severe, chronic masked depressions, particularly those in their fifties or sixties, combined therapy should be limited to mean drug therapy in combination with *direct supportive psychotherapy* and some environmental manipulation, consisting mainly of a reduction of work or social pressures. The therapist must be cautious lest he destroy the benefits that have been obtained by attempting to force an awareness of the underlying psychodynamic mechanisms of the illness upon the patient. Some depressed patients do not have the ego capacities to participate in analytically oriented psychotherapy. As one might expect, the long-term results with this type of patient are more tenuous than with those whose ego capacities permit a more sophisticated type of therapy, the aim of which is to encourage intrapsychic and psychosocial maturation.

With those patients who have the capacities for greater emotional maturation, the extreme positive transference must be reduced, for if it is permitted to continue in an undiluted manner, it paralyzes effective psychotherapy; instead of aiding the patient's depleted ego reserves, it may lead to permanent atrophy of the ego. The therapist deliberately appeals to and in great measure satisfies the patient's infantile magical expectancies during the initial phase of treatment. Indeed, *his ego is the patient's ego, for without it the patient is very likely to commit suicide*. This support is withdrawn at a studied, cautious pace in proportion to the realistic evidence of the patient's increased ego capacity.

In this combined technique, drug therapy is usually continued for many months. Many patients with histories of endogenous depressions have been kept on maintenance drug therapy from one year to as long as fifteen years (attempts at withdrawal sometimes lead to massive depressive exacerbations). Therapy is continued in a face-to-face setting. Careful clinical evaluation of the patient is routine at every session for weeks. In addition to other, more obvious symptoms, the intensity of the hypochondriacal and psychosomatic symptoms must be closely scrutinized, together with the degree of insomnia, anorexia, psychomotor activity, and so on. An increase in these symptoms is an indication of an exacerbation of the depression. Similarly, dream material can be a prime beacon in heralding an exacerbation or improvement (8).

In general, the psychotherapeutic goals for these patients are less extensive than they would be in an intensive reconstructive psychoanalytic procedure. In part this is due to the patient's age group, for severe nonschizophrenic depressions are relatively uncommon in patients under forty years of age. An active attempt is made to promote an understanding of the psychodynamic mechanisms of the patient's illness. He is encouraged to associate freely. However, the therapist *actively* points out various psychodynamic relationships between events, thoughts, and emotions occurring in the patient's daily pursuits and their counterparts from the past as soon as they are evident and as soon as the patient's ego capacity is sufficiently strong to tolerate them. This tends to prevent the development of free-floating anxiety, which early in therapy could be the nidus for an exacerbation of the depression. It is of utmost importance to keep the patient aware of his affective reactions to the here and now, and to his current environmental stresses. A persistent free-floating preoccupation with past events and past emotions without repeated and pointed associations with the patient's affective reactions to current environmental stress is fraught with danger and very unwise in the treatment of any patient who is depressed or who is prone to develop a depression.

An effort is made to relate the psychodynamic mechanisms and psychosocial stresses to the onset of the hypochondriacal complaints or psychosomatic disorders. On occasion, specific events can be related to the onset of these clinical phenomena. On other occasions the patient can be made aware of the fact that he or she had been exposed to intolerable pressures for a period of time prior to the appearance of the "physical" complaints.

To be optimally effective, the patient must become pointedly aware that the hypochondriacal complaints or psychosomatic symptoms are the veneer covering the basic depressive core. The duration of the patient's illness and the multitude of explanations and treatments to which the patient has been exposed by myriad physicians often makes this awareness difficult to come by. As I said earlier, patients who obtain the best results develop a sharp awareness that their "physical" complaints appear repeatedly whenever they are under considerable stress.

When patients with masked depression are studied over a period of many years, one notes that whenever the patient is exposed to excessive stress, the same hypochondriacal complaints or psychosomatic symptoms are the presenting manifestations of the depressive core, no matter how well the patient may have performed during the interim between exacerbations. In addition to developing an awareness that the "somatic complaints" are the presenting symptoms heralding the underlying depressive reaction, the patients are admonished to seek immediate help as soon as these symptoms manifest themselves.

A pointed effort is made to unfold gradually the full degree of the patient's unconscious hostility. *All* depressed patients are very hostile. I have *never* seen a depressed patient of any type who did not have a marked degree of guilt-linked hostility. Many are afraid of the intense degree of their latent anger, which is often tied to unconscious symbolic murderous fantasies. Many of the patients with depression associated with strongly decreased psychomotor activity (endogenous depression) had never been permitted, or permitted themselves, to display anger during their infancy and childhood. Strange as it may seem, many depressed patients must be taught how to express anger and must be made aware of the fact that anger can be a normal and healthy reaction to certain types of stress.

Dream material is encouraged. Indeed, it is one of the main tools used to help the patient become aware of the intensity of his emotional reactions to current and past events.

The patient is actively made to realize that his psychiatric illness is the result of long-standing maladaptation to his environment, and that it is necessary to alter his habit patterns if future periods of emotional decompensation are to be avoided. The therapist repeatedly points out that taking drugs alone and parroting the therapist's psychodynamic formulations do not serve as safe deterrents to future illnesses. The patient becomes sharply aware of the fact that in spite of drug treatment and regardless of the duration, intensity, and degree of immediate success gained by any psychotherapeutic process, there is a dynamically changing threshold of ego strength beyond which he could regress emotionally, and that in general the same patterns of illness could recur if he permitted himself to be exposed to prolonged stress with which he could not cope. At the same time he becomes aware of the very early manifestations of emotional decompensation as they occur in him, and that this process can be reversed if the real stresses of the environment can be confronted as soon as they become evident.

Finally, as an integral part of therapy, an effort is made to help the patient see himself in relation to his socioeconomic and sociopolitical milieu with regard to the sources of the stresses that led to his illness, with regard to the roles he might play in his milieu, and with regard to the mechanisms of adaptation to his culture which are available.

Psychotherapy in combination with antidepressant drug therapy is a very powerful and effective tool in our psychiatric treatment armamentarium. With the development of improved antidepressant drugs and with greater sophistication in the design and application of the psychotherapeutic aspect of the technique, this combined procedure will very likely become the treatment of choice for most patients suffering with moderate to severe depressions, overt or masked. It is also likely that some form of this combined technique will be used as a prophylactic procedure in the prevention of overt depressions (8).

References

1. Lesse, S. Psychotherapy in Combination with Antidepressant Drugs. *J. Neuropsychiat.* 3:154, 1962.

2. Lesse, S. Psychotherapy in Combination with Antidepressant Drugs. *Amer. J. Psychother.* 16:407, 1962.
3. Lesse, S. Psychotherapy in Combination with Antidepressant Drugs in the Ambulatory Management of Severely Depressed Patients. First Conference of the International College of Psychosomatic Medicine, Guadalajara, December 1971.
4. Lesse, S. Psychotherapy Plus Drugs in Severe Depressions: Technique. *Comp. Psychiat.* 7:224, 1966.
5. Lesse, S. The Evaluation of Imipramine Hydrochloride in the Ambulatory Treatment of Depressed Patients. *J. Neuropsychiat.* 1:246, 1960.
6. Lesse, S. Combined Tranylcypromine-Trifluoperazine Therapy in the Treatment of Patients with Agitated Depressions. *Amer. J. Psychiat.* 117:1038, 1961.
7. Lesse, S. Experimental Studies on the Relationship Between Anxiety, Dreams, and Dream-like States. *Amer. J. Psychother.* 13:440, 1959.
8. Lesse, S. Future Oriented Psychotherapy: A Prophylactic Technique. *Amer. J. Psychother.* 25:180, 1971.

16

Accidents as Depressive Equivalents

NORMAN TABACHNICK
and NORMAN L. FARBEROW

In this chapter we shall be examining evidence from a number of sources that bears on the question "Are some accidents manifestations of masked depressive states?" In addition to studying the relationship of masked depression to accidents, we shall also consider data that focus on the issue "Are some accidents manifestations of suicide and/or other self-destructive personality trends?"

We do this with the following rationale: The concept of depression is in some ways vague and amorphous. It touches on and includes many phenomena. Since suicide has traditionally been linked with depression, it seems worthwhile to examine the relationship to accident of both conscious and unconscious suicide (that is, self-destructive trends without conscious awareness of such trends).

Our material includes data from our own researches and the reports of other researchers and theoreticians. We shall also discuss pertinent theoretical issues in order to move toward clarification of the subject.

It is, of course, impossible to review exhaustively all literature and research reports relevant to accident. Accident (particularly automobile accident) has been linked to so many significant factors and has been a topic of research interest for so long that the literature in this field is truly overwhelming. It comprises thousands of epidemiological reports, engineering reports, evaluations of vehicles and roadways, and articles dealing with the significance of climatic conditions and traffic volume.

Psychological issues in accidents have also been the subject of a vast literature. These issues are important as possible independent precursors of accident. In addition, they have meaning as they are studied in relation to other factors closely linked to accident phenomena. (For example, it has been suggested that people in self-destructive frames of mind pay little attention to the mechanical condition of their cars and thus increase the likelihood that defective brakes or steering apparatuses will produce an "accidental" collision.)

For the purposes of this chapter, however, we shall restrict ourselves to the consideration of those researches on accident that deal rather directly with depression, suicide, and other forms of self-destructiveness.

Evaluation of the Term "Masked Depression"

The editor of this book has been a leader in the delineation of the concept of masked depression. As we have already indicated, depression itself is an amorphous group of signs, symptoms, and manifestations. As a result, numerous definitions of depression exist. Most studies include descriptions and evaluations of the affect of depression, but others, such as the important studies dealing with animal models of depression (35), do not. Social withdrawal, somatic aspects, motor aspects, cognitive aspects—all of these are considered important by various clinicians and researchers; yet all have been absent from many descriptions of depression, in both the clinical and the research literature.

Thus we start with a problem of definition when we discuss depression. The concept of masked depression further increases the difficulty of understanding exactly what we are talking about. This term has had numerous definitions, as a recent article by Stanley Lesse documents (23).

In some cases, masked depression means that signs of depression, although present, may be overlooked because (a) they are not specifically evaluated or (b) some other phenomenon has taken precedence. Thus an accident victim might have been suffering from a moderate or even severe depression, but an accident that brings his life close to an end may cause his medical condition to take center stage. Also, if depression is noted following his recovery, it might be assumed that this was a *result* of the accident rather than something that preceded it and may even have contributed to its occurrence.

Such use of the term "masked depression" we find quite valuable because it permits the hypothesis that depression exists where it was not at first seen and encourages the search for objective evidence to substantiate it. However, important problems arise with certain other concepts of masked depression. Most important, in a number of situations the construct "depressive equivalents" has been formulated, apparently to indicate that although none of the objective signs of depression are present, a particular affect or action is, in some way, the same as depression.

What is missing in these formulations is evidence to support the claim that the "equivalent" is the same as depression. It is possible that equivalents exist, but it is also possible that what is called the equivalent is actually an independent personality characteristic that has little to do with depression. Until research studies substantiate a link between the "equivalent" and the "depression" for which it presumably stands, the relationship must remain hypothetical.

Likewise, certain activities such as fighting and destructive behavior in adolescents are interpreted as attempts to "combat depressive manifestations that threaten to become overt" (3). Again, what evidence supports this idea? Is the presence of the fighting and destructive behavior equivalent to depression in all cases, or is it only in some that this is presumed to be true? If so, how are the cases differentiated? We recognize that certain single case studies may suggest this hypothesis, but before it becomes too rigidly established, there should be more objective research findings to substantiate it.

For all these reasons we shall focus on studies of accidents which contain evidence of depression in individuals who contributed to their accidents. We will also include studies that have sought the presence of suicidal and other self-destructive trends in accident victims.

Defining "Accident"

Most people have a strong visceral reaction and a feeling of understanding when the word "accident" is mentioned. Yet before we procede with our discussion, we feel it worthwhile to discuss some of the dimensions of the term.

Frequently "accident" means an unplanned mishap that results in suffering, damage, or destruction of valuable physical or human entities. Most people would agree with the "unplanned" part of this definition. Interestingly, however, when the frequencies of accidents are plotted and the regularities of their occurrence are noted, a paradox becomes apparent. Although we started out investigating a phenomenon defined as chance or unplanned, the results of our efforts indicate that often the "unplanned" or "chance" explanations no longer pertain.

Precisely for this reason, many people who have studied accidents no longer use the term, but prefer to substitute others that merely describe the exchange of physical energy. For example, the word "collision" is used to refer to the striking of one automobile by another.

However, for most people, even for many scientists, the term "accident" remains in favor. Why is this? A number of writers (4) suggest that the choice of the term reflects a cultural value. This value is based on the existence of chance and luck.

These factors are held to have some significance, and indeed, in certain situations, an overwhelming role in the working out of man's destiny.

It has even been suggested that the concept of accident which regards it as an unplanned and perhaps therefore unpreventable aspect of the human condition reflects a tolerance, an acceptance, or perhaps even a positive valuation of the existence of destructive modalities in our world.

At any rate, in this scientific article we shall examine those aspects of depressive and self-destructive functioning which may be highly correlated with collisions characterized by a destructive transfer of energy from one physical object to another. (However, as members of the culture that has evolved the accident mystique, we may at times, against our better judgment, find ourselves using the word "accident.")

Now a word about the "accident" studies we shall be utilizing. For the most part, research on collisions or accidents has focused upon automobile mishaps, probably because they account for the greatest loss of life and property damage. This is true, at any rate, for those nations in which the automobile is widely used. (There are, of course, researches that have been conducted in other areas to which we will refer.)

We assume we can extract certain common psychological features from automobile collisions which apply to the general field of collision or accident. However, here too it has not been demonstrated that such an extrapolation is valid. There may be specific factors as yet unrevealed which make the psychology of automobile accidents a different matter than the psychology of other types of accidents.

Depression in Accident

A crucial formulation dealing with depression as precursor of accident was detailed in a series of articles entitled "The Accident Process" (5, 16, 17). To our knowledge, this is the first series of formulations in modern psychiatric and psychological literature which has pointed to accident as a way of resolving life problems (which often include internal depression). The articles are important because they led to subsequent psychological formulations concerning accident. For example, the idea of a prodromal state that precedes the actual accident has subsequently been used by a number of investigators (14, 37).

The research of Hirschfeld and Behan (17) centered on industrial accidents. A number of individuals (at least several hundred) who had had such accidents were studied in depth. Conclusions were drawn regarding their psychological states and the contribution of those psychological states to the accidents and the chronic disability that followed the accidents.

Hirschfeld and Behan concluded that many of the accident victims had been suffering from combinations of personality difficulties and troubled life situations. A typical example was a woman who had lived an isolated and withdrawn life, which she had been able to accept comfortably because of her marriage. Her husband sheltered and took care of her. When the husband died and it became necessary for her to become more outgoing, she began to have a good deal of difficulty. Hirschfeld and Behan called this "unacceptable disability."

They suggested that people who have such "unacceptable disabilities" can resolve them by a number of mechanisms, such as illness or alcoholism and, most significantly, accident. An accident that provides a justifiable disability gives the victim an opportunity to withdraw and yet not feel uncomfortable about doing so. In other words, an "unacceptable disability" may be transformed by an accident into an "acceptable disability." The woman cited had an accident with an accompanying relief of psychological distress.

An important prodromal feature found in the subjects was depression. It can be seen that even though depression might not have been explicitly revealed by the patients, the reaction might well be formulated as a depressive equivalent.

Hirschfeld and Behan elaborated on these formulations in great detail and presented a convincing case for what *might* be.

However, from the standpoint of valid research, certain important questions must be raised about their work. They used the clinical method; that is, they took histories on their patients and made inferences about the meaning of their findings.

Although such a method is frequently utilized, it has a number of shortcomings. First of all, it incorporates many inferences that may reflect biases on the part of the investigator or interviewer. Second, no comparison groups were utilized, as far as we can tell. Therefore, whether the depression, troubled life situations, and other variables cited existed in a greater degree in those individuals who subsequently had accidents than in appropriate comparison groups is not known. This means there is still a question whether the variables noted—personality difficulties, troubled life situations, and so on—do have some important relationship to accident. Finally, there is no mention of the statistical incidence of the pertinent factors. It would be fairly convincing if some of these variables existed in 60, 70, or 80 percent of the sample, but if they existed in only 5 or 10 percent, significance would be decreased.

In summary, Hirschfeld and Behan present a convincing formulation as to the way in which depression and other personality difficulties can be related to accident. However, important questions must be raised as to the validity of the data upon which their formulations rest.

In 1966 Tabachnick et al. (37) reported a comparative postmortem psychoanalytic investigation of the driver-victims of fifteen one-car automobile accidents and fifteen suicides. Relatives, friends, and business associates of the victims were interviewed extensively. The aim of the study was to discern similarities and differences in the psychological characteristics and psychodynamics of these two types of (presumably) self-destructive individuals.

Some of the results of this study are pertinent in evaluating the issue of masked depression in accident victims. Most striking was the finding that in the group of fifteen accident victims, one-third were rated as having significant trends of depression or self-punishment. Since the issues of loss of significant others or anger toward them are often associated with clinical depression, it is pertinent to note the findings of the Tabachnick study in regard to loss and anger. In the group of fifteen suicides, fourteen had lost or become estranged from a significant other person. This was predictable in view of previous data about suicide. However, in the accident group, only one-fifth (three persons) demonstrated loss of closeness to or anger toward a significant other person.

Later in this article we shall be evaluating the significance of manic or hypomanic trends as indicators of depression or, more properly, defense against depression. This possibility was considered when we devised the study on which we are presently commenting. Increased motor and/or verbal activity was noted in almost equal proportions in both the suicide and the accident group. Nine of the fifteen suicides and ten of the fifteen accident victims demonstrated such increased activity.

The study, however, suffered from a number of shortcomings. First, there were small numbers of cases in both the suicide and accident groups. Therefore, it is quite possible that the results that were obtained could be attributed to chance variation rather than to significant psychological differences in the two groups. Second, the method utilized was one of clinical investigation, and no attempt (besides the choosing of well-qualified psychoanalytic investigators) was made to establish a reliable procedure.

In summary, this study demonstrated a number of significant differences in depressive indices between suicide and accident, as well as one striking similarity (increased motor and verbal activity). It also supported the concept that at least one significant subgroup of automobile accident victims possesses significant depression-linked characteristics.

A third study bearing on depression in accidents was reported in 1970 by Finch and Smith (14). In this study, twenty-five male driver fatalities were compared with twenty-five male controls. (The controls were nonaccident volunteers matched for age and sex from the same neighbor-hoods as the accident victims.) A number of psychological and sociological variables were examined. This was a well-defined and well-executed study. The authors' conceptual approach reflects the Hirschfeld and Behan formulations. They felt that in determining the significant factors affecting a crash, they should investigate the driver's preexisting personality pat-tern, recent stressful events in his life, his utilization of al-cohol, certain nonbehavioral factors (such as a possibly defec-tive automobile), and his emotional state immediately prior to the collision (which they called the "precrash state").

A number of their results are quite interesting in them-selves. Although the majority (twenty-two out of twenty-five) of the controls were considered normal in personality pattern, only five of the driver fatalities were considered normal. One was diagnosed as psychotic and nineteen were felt to possess personality disorders. Of these nineteen, fifteen had "al-coholic personality disorders" and six had "antisocial per-sonalities." The others were distributed among a number of other personality disorders, one or two in each category.

The twenty-one who were categorized as alcoholics and antisocial personalities are important to our present concern because it is possible that these groups would demonstrate more activity and more impulsiveness than others. Activity and impulsiveness may, as we said earlier, represent aspects of a manic state, which is highly correlated with depression. Unfortunately, the data reported by Finch and Smith do not indicate whether there was greater activity in the drivers who fell within these two character disorder groups in comparison with the control group.

Further factors of possible significance are found in the data dealing with precipitating stress. Stress was evaluated for both the six-month and twenty-four hour periods prior to the accident or time of interviewing. In both cases, it was found that there were significantly more indications of precipitating stress among the accident victims than among the controls. Most of the stresses listed could be conceived of as possible losses. They included interpersonal stresses like financial difficulties, job problems, loss of a friend or relative. Although it is not clear from these data that the accident group was more depressed, the data indicate that the kinds of stress that lead to depression were more evident in the accident group.

The data concerning the precrash state yield further evidence in support of the thesis that accidents are manifestations of depressive states. In the judgment of normality and abnormality, only 12 percent of the control group were judged abnormal, whereas 92 percent of the driver fatalities were so judged. Forty percent of the driver fatalities were judged to have been depressed in the precrash state, and a further 12 percent were judged to have been suicidal. The comparative figures for the control group were 4 percent and none.

Uncontrolled anger and impaired judgment or poor impulse control might be indications of manic defenses. In the uncontrolled anger category, 32 percent of the driver fatalities registered positive, whereas only 12 percent of the control group did. In the category of impaired judgment and poor impulse control, 24 percent of the driver fatalities registered positive, as compared to 8 percent of the control group.

In summary, then, a number of findings in this study supported the hypothesis that automobile accidents (at least from the standpoint of drivers who become fatalities) are frequently manifestations of masked depression or suicidal tendency. In addition, the study supports the idea that impulsive, poorly controlled individuals who might have manic defenses against depression are highly represented in accident populations.

Again, some questions must be raised regarding the research methodology of this study. The first is that the methodologies used could not be considered objectively reliable. The use of judgment procedures and consensus procedures without adequate controls still leaves open the possibility that the initial bias or set of the interviewers would tend to make them elicit and interpret data that would confirm their own biases.

Second, the adequacy of the comparison or control group must be questioned. The researchers used as controls only those subjects who agreed to participate. They do not indicate how many individuals approached refused to participate in the research study. Unless that number was quite small, the possibility arises that the people who agreed to participate may have been those least likely to possess "character disorders" of the type described in the study.

Manic Defenses Against Depression

We have previously suggested that increased impulsive activity may be a manifestation of a particular type of defense (manic behavior) against depression. Both epidemiologic studies (19, 21, 24) and psychodynamic theory have concluded that there are important relationships between retarded, depressed, hypoactive individuals and elated, hyperactive, impulsive individuals. Epidemiologic studies of these groups, particularly of those persons who require hospitalization, have indicated that some of them will go through cycles of extreme depression and manic behavior.

From the psychodynamic viewpoint, a number of authors (1, 19, 20, 24) have postulated that manic episodes represent a defense against and denial of depressive affect. Thus, if it could be shown that a significant number of people with histories of manic episodes have been involved in accidents, there would be support for the thesis that accidents are manifestations of, or at least related to, depressive conditions.

In fact, many such correlations do exist. An example is found in the work of Conger et al. (11). This research demonstrated that individuals who were accident repeaters manifested little control over hostility, aggressive behavior, high degrees of separation anxiety, low tension tolerance, and a tendency toward overdetermined acting-out behavior, either in physical belligerence or in verbal form.

Dunbar (12) and Alexander (2) developed the concept of

the accident-prone individual. By studying those who had multiple accidents, ranging from slightly to moderately serious, they developed a profile of individuals who were quick, decisive, independent, and adventurous. "Activity" and "impulsiveness" have been found repeatedly in accident research, particularly in accident-prone groups. But there are some important criticisms of studies of accident-proneness. (We shall summarize these criticisms later.)

From another standpoint, a question has been raised about manic and impulsive behavior as a defense against depressive traits. Although most writers have agreed that manic and depressive states alternate with each other and are part of the same psychopathological condition, it is possible that manic-depressive illness is an artificial construct that has been imposed on clinical data. Cameron (8) has pointed out that the time interval linking depressive and manic episodes has not been specified, and in fact varies from case to case. He therefore raises the issue that many or all such occurrences may represent separate affective disorders occurring in the same person.

In addition, it has been postulated that (in most cases) the mild, hypomanic phase following a depressive episode is a compensatory phenomenon and not a pathological condition (26). There is no good evidence that there are opposite biological substrates for the two poles of manic-depressive illness. Such biological differences as have been found may be secondary to the activity level in the two conditions (7).

From a psychoanalytic and psychodynamic viewpoint, it is possible to postulate the occurrence of impulsive, adventurous, action-oriented life styles that are not defenses against depression. For example, identification with parental models who have these traits, or experiences of success in early life to which this sort of behavior has contributed, could account equally well for such traits.

In summary, caution must be exercised in accepting the notion that impulsive, action-oriented life styles or neurotic traits represent defenses against depression.

The Possibility of Masking in Accidents

It is possible that a number of accidents may have been preceded by severe depressions that have gone unrecognized. First of all, a great deal of attention must necessarily be paid to the medical condition of the accident victim. Second, if some signs of depression are noted, people may assume that depression is the result of the accident rather than a preexisting condition. We do not know if such masking actually does occur, but it is a possibility. Research studies that would shed light on this situation should be constructed and past research studies that might help to clarify it should be reevaluated. In fact, two of the studies on accident already mentioned, the Tabachnick et al. study of accidental and suicidal death (7) and the Finch and Smith study of automobile fatalities (14), bear on this issue.

It is possible that depression is an accompanying characteristic of accident-proneness and is not observed because of a number of possible psychodynamic factors. For example, an individual may feel guilty and depressed about some act or thought, and may unconsciously plan some punishment for himself or may respond to unplanned injury (an accident) by feeling punished. In such a situation, the preexisting state of depression would no longer be seen. It is also possible that a person may be depressed for only a short period of time and become involved in an accident during this period. The lack of any signs of depression upon psychological examination several days later then tells us nothing. All this, however, is speculation. As far as we are aware, there is no strong evidence to support any of these ideas.

Evidence Against Depression in Accident Situations

A research project that tested for the presence of suicidal

and other self-destructive factors in near-fatal accidents (38) has overcome many of the criticisms made about previous researches. A psychoanalytic study, it involved an evaluation of three groups of subjects: (a) a group of drivers who had been involved in near-fatal one-car accidents; (b) a group of suicidal people from the same hospital, matched for age and sex, who had nearly died as a result of their suicide attempts; and (c) a group of subjects from the same hospital, matched for age and sex, who underwent emergency appendectomies. The method of interviewing was first tested so that it had high reliability. A check was also made for possible bias of the interviewers, and it was determined that any bias present did not affect the results.

Depressive, counterdepressive, and impulsive manifestations in each subject were noted. A rigorous search was made for any loss suffered by the subject prior to the situation that led to hospitalization. Tentative conclusions (results await more refined evaluation) are that significantly greater indications of loss and depression, as well as a number of other self-destructive manifestations, are found in the suicide group than in the accident group. In regard to loss, depression, and self-destructive manifestations, the accident and appendectomy group were low and similar to each other.

In summary, a number of studies indicate that depression does exist in accident victims to some degree; however, other studies do not support this point of view, so that the question should remain open. At this time there seems to be little support for the hypothesis that impulsive, antisocial, hypomanic characteristics are significantly in evidence just prior to an accident.

Intentional and Unintentional
Self-Destructive Trends

Depression and suicide have traditionally been linked. A number of theorists, such as Sigmund Freud (15) and Karl

Menninger (29), have postulated that suicide is a frequent end point for severe depression. Their theorizations rest on the keystone of the "death instinct," that is, that within each individual there is a biological tendency toward death which focuses hostility upon the self. In this situation, much depression becomes manifest; one of the final outcomes of a highly activated death instinct is suicide. There are many other psychoanalytic and psychodynamic formulations that link depression and suicide.

That depressive patients are highly likely to commit suicide is supported by many statistical studies. Some quotations from Aaron Beck's recent book *Depression* (4) bear out this point: "At the present time, the only important cause of death in depression is suicide."

> Pokorny investigated the suicide rate among former patients in a psychiatric service of a Texas veterans' hospital over a 15-year period. Using a complex actuarial system, he calculated the suicide rates per 100,000 per year as follows: depression, 566; schizophrenia, 167; neurosis, 119; personality disorder, 130; alcoholism, 133; organic, 78. The suicide rate for depressed patients, therefore, was 25 times the expected rate and substantially higher than that of other psychiatric patients [32].

As we pointed out earlier, there is reason to question whether the amorphous and global concept of depression does indeed constitute a unity so that it is possible to define a link between it and another condition—for example, suicide. A study in Los. Angeles indicated that various aspects of depression—for example, somatic, affective, and social withdrawal signs—are differentially related to suicide rates (39).

All the same, it is still possible to evaluate the degree to which suicide is found in situations first called accidents. There are endless anecdotes that support this point of view. A middle-aged woman, for example, died when her car went over a cliff, falling many hundreds of feet into a canyon below. An investigation of the accident site revealed no skid marks.

This brought up several possibilities: (a) The car did not have good brakes. (This possibility was not supported by the evidence of her husband.) (b) She went over the cliff while asleep. (Since she was alone, no one could answer this question.) (c) She deliberately drove her car over the edge of the cliff. This last view was supported by her husband's statement that she was supposed to be on her way home at the time the accident occurred, and the fact that the particular route that took her past the fatal cliff was neither the most direct nor the usual way home.

Further interviews with the husband and business associates developed the following history: The woman had been in jail early in her life, a fact she had not revealed to her husband when they were first married. When he did learn about it, he was quite angry and told her that if she were ever again to be involved in criminal activity, he would divorce her. Fifteen years later, the woman embezzled funds from her employer. He was willing not to press charges if she returned the money. However, she could see no way of returning the money without having the facts revealed to her husband. During the week or ten days prior to the "accident," she became increasingly depressed. The deadline for returning the money was the day after she died. Impression: the "accident" was an intentional suicide that represented the woman's choice of conflict resolution.

A number of authors have detailed similar situations in the psychiatric literature (31, 39). MacDonald (27) reported a statistical evaluation of automobile accidents causing death of the driver or of others, with the entire number of Colorado license holders used as the comparison group. His conclusion was that the incidence of fatal accident drivers in the population of psychiatric hospitals was over thirty times greater than would be expected. He further suggested that this disproportionate representation might be related to the greater risk of suicide in persons who have been in psychiatric hospitals. Although the numbers involved in the study are relatively small, the results support the hypothesis that accident may be a manifestation of suicide.

A sophisticated statistical study was performed by Porterfield in testing the hypothesis that the motor vehicle death rate followed a pattern similar to the suicide and homicide rates (33). The reasoning underlying this hypothesis was that motor vehicles are deadly weapons and that the same social forces that lead to suicide and homicide may manifest themselves in the production of automobile accidents. The study compared the rank order of metropolitan areas in the United States according to indices of suicide, homicide, crime, and motor traffic deaths. The correlations obtained supported the hypothesis. Porterfield concluded that "aggressive hazardous driving is likely to be characteristic of persons similar to those who have suicidal or homicidal or both tendencies." Thus, although it is not proved that accident is the same as suicide, it is suggested that the same type of people are involved in both.

We can refer also to our comparative psychiatric study of deaths by accident and suicide, cited earlier (37), in which we found certain similarities and differences in the psychological data developed around subjects who had died in these two ways. We did not, however, conclude that accident was equivalent to suicide.

Barmack and Payne (3) studied injury-producing motor vehicle accidents among airmen. On the basis of interviews with airmen who had been involved in these accidents, they generated certain hypotheses in regard to psychological events. Of particular interest is their consideration of certain unconscious directing processes. They state, "The interview protocols do not support the view that the aim of these processes was necessarily to achieve a self-aggressive, destructive end" (p. 522).

Many questions can be raised about the control groups, depth of interviewing, and other research procedures of these studies. We consider them suggestive but not conclusive. Like many earlier studies, they suggest that although there may be certain relationships between accident and suicide, and although in a small subgroup there may be individuals who actually attempt suicide by automobile and conceal their true intentions, a high correlation between suicide and accident cannot be supported.

Indirect Self-Destructive Trends

We have been discussing the possibility of suicidal trends in certain accidents. The rationale for this hypothesis is that since suicide is often linked in a statistical and dynamic way to depression, suicidal trends in accidents would be evidence for the existence of depression. Now we propose to go one step further in an attempt to discover whether accident may sometimes be an indirect manifestation of depression. Self-destructive personality trends other than suicide could be designated "indirect suicide." "Indirect suicide" is both a highly abstract and a relatively new term in psychological literature.

Of all the conditions met by the physician and psychiatrist, it would seem that the indirect suicide would be most likely to contain masked depression, or even to exemplify it. Indirect suicide implies inappropriate, unexpected, and difficult to identify emotional components in activities that vary widely but which have in common the motivation of self-destruction, usually unconscious.

The conditions seem closely related to those referred to by Lesse (22), such as hypochondriasis and psychosomatic disorders, in which he finds a disproportional incidence of psychiatric depressive affect. He says:

"It may occur simply as an expression of an underlying depression without an organic process being present. At other times, the patient may have a true organic deficit with a masked depression superimposed. Thus, a minor organic illness may be magnified to a great extent by this psychogenic overlay and superficially, to the uninitiated, may appear as a major organic disorder. . . . On the other hand, a patient with a major organic lesion also may be plagued by hypochondriacal or psychosomatic complaints. In this instance, if the physician becomes preoccupied with the psychogenic aspects of the problem and fails to give adequate emphasis to the organic lesions, serious, even tragic consequences may result" [p. 610].

Again on the same page he states, "The hypochondriacal and psychosomatic symptoms are referred to many organic systems including the central and peripheral nervous systems, cardiovascular, respiratory, gastrointestinal, genitourinary, endocrine, otolaryngologic, and dental systems."

Depression has often been cited as the primary characteristic of overt suicide. One might expect it to be present in any form of self-destruction. Thus, a glance through the *Bibliography of Suicide and Suicide Prevention* (13) reveals that depression is referred to as a prominent affective characteristic in fully two-thirds of the references. This does not mean, of course, that a typical neurotic-depressive reaction or psychotic-depressive state was actually present. It has been determined that depression is not the only pathway to suicide, although the depressive affect may often be present. It is important to distinguish between the presence of the affect and the indication of a psychiatric syndrome.

Indirect Self-Destruction

What is the likelihood of finding a depressive state in indirect suicide? By its very definition, indirect suicide indicates that the self-destructive behaviors involved are covert and unconscious, and that the self-destructive or self-injurious factors may take a long time to surface. The activities may result in death, physical injury, damage to any of the physiological systems, or the threat or actual loss of functioning in society, status, prestige, position, and future.

A number of people have written about indirect suicide, some without actually using the term. Menninger developed the concept of indirect self-destruction through the application of Freud's theory of the death instinct. For him, there is a state of balance between the opposing and fluctuating forces of the life and death instincts. Self-destruction may occur when the death instinct gains temporary ascendance, usually under the influence of diverse patterns of motivation such as guilt, depression, and eroticism. Menninger does not postulate any depressive state in the various conditions he describes in his book *Man Against Himself* (30). He describes focal, partial, and organic suicide, and in almost all instances infers guilt, aggression, and eroticism combined in various patterns to produce the self-limiting and self-injurious behaviors. In some situations he considers the indirect self-destructive behavior to be a form of partial sacrifice offered by the self to avoid greater or perhaps complete self-destruction.

Meerloo (28) has called indirect suicide "hidden suicide," and refers especially to such behaviors as drug addiction, accident-proneness, courting of disaster, and psychosomatic illnesses. Blachly (6) has used the word "seduction" as a synonym for partial or indirect suicide, referring especially to behaviors such as alcoholism, drug abuse, gambling, sexual indiscretions, and rioting. Neither Meerloo nor Blachly, however, refers to a psychiatric state of masked depression in order to explain these behaviors.

Schema of Indirect Self-Destructive Behavior

Our own conceptualization of indirect suicide includes a comprehensive schema that incorporates most of the conditions in which indirect self-destruction have been identified. In general, the conditions seem to fall along two main axes. Along one axis are those activities or conditions in which the primary objects of the activity is either the body or the self. The other axis designates the source of the activities as either internal (that is, behavior originating within the individual, apparently out of psychological needs) or external (that is, as a result of illness or accident occurring to the body, causing the individual to adjust his functioning in relation to it). Four main cells emerge: conditions, activities, or behaviors that are (a) internally initiated with damage to the body, (b) internally initiated with damage to the self, (c) externally initiated with damage to the body, and (d) externally initiated with damage to the self. Within the cell designated "internally initiated with damage to the body," a further subdivision indicates a limited target (that is, a part, section, limb, or specific organ of the body is affected) and a generalized target (that is, the entire body or complete systems in the body are affected). A chart with the cells identified and an example in each cell illustrates the schema (*Figure 1*).

Examples help indicate the various kinds of indirect self-destructive activity found in each category. Thus, in internally initiated conditions where limited body damage occurs, one finds such activities as tattooing, self-mutilations, and polysurgery. Generalized body damage includes such behaviors as drug addiction, alcoholism, obesity, smoking, and accidents.

Sometimes the damage is potential rather than actual, and one finds stress-seeking activities, often described as counter-phobic, such as mountain climbing, sky diving, scuba diving, "death-defying" circus acts, automobile and boat racing, and criminal, violent, and riotous behavior.

"Internally initiated self-damage" refers to behavior resulting in damage to the self in personal functionings, status, prestige, career, or relationships: malingering, asceticism and martyrdom, severe mental disorders. Sexual problems, such as impotence, frigidity, nymphomania, satyriasis, and homosexuality, classified as focal by Menninger, fall in this category as well. Another example is the man who overworks at his job, spending so much time at it that his relationships with his family are ruined.

The third major category is composed of a group of conditions in which an illness or some deleterious change has occurred within the body. This illness or change becomes the focus for behavior generally recognized as life-threatening, life-shortening, and often further body-damaging. The most frequent examples in this category are psychosomatic conditions such as ulcer, colitis, dermatitis, and asthma. One may also find in this group some disorders of the skeletal system, hypochondriacal conditions, invalidism, and intractable psychogenic pain. Menninger has called these forms of behavior organic suicide.

Externally initiated self-destructive conditions are exemplified by cases in which injury or illness resulting in limitation of mobility or damage to the body image is used by the individual to declare his own ineffectiveness and incapacity. Actually the condition seems to represent more a violent blow to the self-concept than a realistic limitation of functioning. A woman who suffers a mastectomy or hysterectomy may, as a result of the blow to her self-concept, feel unable to function any more as a whole woman and be unable to carry out her roles of wife and mother.

Research Studies Dealing with "Indirect Suicide" in Accident

Barmack and Payne (3) looked for self-destructive (they called it "self-aggressive") trends in the personalities of automobile accident victims, and concluded that they could find no evidence for such trends. However, they did note something that they called "passivity of the ego." They found evidence for this concept in the occurrence of impaired consciousness, falling asleep, memory deficit, and degraded anticipation (that is, just before the accidents the drivers did not seem to be as alert to the possibility of mishap as they ordinarily were). The authors quote the psychoanalyst Rapaport, who suggested that a reduction in ego autonomy or surrender of active processes may itself be an instrument of self-destruction.

A similar line of thinking was developed by Litman and Tabachnick (25) in a psychoanalytic evaluation of automobile accident processes. They theorized not only that accident might occur in a passive manner, as suggested by Barmack and Payne and Rapaport, but that one might also think of an "active" type of accident process in which a tendency to be hyperactive, impulsive, and thus free of the usual judgmental and monitoring apparatuses could be an important factor leading to automobile accidents. However, as we have noted, neither Barmack and Payne nor Litman and Tabachnick attempted to correlate these inferred mechanisms with depression.

The concept of accident-proneness was a limited one for the investigators who first developed it, but it seemed to challenge the imagination of subsequent researchers and writers and became quite popular. Subsequently, serious criticisms of the concept have severely limited its applicability.

The classic paper in the field was written in 1919 by Greenwood and Woods (16). Using a statistical method, the two authors studied accidents among workers in a British munitions factory during the First World War. They found that a relatively small percentage of the workers had most of the accidents, and suggested there might be an unequal initial liability, that is, that some individuals were inherently more likely to have accidents. They tested a number of alternate hypotheses and concluded that their initial hypothesis could best explain the observed facts. Appropriately cautious, they indicated that, for a number of sound experimental reasons, the studies would have to be repeated in a variety of environments.

The hypothesis of accident-proneness has severe limitations, many of them summarized by Suchman and Scherzer (36). They classify the objections to the theory as statistical, methodological, and theoretical.

From a statistical standpoint, follow-up studies have indicated that a relatively small number of people do seem to have a disproportionately large number of accidents. However, an interesting situation develops if the groups are studied over long periods of time. Although the accident-prone group continues to exist, *its membership changes;* that is, in the second and third years of the study, the people in the accident-prone group are not the same as the ones who comprised the group in the first year. Those who were in the group originally are no longer there, and new members have taken their places. One can speculate either that accident-proneness is a temporary state or that chance has caused many people to be considered accident-prone. In addition, statistical correlations between present and future accidents are usually low. Obviously, the relatively crude statistical surveys upon which the concept of accident-proneness is based cannot take into consideration the multitude of possible intervening factors.

Methodologically, the evaluation of the concept of accident-proneness has suffered from a number of inadequacies. One of the most important is that certain individuals may be more exposed to the possibility of dangerous mishaps than others. An increased number of accidents for such a person does not necessarily reflect some psychological tendency toward accident-proneness, but merely that the exposure risk has been higher.

From a theoretical standpoint, there is little agreement among the various formulations of the concept as to what the accident-prone person is actually like. Some investigators describe him as overly timid, others as aggressive. While it is possible that there are a number of accident-prone personalities, when there are a number of theoretical and often opposing formulations for the same syndrome, one begins to question whether in fact such a syndrome actually exists. It seems, therefore, that while accident-proneness may exist in a small number of individuals, the hypothesis is not useful for an understanding of large numbers of accidents.

In summary, although "indirect self-destruction" has been and remains an intriguing hypothetical approach, research data that support its relevance to accident are minimal.

Figure 1

EXAMPLES OF INDIRECT SELF-DESTRUCTION

Source		Primary Damage		
		Body Limited (part of body involved)	**Body** Generalized (whole body involved)	Self
Internal: Self-initiated activity with actual or potential harm	Damage occurred	Polysurgery	Alcoholism	Asceticism, martyrdom
	Damage potential	Risk-taking Crime Mountain-climbing		Risk-taking Compulsive gambling
External: accident, injury, or illness in body is used to produce actual or greater harm		Diabetes		Loss requiring change of self-concept

Conclusion

At this point there are some well-conducted researches that suggest the presence of masked depression in a number of accident situations. It is thus possible that there are important correlative links between depression and accident. However, there is little indication that depression is a general factor in many or most accidents. This impression fits in with the fact that many factors of both psychological and nonpsychological nature have been demonstrated to be important in the occurrence of particular types of accidents. It would be contradictory to this multifactoral nature of accident situations to find that any single factor is linked to many types of accidents.

There is little evidence to support the hypothesis that a significant number of "accidents" are in fact concealed suicides, and even less that "indirect suicide" is an important issue in accident situations.

References

1. Abraham, K. "A Short Study of the Development of the Libido." In *Selected Papers on Psychoanalysis.* New York: Basic Books, 1960.
2. Alexander, F. The Accident Prone Individual. *Public Health Report* 64:357, 1949.
3. Barmack, J. E., and Payne, D. E. Injury-Producing Private Motor Vehicle Accidents Among Airmen. In *Accident Research*, ed. Haddon, E. A. Suchman, and M. Klein. New York: Harper & Row, 1964.
4. Beck, A. T. *Depression: Clinical, Experimental; and Theoretical Aspects.* New York: Paul B. Hoeber, Harper & Row, 1967.
5. Behan, R. C., and Hirschfeld, A. H. The Accident Process: II. Toward a More Rational Treatment of Industrial Injuries. *JAMA* 186:300, 1963.
6. Blachly, P. H. Suicide as Seduction. *Hosp. Med.* 5:117, 1969.

7. Cameron, N. The Place of Mania Among the Depressions from a Biological Standpoint. *J. Psychol.* 14:181, 1942.

8. Cameron, N. The Functional Psychoses. In *Personality and the Behavior Disorders*, ed. J. McV. Hunt. New York: Ronald Press, 1944.

9. Clayton, P. J.; Pitts, F. N.; and Winokur, G. Affective Disorder: IV. Mania. *Comprehens. Psychiat.* 6:313, 1965.

10. Cohen, M. B.; Baker, G.; Cohen, R. A.; Fromm-Reichman, F.; and Weigert, E. V. An Intensive Study of Twelve Cases of Manic-Depressive Psychosis. *Psych.* 17:103, 1954.

11. Conger, J. J.; Gaskill, H. S.; Glad, D. D.; Hassell, L.; Rainey, R. V.; and Sawrey, Psychological and Psychophysiological Factors in Motor Vehicle Accidents. *JAMA* 169:1581, 1959. Reprinted in *Accident Research*, ed. Haddon, E. A. Suchman, and M. Klein. New York: Harper & Row, 1964.

12. Dunbar, H. F. *Psychosomatic Diagnosis*. New York: Paul B. Hoeber, Harper & Row, 1943.

13. Farberow, N. L. *Bibliography of Suicide and Suicide Prevention*. National Clearinghouse for Mental Health Information, Publication 1970, 1967.

14. Finch, J. R., and Smith, J. P. *Psychiatric and Legal Aspects of Automobile Accidents*. Springfield, Ill.: Charles C. Thomas, 1970.

15. Freud, S. *Beyond the Pleasure Principle*. Vol. 18 of *The Standard Edition of the Complete Psychological Works of Sigmund Freud*, ed. J. Strachey. London: Hogarth Press, 1953–1965.

16. Greenwood, M., and Woods, H. The Incidence of Industrial Accidents Upon Individuals with Special Reference to Multiple Accidents. In *Accident Research*, ed. Haddon, E. A. Suchman, and M. Klein. New York: Harper & Row, 1964.

17. Hirschfeld, A. H., and Behan, R. C. The Accident Process: I. Etiological Considerations of Industrial Injuries. *JAMA* 186:193, 1963.

18. Hirschfeld, A. H., and Behan, R. C. The Accident Process: III. Disability: Acceptable and Unacceptable. *JAMA* 197:125, 1966.

19. Jacobson, E. Contribution to the Metapsychology of Cyclothymic Depression. In *Affective Disorders*, ed. P. Greenacre. New York: International Universities Press, 1953.

20. Klein, M. A Contribution to the Psychogenesis of Manic-Depressive States. In *Contributions to Psychoanalysis 1921–1945*. London: Hogarth Press and the Institute of Psychoanalysis, 1948.
21. Kraeplin, E. Manic-Depressive Insanity and Paranoia. In *Textbook of Psychiatry*, trans. R. M. Barclay. Edinburgh: Livingstone, 1913.
22. Lesse, S. Hypochondriasis and Psychosomatic Disorders Masking Depression. *Amer. J. Psychother.* 21:607, 1967.
23. Lesse, S. Masked Depression: A Diagnostic and Therapeutic Problem. *Dis. Nerv. Syst.* 29:169, 1968.
24. **Lesse, S. The Multivariant Masks of Depression.** *Amer. J. Psychiat.* 124:11, 1968.
25. Litman, R. E., and Tabachnick, N. Fatal One-Car Accidents. *Psychiat. Quart.* 36:248, 1964.
26. Loftus, T. A. *Meaning and Methods of Diagnosis in Clinical Psychiatry*. Philadelphia: Lea & Febiger, 1960.
27. MacDonald, J. M. Suicide and Homicide by Automobile. *Amer. J. Psychiat.* 121:366, 1964.
28. Meerloo, J. A. M. Hidden Suicide. In *Suicidal Behaviors: Diagnosis and Management*, ed. H. L. P. Resnik. Boston: Little, Brown, 1968.
29. Menninger, K. A. Purposive Accidents as an Expression of Self-Destructive Tendencies. *Int. J. Psychiat.* 17:6, 1935.
30. Menninger, K. A. *Man Against Himself*. New York: Harcourt, Brace, 1938.
31. Moseley, A. L. *Research on Fatal Highway Collisions*. Harvard Medical School, 1963.
32. Pokorny, A. D. Suicide Rates in Various Psychiatric Disorders. *J. Nerv. Ment. Dis.* 139:499, 1964.
33. Porterfield, A. L. Traffic Fatalities: Suicide and Homicide. *A. Sociol. Review* 25, 1960. Reprinted in *Accident Research*, ed. Haddon, E. A. Suchman, and M. Klein. New York: Harper & Row, 1964.
34. Rennie, T. Prognosis in Manic Depressive Psychoses. *Amer. J. Psychiat.* 98:801, 1942.
35. Seligman, M. Depression and Learned Helplessness. In *The Psychology of Depression: Contemporary Theory and Research*, ed. Friedman and Katz. In press.

36. Suchman, E. A., and Scherzer, A. L. Accident Proneness. In *Current Research in Childhood Accidents*. New York: Association for the Aid of Crippled Children, 1960. Reprinted in *Accident Research*, ed. Haddon, E. A. Suchman, and M. Klein. New York: Harper & Row, 1964.
37. Tabachnick, N.; Litman, R. E.; Osman, J.; Jones, W.; Cohen, J.; Kasper, A.; and Moffat, J. Comparitive Psychiatric Study of Accidental and Suicidal Death. *Arch. Gen. Psychiat.* 14:60, 1966.
38. Tabachnick, N.; Litman, R. E.; Gussen, J.; Wold, C. I.; Peck, M. L.; and Tiber, N. *Suicide or Accident*. Springfield, Ill.: Charles C. Thomas, in press.
39. Wold, C. I., and Tabachnick, N. Depression as an Indicator of Lethality in Suicidal Patients. In *The Psychology of Depression: Contemporary Theory and Research*, ed. Friedman and Katz, p. 524. New York: Harper & Row, 1964.

17

Atypical Facial Pain
of Psychogenic Origin:
A Masked Depressive Syndrome

STANLEY LESSE

In previous chapters I have pointed out that many depressive syndromes are initially manifested clinically as hypochondriacal complaints or psychosomatic disorders referred to various organ systems, with the depressive affect being masked by these symptoms and signs to such an extent that the physician may be unaware of the fact that a serious psychiatric disorder is at hand until a massive, full-blown depression erupts. I also pointed out that as a result of these diagnostic errors, the patient is often subjected to unnecessary and inappropriate treatment, even surgery.

Facial pain that does not fall into well-defined patterns, such as trigeminal neuralgia and the less frequently seen glossopharyngeal neuralgia, the dental syndromes associated with infected or impacted teeth, and the otolaryngological syndromes associated with sinusitis and otitis has been categorized in general as "atypical facial pain syndrome."

In the vast majority of instances these atypical facial pain syndromes are of psychogenic origin and they are classical examples of masked depression.

Patients with atypical facial pain pose a challenge to physicians of many specialties and to dentists. Yet this syndrome can be diagnosed readily by physicians and dentists alike early in the course of illness, for there are usually definite symptoms and signs present to alert the knowledgeable clinician to the fact that he is dealing with a psychologically ill individual.

Methods

The material for this report consists of data gathered over a period of ten years from 225 successive patients. Some patients were observed for more than six years.

All patients were examined neurologically and by one or more dentists. In addition, most were evaluated by dental surgeons especially interested in temporomandibular joint difficulties. All but eleven of the patients had been seen by an otolaryngologist. Finally, all patients were studied intensively on a psychiatric basis.

Laboratory examinations included skull films (base views were routine), sinus films, dental X-rays, and in most instances roentgen surveys of the temporomandibular joints. These were only the baseline investigations. Many patients had additional laboratory studies.

The patients were referred to me from various sources. One hundred and three were referred by dentists, fifty-five from other neurologists, forty-one from general practitioners, fourteen from otolaryngologists, and the remaining twelve from other sources.

Delay in Diagnosis

I rarely saw one of these patients in an acute state and very rarely even in a subacute state. Of the patients in this study series, 172, or 77 percent, had their facial complaints for more than a year before I first saw them. One hundred and sixteen patients (52 percent) had facial pain symptoms for more than two years. It was not rare to see patients who had been ill for five or more years, and a few had been under various treatments for more than ten years. Two patients had been ill for twenty years.

Etiology of the Atypical Facial Pain Syndromes

I found organic causes to account for the atypical pain syndromes in only twenty-seven (12 percent) of the patients in this study. Five of the patients with organic lesions had neoplasms, two had malignancies of the tongue, and two others had nasopharyngeal tumors. A fifth patient had a meningioma lying at the base of the skull in the middle cranial fossa which compromised the trigeminal nerve. Five patients were chronically ill with multiple sclerosis and had evidence of widespread areas of demyelination. They experienced severe, diffuse, unilateral facial pain presumably due to pontine lesions. Five patients had chronic, severe facial pain in the postherpetic phase of herpes zoster. The remaining twelve patients in the "organic" group had documented histories of true trigeminal neuralgia, which had been treated by either alcohol injections or sectioning of the sensory roots. The original paroxysmal quality of their pains had disappeared and were replaced by constant nagging discomforts.

Finally, 198, or 88 percent, of the patients studied had no specific anatomic lesions to account for their atypical pain patterns. (I have not included in this group patients who had autonomic components to their syndromes of the type that has been described as "cluster headaches.")

Age and Sex

One hundred ninety-four, or 86 percent, of the 225 consecutive patients who made up this series were women.

Table 1 summarizes the age distribution of male and female patients at the onset of facial pain. It should be noted that only nine patients, or 4 percent were under thirty years of age at the onset of facial pain syndromes. Similarly, pain began past the age of sixty in only eighteen patients (8 percent). In other words, 88 percent of the total group were between thirty-one and sixty years of age.

If these figures are further corrected so that only the 198 patients who had *no* organic lesions to account for their facial pains are included, some very striking observations appear, as summarized in *Table 2.* I found that 180 (91 percent) of the 198 patients who had atypical facial pain syndromes in the absence of organic lesions were women. I further noted that in 163, or 91 percent, of the 180 female patients who had no demonstrable organic lesions, the onset of facial pain occurred between the ages of thirty-one and sixty. I can be more specific and report that almost all of these 163 patients were between thirty-five and fifty-five years old. There were only eighteen male patients with atypical facial pain without any demonstrable organic lesions. Of these, sixteen first experienced facial pain between the ages of thirty-one and sixty.

TABLE 1 *Age of Patients at Onset of Atypical Facial Pain* (Organic and Nonorganic Causes)

Age	Number of Patients	
	Male	Female
11–20	0	1
21–30	1	7
31–40	6	38
41–50	13	81
51–60	6	54
61–70	5	12
71–80	0	1
TOTAL	31	194

TABLE 2 *Age of Patients at Onset of Atypical Facial Pain* (Nonorganic Causes)

Age	Number of Patients	
	Male	Female
11–20	0	1
21–30	1	7
31–40	5	37
41–50	6	80
51–60	4	46
61–70	2	8
71–80	0	1
TOTAL	18	180

As one reviews *Table 2*, it is obvious that in the vast majority of patients the onset of pain occurred between the ages of forty-one and sixty. Most of the patients who experienced the onset of pain before the age of forty were between thirty-six and forty. We therefore can say that this syndrome is primarily found in middle-age women.

Of the twenty-seven patients who had organic lesions to account for their pain, thirteen were men and fourteen were women.

Clinical Findings

In my descriptions I will deal only with the 198 patients who had no discernible organic lesions to account for their pain syndromes.

Onset

The patients invariably claimed to have definite organic lesions. Many specifically associated the pain with minor dental or facial traumas. The initial complaints of pain followed simple dental or otolaryngological procedures in seventy-nine patients and followed minor facial traumas in thirty-two patients. There was no history of precipitating surgery or trauma in the remaining patients. It should be noted that none of these patients had massive facial injuries prior to the onset of facial pain.

The pains usually began gradually. If they followed a dental procedure or facial trauma, the initial pains were localized to the site of injury. Pains were commonly described as being aching in nature and lasted for long periods, with some spontaneous remissions. Rarely were trigger points described.

After a few days or weeks, the pain became constant and more intense. A dentist was commonly consulted at this point. By this time the patient was preoccupied by the facial region. If the patient was questioned about the intensity of the pain at this point, he or she would usually say, "It's bad, but I can stand it."

As the weeks extended into months, the patient became obsessed with her face. It became her sole topic of conversation. The pains were then described as being very severe, usually "agonizing," and constant, with occasional fluctuations in degree but without significant relief even after taking analgesics. At the same time, the pain was commonly characterized as razor-sharp and burning or stabbing in addition to aching. The description was usually mixed.

Slowly the pain spread to involve wider areas of the face. Often the entire side of the face became involved, together with the eye, the ear, and the dorsal cervical and suprascapular regions. In more than half of these patients the facial pains became bilateral at some time during the course of the history. The original focus of pain almost always remained, but at times other areas became the major points of concern. This was usually just a shifting of emphasis.

There was gradual but progressive interference with function. Initially it was described as interference with chewing, talking, cleansing the face, or brushing the teeth. The patient gradually retreated from social relationships and working became increasingly difficult. Frequent absences from work were common. In the chronic state, many patients lay about the house protesting that their pain prevented them from assuming any responsibilities.

These patients literally spent all of their money on dentists and physicians. The dentist, who was usually the first person to be consulted, was plagued by repeated visits and telephone calls. Usually the dentist, or less commonly the otolaryngologist, was coerced by the patient's persistent and urgent appeals for help into making a diagnosis of an organic lesion to account for the pain syndrome.

If the first dentist or physician diagnosed no organic lesions, the patient deserted him to seek another. A safari that led to many dentists, general practitioners, otolaryngologists, and finally neurologists began, and along the route she invariably found one or more consultants who made the diagnosis of an organic lesion and who instituted organic therapy.

All mechanical manipulations or injections added to the patient's facial fixation. This resulted in a progressive spreading of the pain. In rare instances mechanical interventions, which in retrospect did nothing specific, were followed by brief remissions of pain, but this was the gross exception and definitely not the rule. These remissions were due to placebo effects.

Most patients with pain in the mouth region were subjected to many dental manipulations. Teeth were often pulled and others were "ground down." Gingival biopsies were commonly performed. The diagnosis of dental malocclusion (bad bite) was often made, and followed up by extensive work to correct the bite.

Complete "mouth rehabilitations" were often done, with recapping of the teeth. Others had new dental prostheses made. Many patients had all their teeth extracted and dentures made.

All dental manipulations failed, and indeed aggravated the initial complaints. The patient became an expert in dental terminology. One dentist's diagnostic impressions were pitted against another's. In many cases, after mechanical manipulations had failed, a diagnosis of trigeminal neuralgia was commonly made, and the typical character of a "tic" described to the patient. This description, gathered from the dentist or in some instances from medical books, was often incorporated into the patient's clinical picture.

The general practitioner usually was at a loss as to the nature of the difficulties, and often mistakenly diagnosed trigeminal neuralgia. Often vitamins, particularly parenteral vitamin B_{12}, were given in massive doses. The patient might be given various analgesics, including large doses of narcotics. I have seen opium habituation and addiction in a few patients as a result.

As I mentioned earlier, the neurologist commonly does

not see this type of patient until one or more years after the onset of pain. By the time he does see her, her social and vocational functioning have become severely limited. She is convinced that she has a severe organic illness and is hostile to anyone who will not confirm her opinion.

Multiple trigger points are often described over various sites, but as we shall see, these cannot be confirmed by careful neurologic examination. The neurologist often makes a diagnosis of a variant of trigeminal neuralgia. Various medications are administered, including trichlorethyline inhalations, vitamin B12, analgesics, ergotamine preparations, Dilantin, and more recently Tegretol.

Some of my patients had been given alcohol injections and some had had trigeminal nerve sectionings. One patient had had a lobotomy. Stellate ganglion blocks and strippings of the adventitia over the carotid arteries were performed on others. Histamine desensitization was also used. Any hypalgesia or hypesthesia produced by a trigeminal injection or section was interpreted by these patients in a distorted fashion. Most complained of an agonizing increase in their pain, and there was often a delusional quality to their descriptions. After long periods of therapy, many of these patients were quite referential toward various dentists and physicians, and frank paranoid trends were not uncommon.

Further probing, with few exceptions, revealed that the patient's pain was markedly affected by emotional stress. The patients complained of ready fatigability, insomnia, difficulty in concentrating, loss of interest in their surroundings. They had become rather seclusive socially and were isolated to a great extent from their friends. Irritability and restlessness were very common. Anorexia was a universal problem, which the patients blamed on their facial pain.

Without exception these patients were depressed. Crying spells were frequent. Feelings of hopelessness were usual. At one time or another in the history, suicidal preoccupations were recorded in 71 (32 percent) of the 198 patients. Suicide attempts had been made by five patients.

As I pointed out in earlier chapters, gentle interrogation was necessary if one was to piece together this rather characteristic clinical picture. These patients described agitated states characterized by restlessness, pacing, and persistent fatigue, particularly in the morning. They constantly referred back to their "physical illnesses," but with patience and with increasing pointedness one could usually elicit a statement that the patient was feeling blue. She would then ask, "But Doctor, isn't it natural that I'm depressed with all this pain?"

As with most types of depression, careful questioning usually revealed a close correlation between the onset of the patient's symptoms and socioenvironmental traumas. This discovery required a point-by-point account of the patient's life situation before, during, and after the onset of the "physical complaints."

Personality Profiles

A very typical and predictable personality profile was obtained without exception among the women in the forty-to-sixty age group. They were characteristically very intelligent, meticulous, hard-working, ambitious, and usually very aggressive individuals. In general, they had a need to dominate their environment, either in the form of their households or their immediate communities. They were quite domineering and very critical, particularly of themselves. The meticulous, perfectionistic, obsessive-compulsive patterns were highly developed and dominated the personality profile. In the main, they were intolerant of their own failures and extremely critical of the failures of others. Very often they were overbearing and alienated those around them, both relatives and acquaintances.

These patients were constantly fighting against imagined feelings of worthlessness and inadequacy. However, any expression or admission of these conflicts was slow in coming to the surface clinically. The patient literally had spent a lifetime fighting against this negative image. Highly intellectualized defensive mechanisms were utilized throughout life in an attempt to compensate for these feelings of self-derogation.

A history of hypochondriacal manifestations was not unusual. On occasion it was initially projected as concern about other members of the family. However, further questioning would usually elicit the fact that these patients lived in dread of being physically incapacitated. The psychodynamic explanation of this fear related to the patients' need to prove themselves, which required physical well-being.

Family History

A review of the patients' family histories, with only two exceptions, revealed that there was a very aggressive, domineering, critical parent in the background. The dominant parent was nearly always the mother, while the father was rather passive. The husbands of these patients were routinely passive and dependent in the home. Very commonly the husbands accompanied the patients to the initial interviews. In almost all instances they echoed and reinforced their wives' accounts of the painfulness of their symptoms. In some situations, particularly when the hypochondriacal manifestations took on the characteristics of somatic delusions, the husband-patient relationship bordered upon a *folie à deux* syndrome.

Very often there was evidence of strong guilt feeligs on the part of the patient in relation to a conflict between the patient and the dominant parent. Usually the patient saw the mother as an aggressive, critical person whose negative attitudes had filled the patient with anxiety and feelings of inadequacy and worthlessness. The patient was usually quick-tempered, irritable, and opinionated, with strong guilt-linked retroflex rage mechanisms.

The reader will note that this is the classical description of an agitated depression seen most commonly during the involutional period of life. Indeed, these patients in the forty-to-sixty age group had agitated depression, moderate to severe in degree, masked by their excessive fixations on the facial area. The facial pain could be described in the main as being a hypochondriacal expression of the underlying depression.

In those relatively few patients in whom the atypical facial pain syndrome began while they were in their twenties or early thirties, schizoid personality matrices were noted. In this younger group, the symptom patterns were usually more bizarre and very often had qualities suggesting somatic delusions. Ten patients in this younger group were actively schizophrenic.

Initial Examination

The patients with atypical facial pain patterns were characteristically very garrulous, and minutely circumstantial. Their histories were filled with highly intellectualized technical dental and medical jargon that had been accumulated through the months or years. They were often very hostile toward previous doctors or dentists. Many complained of a "bad bite," or said their faces were out of shape. While they were complaining of severe facial pain, they usually had inappropriate facial expressions. A flat, bland facies was often seen. Other patients, in spite of complaints of pain, smiled inappropriately through most of the interview. Some patients did appear overtly depressed.

Some patients repeatedly localized the area of pain very epicritically. More commonly, the borders of the zones of pain were somewhat vague and even inconsistent. Rarely did they follow true anatomic neurologic lines. With their pent-up hostility, the patients were ever ready to do verbal battle with the examiner, necessitating a great deal of patient persistence on the part of the examining physician.

On neurologic examination, the "abnormalities" were almost always limited to the head and neck areas. A few patients complained that malocclusion of the jaws caused disalignment of the spine with resultant low back pain.

The head was usually held in a rigid position. The dorsal cervical muscles and the sternocleidomastoid muscles were commonly under increased tension, most marked on the side corresponding to the facial pain. These muscles were described as being very tender on palpation.

The examination of the head and face was usually attended by severe grimacing or a very bland facial expression. In either instance, there were protestations of severe pain on palpation. The area in which the painful symptoms were described as occurring was tender to the touch. Trigger points were often found. However, these did not induce the exquisite changes noted when a true tic douloureux is fired off. Rather, there were marked verbal protestations without much defensive withdrawal.

The muscles of mastication, particularly the masseters, often were hypertrophic and tender (the hypertrophy is caused by chronic clenching of the jaws and bruxism, which is very common in these patients).

There was frequently tenderness over the temporomandibular joint on the side where the pain was felt. In a few instances, crepitus was noted over the joint. The internal pterygoid muscles on the painful side were at times slightly tender. This too is due to long-standing clenching of the jaws. (The internal pterygoid muscles may be readily palpated if the examiner places his thumbs just behind the anterior pillars of the tonsils, and the forefingers over the temporomandibular joints and then exerts pressure between them.) In all instances the tongue, mouth, and oral pharynx must be carefully visualized and palpated lest neoplasms be overlooked. The external auditory meati should also be examined very closely to rule out sources of referred pain.

Inconsistent areas of hypasthesia and hypalgesia were found in thirty-eight patients. These did not follow normal neurologic sensory patterns. Alleged trigger points and even some areas of tenderness disappeared when the patient was distracted by various means.

Twenty-seven patients exhibited severe limitation in opening their jaws. This was due to the chronic contraction of the jaw muscles. As in other areas of the body, chronically contracted muscles become hypertrophied, fatigued, and tender. However, this aspect of the pain was not the prime cause of the patient's complaints.

On occasion the histories and examinations were extremely complicated, particularly when the patients had once had true trigeminal neuralgia and had been exposed to various treatments such as Dilantin, Tegretol, alcohol nerve blocks, and nerve sectionings. In some of these patients, inconsistent trigger points were found, but the descriptions of the pains contained elements not incompatible with a true tic. In these patients the overlays were compatible with a psychogenic process. In other words, there are patients who have had treated or untreated trigeminal neuralgia and have atypical facial pain of psychogenic origin superimposed on it.

A few patients manifested long track motor and sensory deficits. These invariably were on the side of the facial pain. In all instances the pyramidal track signs had a dramatic quality, were inconsistent, and could readily be discerned as not being organic in origin. The sensory deficits were usually totally unilateral in the side of the facial pain and usually involved all modalities, including pain, touch, vibration, and position sense. The discomforts would extend exactly to the midline. Vibratory sense would be decreased on one side of the dorsal spinous processes and over the head. This, of course, was impossible to explain on an organic basis, and enabled one to rule out any true sensory deficits.

In five patients I found spasmodic torticollis, with the head tilted to the side of the alleged pain. In one patient there was a tortipelvis in addition to the torticollis.

Complications and Cautions

In most instances the diagnosis of atypical facial pain of psychogenic origin is readily made. However, as I have cautioned in earlier chapters, whenever the diagnosis of a masked depressive syndrome is made, the examiner must be extremely careful that he is not overlooking a true organic lesion that may be hidden behind the masked depression.

The examiner must also be sharply aware of the fact that a sizable number of patients with atypical facial pain of psychogenic origin have very severe underlying depressions with suicidal propensities. In other words, by the time these syndromes are correctly diagnosed, they often pose urgent or even emergency situations.

The diagnosis and particularly the treatment are complicated by the iatrogenic factors. These factors are secondary to the multiple exposures to the veritable cornucopia of somatic treatments to which the patients have been exposed prior to the neuropsychiatric consultation.

It is not unusual to see patients who have consulted twenty-five or thirty dentists and physicians. Two had spent more than $100,000 in ill-advised attempts at somatic corrections. To be sure, the duration and cost of these treatments enhanced the patient's hypochondriacal fixations upon their faces.

Treatment

In Chapter 15, I described in detail the treatment procedure that I have utilized in the management of patients with masked depressions. The treatment that offers the greatest success is psychotherapy in combination with antidepressant drugs.

The treatment results were inversely proportional to the duration of illness. Approximately 75 percent of those patients who had symptoms of atypical facial pain for six months or less had complete remissions. Approximately half of those who had the syndrome for twelve to eighteen months obtained remissions. In contrast, only one-third of those who had been ill for two or more years obtained significant ameliorations of their depressions and facial pain patterns.

As I noted before, treatment results are massively compli-cated by iatrogenic factors. Therapeutic results were poorest when true sensory deficits had been caused by alcohol blocks or nerve sectionings. In many of these patients the complaints of pain took on a delusional character.

At no time should the physician lose sight of the fact that he is treating a severely depressed patient. Those patients who obtained significant improvement in response to psy-chotherapy combined with antidepressant drugs usually man-ifested the same patterns of masked depression in the form of facial pain if they were once again placed under pressures they could not tolerate. Recurring facial pain patterns are usually more difficult to treat than the initial episodes.

I often find it necessary to work closely with a dentist who has great expertise with the temporomandibular joint. Very frequently it is necessary for the dentist to relieve the chroni-cally contracted masseter and internal pterygoid muscles to permit the patient to eat and to relieve the true pain associated with persistent muscle contraction. If the dentist has no in-sight into the psychogenic aspects of the problem, however, he is likely to do more harm than good. (I have had the good fortune to work closely with two dentists who have been pioneers in this field, Joseph Marbach and the late Laszlo Schwartz.) No definitive dental work should be attempted until the underlying depression has been significantly ameliorated. The insertion of any mechanical devices or the changing of the character of the bite will fail and produce adverse results no matter how brilliant the technical proce-dures may be.

Patients with atypical facial pain of psychogenic origin are usually easy to diagnose but very difficult to treat, as I have described in some detail. The answer lies in prophylaxis, which in turn depends upon early diagnosis. Unfortunately, there are very few dentists, internists, otolaryngologists, neurologists, or psychiatrists who can recognize this syn-drome, let alone understand its psychophysiologic and psychodynamic bases. To my knowledge, definitive instruction in the atypical facial pain syndrome of psychogenic origin is limited to the training offered by me in the School of Dentistry of Columbia University and in the Neurological Institute of New York. It is my hope that these chapters will stimulate increased awareness of this problem.

18

The Relationship of Depression to Alcoholism

MAX HAYMAN

For more than half a century it has been axiomatic that there is a close relationship between alcoholism and depression—that underlying excessive drinking there is depression. In recent years questions have been raised concerning this concept. The discussion is more than academic, since it has an important bearing not only on nosological factors, but on theoretical concepts of the nature of alcoholism and depression and practical aspects of the management and treatment of alcoholism.

It is of interest, therefore, to review evidence on the association of alcoholism and depression: alcoholism as a mask for depression, alcoholism as a precipitant of depression, depression as an incident during the course of alcoholism, and alcoholism as a diagnostic category.

Does Depression Induce Alcoholism?

A number of clinical, experimental, and genetic studies

support the view that depression underlies alcoholism or that alcoholism masks depression. From their study of the effects of intravenous alcohol on alcoholics and depressives, Mayfield and his associates have found, on the basis of psychological tests, that alcohol acts as an antidepressant for a depressive and, to a somewhat lesser degree because of tolerance, for an alcoholic (30, 31). They reach the conclusion that the alcoholic has a depression and that alcohol lessens this depression in the doses used, but that its value is limited because of the development of tolerance. They also found that normal individuals too exhibit a lessening in the depressive scale. They consider alcohol a calmative rather than a euphoriant. At the same time, they make the interesting statement that the incidence of excessive drinking during periodic depression has been overstated in the literature.

In a review paper, Freed (11), discussing the issue of functional depression and depression of function by alcohol, brings up the question of whether increased drinking produces depression. He cites Gross (14), who notes that some alcoholics do suffer from psychotic depressions, and who speaks of manic-depressive psychosis "masquerading" as alcoholism. Hoff's extensive experience leads him to believe that there is a reciprocal relationship between drinking and depression (19). Curiously, Freed had to search the literature exhaustively to find evidence that manic patients often drank to excess. My own experience suggests that a large percentage of manic patients have been heavy drinkers. Such drinking appears to be an attempt to maintain the manic state and prevent the onset of depression.

Kielholz (22) feels that depression, often of long duration, may be a contributory cause of alcoholism. He writes of "exhaustion depression" following years of strain, and advises intensive and prolonged use of antidepressants. Sclare (49) emphasizes that women give histories of depression more frequently than men, but mentions crises of despair or depression in alcoholics of both sexes.

The Psychoanalytic Review of Alcoholism

The psychoanalytic school has provided us with considerable information on the psychopathology of the alcoholic (1, 3, 33, 34, 42, 47, 50, 56). Much of the psychodynamic information we have about alcoholism and alcoholics stems from their work. Their findings, however, encompass most of the developmental phases of the individual. In an attempt to organize the material, I reconstructed a schema of drives, defenses, and personality characteristics applicable to alcoholics (15). It should be noted that most of the psychoanalysts emphasized the regression to the passive-receptive or oral stage of development, but frequently it was most difficult to assign any particular stage of developmental disturbance to the alcoholic, and other libidinal stages were also importantly emphasized.

The psychoanalytic viewpoints were primarily based on unconscious factors, and the depression was most often considered to be unconscious. Even the evidences of unconscious depression were often indirect and not clearly delineated. While their constructs can be recognized by anyone who treats alcoholics intensively, evidence of a clinical depression rarely appears during the psychoanalytic therapy of alcoholics. Excessive dependence (62) and the important influence of the mother (31) have been observed. Psychoanalysis as a treatment method, however, has been found effective with only a small percentage of alcoholics (24).

Genetic Factors in Depression in Alcoholism

Recently, interest has been renewed in genetic factors in alcoholism. At a meeting devoted to "Nature and Nurture in Alcoholism," evidence was adduced that chromosomal aberrations can be observed in the blood cells of alcoholics, and claims were made that twin studies supported the hypothesis of a hereditary mechanism in alcoholism (43). In the discussion periods at these meetings it was brought out, however, that some of the effects may have been secondary, the results of prolonged alcoholism. There was some indication, nevertheless, that genetic factors should not be ignored in the assessment of alcoholism.

Winokur and his associates (61) offer further data on the genetic factors that link affective disorders and alcoholism. They state that they cannot distinguish in their genetic studies among neurotic-depressive reaction, psychotic-depressive reaction, manic-depressive disease, and involutional depression. As far as the family history is concerned, all of these groups, he says, make up a homogeneous population. He finds that women are more prone to depression than men; in men, however, alcoholism and personality disorders occur where an affective disorder might be expected. He says that if one combines the prevalence of alcoholism and affective disorders in fathers of affective-disordered patients, the total (23.1 percent) closely approximates the combined prevalence in women (24 percent). He is convinced that depression and alcohol are closely related and states that depression lasting for months follows withdrawal from alcohol (60). This observation cannot be confirmed clinically in my own experience. He emphasizes the incidence of suicide and states that in no other psychiatric illness is there such a high termination in death by suicide. His linking of alcoholism and sociopathy is interesting (59).

The therapeutic test using drugs as a diagnostic instrument to determine the presence of depression in alcoholism is an inadequate indicator. Travis (53) claimed improvement in alcoholics through the use of iproniazid, a drug with antidepressant properties. Of twenty alcoholics treated from five to thirteen weeks, he reported sixteen had fair to excellent reversal of depression. This was an uncontrolled study and was not replicated. Kissin and Charnoff (23) used many different drugs with 1,500 alcoholic patients and found that no drug was superior to placebos. They used three antidepressants and major and minor tranquilizers. Since alcoholics have both depression and anxiety, they reason, a combination of chlordiazepoxide and imipramine should make for improvement, and they believe that such evidence will eventually be found.

Evidence Against Depression Underlying Alcoholism

We cannot take it for granted that suicide is always associated with depression. Rushing (46) has written a paper on suicide and alcoholism without once mentioning depression. However, we also cannot say that the proximate cause of suicide may not be an unconscious depression, an unrecognized depressive episode, or even a "flash" of depression. Rushing suggests there may be common causes for alcoholism and suicide, although one cannot say what these are. He suggests that alcoholism contributes to suicide and gives evidence of this in his hypothesis of "social reaction to deviance." Social relations are disrupted, and this leads to loss of love objects, which in turn leads to suicide, as Murphy and Robins have noted (36).

There is also considerable evidence against an integral association between alcoholism and depression. Faulstick (8) feels that most of the depression comes directly from the alcohol. He writes of the drunkenness of depressive psychopaths and neurotics, of "depression due to organic cerebral changes caused by excesses of alcohol, reactive depressions connected with social or economic consequences of alcoholism, or resulting from strong guilt feelings, or even the reactive depressions that come on during the 'sobering down' stage of the withdrawal treatment of alcoholism."

Although Zwerling (64) finds depression occurring in the alcoholic in his clinical diagnosis of forty-six closely studied alcoholics, he lists only one case as a manic-depressive psychosis. Most frequent are schizoid characters and passive-aggressive characters. Zwerling himself believes that there is an oral depressive core to the alcoholic (65). Gillis and Keet (12) found that only 13 percent of their alcoholics had depressive reactions. The majority (85 percent) had personality disorders, mainly of the inadequate and passive-aggressive types. It is interesting that Grinker and his co-workers (13), in describing the borderline syndrome, have given a description that accords very well with the description of alcoholics; for example, hostility, poor sense of identity, depressive loneliness, acting out, reaching for a mother figure, and passivity.

The high suicide rate among alcoholics has been cited as an indication of the existence of a covert or overt depression in the alcoholic. The high suicide rate is well established, but it is also well known that a clinical depression is not always a component of attempted suicide. Philip (40) found character disorders in almost half of her patients. She found that alcoholics who attempted suicide were more hostile and anxious than normal or neurotic individuals. They were also characterized by impulsiveness.

Rotov (45), in describing twenty hospital suicides, stated that the patients were often compulsive and repetitive, and that such suicides often occur in people who do not appear to be depressed. Sometimes, he says, they will go into a state of "dissociation," and they can commit suicide impulsively if the means present themselves. In a report from Sweden, Bjurulf (4) states that 33 percent of suicides were intoxicated at the time they killed themselves.

It is difficult to judge the presence of depression during an acute alcoholic episode (21). Nathan and his co-workers (37) and McNamee and his associates (32) have shown that alcoholics, after a preliminary period of relief of tension and even euphoria, develop increased anxiety and depression. Finally, Palola and his co-workers (39) reported that 80 to 90 percent of fifty alcoholics attempted or committed suicide while intoxicated. Such reports suggest that depression and suicide are precipitated by alcoholism. This view is also attested to by the preponderance of suicides by alcoholics while they are in the drinking phase, with a lesser number in the hangover phase, when they are full of guilt and remorse over their behavior.

Paffenbarger and his associates (38) in a study of persons who died by suicide or accident from seventeen to fifty-one years after their student days, found that alcohol was related to accidental deaths, but that suicide was often a result of drinking to excess. In Paffenbarger's opinion, however, although alcohol "is not an early precursor of suicide . . . it may be involved as a prodromal symptom—removing inhibitions, clouding judgment, causing depression or acting organically."

Fox (9) notes the diverse underlying psychopathology of alcoholics in spite of common difficulties. Although their criteria differ from ours, a group of English workers (2) found that a significant number of Irish alcoholics had one to three schizophrenic symptoms and a number were overtly schizophrenic. They stated that this supports the hypothesis that alcoholism masks schizophrenia. Hoffer (20) states that 33 percent of alcoholics are basically schizophrenic on the basis of the adrenochrome urine test.

In the electroencephalographic study of sleep and dreams (48), depressed patients have significantly less REM sleep, less stage 4 sleep, and less total sleep than nondepressed controls. This finding has been linked with the catecholamine hypothesis of affective disorders. Vogel (55) suggests that the reaction to alcohol is quite different and that alcohol is a REM depriver and increases the propensity for REM sleep but inhibits discharge. These interesting leads, particularly the study of the biogenic amines, may provide further information regarding the relationship of depression and alcoholism.

In the area of psychological tests, no additional evidence was found for a depression or depressive type in alcoholics. When Rosen (44) compared the responses of psychiatric patients in general with those of alcoholic patients on the M.M.P.I., he found that both types of patients showed substantially the same constellation of psychiatric symptoms. The only difference was a greater frequency of antisocial or asocial impulses in the alcoholic, as measured by the psychopathic deviate scale. Rosen concluded that alcoholics do not represent a unique personality type or a unique psychiatric nosological group.

MacAndrew and Geertsma (26, 27) found that the M.M.P.I. could not differentiate alcoholics from nonalcoholic psychiatric patients to any significant degree. MacAndrew developed a scale from the M.M.P.I. which did, however, differentiate between alcoholics and nonalcoholics to a certain extent (28). Vega (54) suggests that the MacAndrew scale can differentiate the alcoholic from other psychiatric patients to a significant degree, but is poor in discriminating them from nonpsychiatric control subjects.

Lisansky (25) notes that testing the alcoholic during a period of intoxication or withdrawal does not give an estimate of intelligence factors, brain damage, or other variables. She agrees with Zwerling (64) that the alcoholic may have a constellation of traits which is embedded in a variety of personality structures.

Williams (57) found that alcoholics scored highest on the psychopathic deviate scale and that depressives were second. Most of the scales were elevated, however, and the M.M.P.I. gave only a limited indication that a depressive type occurred more frequently than others. In a study of 795 alcoholics, Williams also found that 95 percent were diagnosed as personality disorders, 11 percent were suicidal, and only 3 percent had a chronic marked depression (58).

Ruth Fox (10) states that neither depression nor alcoholism can be considered clear-cut clinical entities, and that depression may occur in any psychiatric condition. In considering depression in relation to the use of alcohol, she divides depressives into five classes: (a) retarded depressives, who give alcohol up quickly, if they use it at all; (b) tension depressives, who turn to alcohol as a relaxant (I have seen this frequently in menopausal women, who sometimes drink for several years until they spontaneously recover from their underlying depression); (c) schizo-affective depressives, whose depression masks a serious underlying disorder—patients who drink to relieve their loneliness, emptiness, and depression, which are actually aggravated by alcohol; (d) those whose depression is secondary to a problem in living, which alcohol assuages; and (e) those whose depression is due to organic illness.

Fox does not consider in this classification those whom Knight has called "essential alcoholics" and who have been categorized in the literature under character disorder, psychopathic deviance, and the like. Her experience has generally been the same as mine: whatever depression the alcoholic patient has is quickly dissipated when he stops drinking, especially when he receives appropriate treatment for the specific condition.

Murphy and Robins (36) studied 134 suicides, the majority of whom were either depressives or alcoholics. They felt that the affective disorders were in general a response to an endogenous depression, while in alcoholics they were a response to a social disturbance, namely, the loss of a love object. Thirty-two percent of alcoholics had lost love objects within six weeks before they committed suicide, as compared to 3 percent of the depressives; and 48 percent of the alcoholics had lost love objects one year before the suicide, as opposed to 15 percent of the depressives. In their opinion, there were clear-cut differences between them. This is interesting, since the recent loss of a love object has been considered a trigger for the recurrence of an endogenous or reactive depression.

Freed (11) summarizes his considerable material on alcoholism and affective disorders in this way: "The evidence for causal relationships between alcoholism and affective disorders is unimpressive although there is substantial evidence that many manic-depressive patients use alcohol intemperately . . . manic-depressive reactions may initially masquerade as alcoholism because . . . the alcoholismic symptomatology is blatant and predominant."

In my own experience, an association between alcoholism and overt depression has not been sufficiently marked to justify a separate classification for those in whom the two disorders are combined (15). A few alcoholics exhibit a psychotic or neurotic type of depression, but the great majority of alcoholics can be classified under "character disorders." (See *Figure 1*, which includes the parallel sociological classification and treatment type.)

CHRONIC ALCOHOLICS
TREATMENT AND CLASSIFICATION

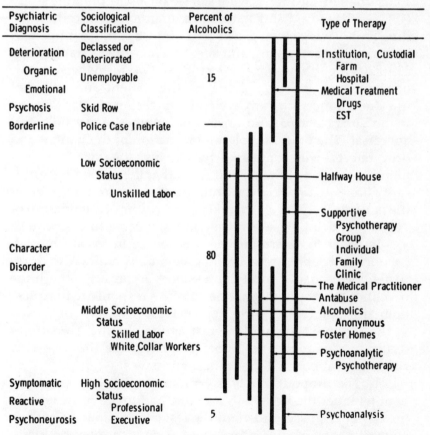

Psychiatric Diagnosis	Sociological Classification	Percent of Alcoholics	Type of Therapy
Deterioration	Declassed or Deteriorated		Institution, Custodial
Organic	Unemployable	15	Farm Hospital
Emotional			Medical Treatment
Psychosis	Skid Row		Drugs EST
Borderline	Police Case Inebriate	—	
	Low Socioeconomic Status		Halfway House
	Unskilled Labor		
			Supportive Psychotherapy Group
Character		80	Individual Family
Disorder			Clinic
			The Medical Practitioner
			Antabuse
	Middle Socioeconomic Status		Alcoholics Anonymous
	Skilled Labor		Foster Homes
	White Collar Workers		Psychoanalytic Psychotherapy
Symptomatic	High Socioeconomic Status	—	
Reactive	Professional		
Psychoneurosis	Executive	5	Psychoanalysis

From Max Hayman, *Alcoholism: Mechanism and Management* (Springfield, Ill.: Charles C. Thomas, 1966). Reproduced by permission.

A Therapeutic Test of Depression in Alcoholism

At the Alcoholism Research Clinic at U.C.L.A. several years ago, a large number of drugs were tested in a series of controlled studies. None of these proved to be better than placebos, and the only finding was that chlordiazepoxide influenced the clinic patients to return more frequently. It did not prevent excessive drinking, however.

On the theory that depression was a feature of alcoholism, 195 outpatient alcoholics were started on an imipramine study (18). One hundred and sixteen were randomly placed on the drug and 79 were given placebos. The dose of imipramine was 100 mg. a day at the start, and later was modified to range from 25 to 200 mg. daily. For these studies, two forms were used, one of which was completed by the patient and included questions concerning anxiety and depression similar to those in the Zung tests (63) and various other types of psychological appraisal. The other, involving evaluation of the patient and drug effects, was completed by the investigator (7). It was found at the end of the second week that there was no significant difference between the drug and placebo groups, whether the patients were "wet" (drinking at the time of attendance) or "dry" (not drinking when they initially came to the clinic).

In order to determine the differences in response of alcoholics and depressives, I compared the alcoholics with thirty patients who had clinical depressions, according to both the psychiatrist's appraisal and the patient's response to the questionnaire (18). Of the thirty depressives, two were diagnosed as the reactive type and the rest as the chronic, sometimes recurrent, "endogenous" type. We can make the following statements about this group of depressives:

1. The dropout rate was very small. One depressed patient left after the first visit, and one had to move away from the city after the second visit; the rest continued to keep their appointments. Alcoholics present a serious dropout problem.

2. The depressed patients were seen weekly for many months, and their doses of imipramine had to be readjusted

primarily because of side effects. Alcoholics would often decide for themselves whether they would take the medication, and if so, the amounts they would take.

3. In the first week the depressives showed reduced irritability; in the second week insomnia lessened; and in the third and subsequent weeks the depression was alleviated. The responses of alcoholics depended on whether they resumed or continued drinking.

4. Improvement rates ranged from moderate improvement to recovery. (See *Table 1*.).

The alcoholics who showed improvement improved more rapidly than the depressives, but in most of these the im-

TABLE 1   Improvement Rates of Depressed
Patients Treated with Imipramine

Improvement	No. of Patients	Percent
None	4	14.3
Mild improvement	4	14.3
Moderate improvement	6	21.4
Considerable improvement	7	25.0
Recovery	7	25.0

provement consisted of relief from withdrawal symptoms, and it made no difference whether they were given imipramine or a placebo. The nonalcoholic depressed patients responded more slowly. When the alcoholics were compared with the nonalcoholic depressed patients, it was difficult to distinguish them on the basis of their responses to self-rated items. There was a tendency only for the nonalcoholic depressed patients to check more "unsociable" items and to indicate a more unsatisfactory sexual life.

In their appraisals, however, the psychiatrists had no difficulty in distinguishing between the two groups. The nonalcoholic depressed patients had a morbid expression; the depression was deeper; their speech was slowed, they lacked energy, their sleep was impaired, and their general retardation was obvious. This suggests that there is both a qualitative and a quantitative difference between the alcoholic and the depressed patient. The alcoholics were often anxious to have medication and therefore exaggerated their complaints. This depended partly on whether they were "wet" or "dry" or were suffering from withdrawal symptoms. Unless the alcoholic was actually in severe withdrawal, he could express intense depression without evidence of suffering.

One can understand that the alcoholic is often a despairing and miserable person, but he does not often show the clinical picture presented by the depressed patient. Ditman (7) cites two patients who did not drink during their depressed stage, but resumed drinking after recovery through imipramine treatment. Relatively few patients will drink during a deep depression.

The response of the patients to our questionnaire brings up the question of the response of alcoholics to depression scales such as the Zung (63) and M.M.P.I. If the responses to these are similar to the responses to our questionnaire, the alcoholics would have a high rating on both the depression and anxiety scales. They might be rated the same as depressed and anxious patients, and if they were not seen by a trained worker, or if they took the test in seclusion, they might be considered qualitatively and quantitatively the same.[1]

In spite of the failure of drugs in chronic alcoholism up to now (17), a survey of psychiatrists conducted at the U.C.L.A. Alcoholism Research Clinic (16) showed that alcoholism was the second most frequent condition in which psychoanalysts used drugs and the third most frequent condition in which general psychiatrists used drugs. Fifty-seven percent of psychoanalysts used drugs in classical psychoanalysis of alcoholics and 85 percent used them in conjunction with psychoanalytically oriented psychotherapy. Among general psychiatrists the frequency was higher: 81 percent used drugs with intensive psychotherapy and 87 percent with supportive psychotherapy of alcoholism. Family physicians, of course, use drugs with alcoholics a great deal more often than psychiatrists. Some reasons were given for this frequent use of drugs without adequate evidence of therapeutic effect (17).

Overt vs. Unconscious Depression in Alcoholics

We have touched on an area that may be of considerable importance in alcoholics, the area of defense mechanisms. Most of the defense mechanisms used by alcoholics have been listed and described elsewhere (15). Alcoholics—and we are indebted to the psychoanalysts for these data—use especially primitive defense mechanisms. These include introjection, projection, denial, and acting out as basic mechanisms, although some of the more mature defense mechanisms, such as rationalization and repression, are also used to a limited ex-

1.The Palm Springs Mental Health Clinic has carried out a drug evaluation, using as instruments the Zung self-rating depression scale, the Zung anxiety scale, and the Hamilton scale. The data are currently being reduced, but it appears that the alcoholics will rate high on depression and anxiety on the Zung scales and less so on the Hamilton, which is completed by a trained worker.

tent. Moore (35) has written on what is probably the major defense mechanism in alcoholism, denial. Aided by his defense mechanisms, the alcoholic has been able to maintain his narcissism, his feelings of omnipotence, his passivity and dependency, and other psychopathologic traits. It is particularly when stresses occur that defenses are needed, and when defenses fail or are threatened, the alcoholic resorts to alcohol. He clouds his consciousness and provides himself with euphoria to boot. Thus awareness of depression or anxiety and the need to do something about them is successfully avoided either temporarily or for a long period.

In reviewing the relationship of alcoholism to depression, we must conclude that *overt* depression is not intrinsic to alcoholism; and if we regard alcoholism as a symptom, we cannot say it is symptomatic of depression in a psychiatric sense. It is far more likely that the great majority of alcoholics come under the heading of character disorder or sociopathic personality, or one of the synonyms for this type of behavioral reaction. For the alcoholic, the process of drinking is the equivalent of the acting-out behavior of the nonalcoholic person with character disorder. Neither the latter nor the alcoholic is likely to tolerate a prolonged clinical depressive reaction or a great deal of anxiety. Both will dissipate it by any means at their command. The person with a clinical depression, on the other hand, can ordinarily tolerate overt depression for days, weeks, even years.

Thus there are two principal factors at work in alcoholics which are not sufficiently emphasized: the unconscious nature of any depression or anxiety and the strength of their defenses.

Recent work in the biochemistry of depression may give some help in understanding these processes. Relatively little of this information has yet been applied to the alcoholic, but gradually the depressive mechanisms involved are becoming clearer (6, 51). It has been noted that 17 hydroxycorticosteroids rise with the onset of depression and fall as it becomes resolved. It has been noted also that the defense mechanism of denial is often most intense with a rise of 17 OHCS. When the denial breaks, five times the amount of 17 OHCS is present. This would suggest that the mechanism of denial itself is associated with hormonal factors (5). If this is supported, we have a partial biochemical explanation of the defense mechanism that is perhaps most commonly used by alcoholics. Additional factors involved in the biogenic amine theory of depression and the effects of the neurochormones are under investigation by several groups of investigators. The implications of such findings hold great significance for psychiatry generally.

Conclusions

Depression and anxiety in the alcoholic are primarily unconscious, although it is very frequently claimed that they are overt.

Developing depression and anxiety in the alcoholic are pushed into the unconscious by the defenses, notably denial. Energy is required to maintain these defenses, but they may be successful in blocking the unconscious anxiety from reaching consciousness and becoming overt, thus maintaining the equilibrium of the individual. If, because of defensive deficiencies, a drink becomes "necessary" at this time, relief is obtained partially and temporarily, though probably enough to establish a positive reinforcement. At a certain point, as drinking continues, alcohol use is followed by depression. The depression is probably caused by the alcohol, and now it becomes overt and conscious (37, 52). Suicide may then follow. The hangover is another development. It may be aborted by further drinking, or, if the alcoholic does not resume drinking at that time, he eventually recovers from his hangover and again an equilibrium is attained. With the next stress the cycle is repeated and the depression and anxiety are again denied or a drink taken whenever they threaten to become conscious.

In my clinical work with chronic alcoholics, which has run the gamut of psychotherapy from classical psychoanalysis to supportive treatment, not one patient has developed a clinical depression after achieving abstinence. The depressions these patients do occasionally develop are short-lived, and depend on current interpersonal factors.

There are three factors, I believe, which prevent the occurrence of depression in successfully treated alcoholics: (a) Alcohol often prolongs or initiates depression; abstinence shortens it. Accordingly, the goal in therapy should be abstinence. (b) In psychotherapy of alcoholism we note that the patient utilizes his defenses in the transference situation and, to a certain extent, is permitted to do so. He "introjects" the therapist (reversing projection to introjection). The therapist permits the introjection without allowing himself to be "swallowed up." The therapeutic agent, whether an individual, group, or Alcoholics Anonymous, become the love object. The feeling of self-worth in the alcoholic increases, which would tend to dissipate any depression. (c) The need for defense mechanisms such as denial decreases as therapy proceeds and the alcoholic develops trust in the therapist. The energy thus freed can be utilized to combat various types of stresses.

The relationship between alcoholism and depression is not established, nor can we speak of alcoholism as a mask for depression. Any reaction to stress may induce depression, anxiety, or alcoholism in varying measures. There is increasing evidence, however, that alcohol itself precipitates depression after an early euphoriant effect. To the extent that depression is associated with alcohol, it is likely to be unconscious until the main defense mechanism of the alcoholic, denial, breaks down and the early alleviating effect of alcohol is dissipated.

The alcoholic chooses to fortify the defense mechanism of denial with alcohol, but this paradoxically produces a release of the very impulses that he tries to hold in check. In addition, there may very well be a biochemical depressant effect that further entangles the alcoholic in sequences of depression and anxiety, drinking, and further depression.

References

1. Abraham, K. L. Psychological Relations Between Sexuality and Alcoholism. In *Selected Papers.* London: Hogarth Press, 1927.
2. Bagley, C., and Binitie, A. Alcoholism and Schizophrenia in Irishmen in London. *Brit. J. Addict.* 65:3, 1970.
3. Bergler, E. Personality Traits of Alcohol Addicts. *Quart J. Stud. Alcohol.* 7:356, 1943.
4. Bjurulf, P.; Sternby, N. H.; and Wistedt, B. Definitions of Alcoholism: Relevance of Liver Disease and Temperance Board Registrations in Sweden. *Quart. J. Stud. Alcohol* 32:393, 1971.
5. Bunney, W. E., Jr.; Mason, J. W.; Rostch, J. F.; and Hamburg, D. A Psychoendocrine Study of Severe Psychotic Depressive Crisis. *Amer. J. Psychiat.* 122:72, 1965.

6. Costa, E. The Neuropharmacological Background of Antidepressant Drugs. *Psychosomatics* 7:99, 1966.
7. Ditman, K. S. The Depressed Alcoholic. Symposiums on Depression, Michigan and Wayne County Academies of General Practice, Detroit, September 7, 1960.
8. Faulstick, H. R. Combined Amitriptyline and Perphenazine in the Withdrawal Treatment of Alcoholics. *Ther. Umsch.* 23:55, 1966.
9. Fox, R. The Dynamics of Alcoholism. *Southern Med. J.* 57:914, 1964.
10. Fox, R. Alcoholism and Reliance Upon Drugs as Depressive Equivalents. *Amer. J. Psychother.* 21:585, 1967.
11. Freed, E. X. Alcoholism and Manic-Depressive Disorders: Some Perspectives. *Quart. J. Stud. Alcohol* 31:62, 1970.
12. Gillis, L. S., and Keet, M. Prognostic Factors and Treatment Results in Hospitalized Alcoholics. *Quart. J. Stud. Alcohol* 30:426, 1969.
13. Grinker, R. R. Sr.; Werble, Bond Drye, R. C. *The Borderline Syndrome: A Behavioral Study of Ego Functions.* New York: Basic Books, 1968.
14. Gross, M. M. Management of Acute Alcohol Withdrawal States. *Quart. J. Stud. Alcohol* 28:655, 1967.
15. Hayman, M. *Alcoholism: Mechanism and Management.* Springfield, Ill.: Charles C. Thomas, 1966.
16. Hayman, M., and Ditman, K. S. The Influence of Age and Orientation of Psychiatrists on Their Prescription of Drugs. *Comprehen. Psychiat.* 7:152, 1966.
17. Hayman, M. Failure of Drugs in Chronic Alcoholism. *Int. J. Psychiat.* 3:260, 1967.
18. Hayman, M. Comparison of Response of Depressed Patients and Alcoholics. Unpublished data.
19. Hoff, E. C. Newer Concepts of Alcoholism and Its Treatment. *Quart. J. Stud. Alcohol,* supplement no. 1, 1961.
20. Hoffer, A. Niacin Therapy in Psychiatry. Springfield, Ill.: Charles C. Thomas, 1962.
21. Kapamadzija, B. Alcohol and Suicide. *Alkoholizam* 9, no. 3:23, 1969.
22. Kielholz, P. Alcohol and Depression. *Brit. J. Addict.* 65:187, 1970.
23. Kissin, B., and Charnoff, S. M. Clinical Evaluation of Tran-

quilizers and Antidepressant Drugs in the Long-Term Treatment of Chronic Alcoholism. In *Alcoholism Behavioral Research: Therapeutic Approaches*, ed. R. Fox. New York: Springer, 1967.

24. Knight, R. P. Evaluation of the Results of Psychoanalytic Therapy. *Amer. J. Psychiat.* 98:434, 1941.

25. Lisansky, E. S. Clinical Research in Alcoholism and the Use of Psychological Tests: A Reevaluation. In *Alcoholism Behavioral Research: Therapeutic Approaches*, ed. R. Fox. New York: Springer, 1967.

26. MacAndrew, C., and Geertsma, R. H. An Analysis of Responses of Alcoholics to Scale 4 of the M.M.P.I. *Quart. J. Stud. Alcohol* 24:23, 1963.

27. MacAndrew, C., and Geertsma, R. H. A Critique of Alcoholism Scales Derived from the M.M.P.I. *Quart. J. Stud. Alcohol* 25:68, 1964.

28. MacAndrew, C. The Differentiation of Male Alcoholic Outpatients from Nonalcoholic Psychiatric Outpatients by Means of the M.M.P.I. *Quart. J. Stud. Alcohol* 26:238, 1965.

29. Mayfield, D. G., and Allen, D. Alcohol and Affect: A Psychopharmacological Study. *Amer. J. Psychiat.* 123:1346, 1967.

30. Mayfield, D. Psychopharmacology of Alcohol: I-Affective Change with Intoxication, Drinking Behavior, and Affective State. *J. Nerv. Ment. Dis.* 146:314, 1968.

31. McCord, W., and McCord, J. *Origins of Alcoholism*. Stanford: Stanford University Press, 1960.

32. McNamee, H. B.; Mello, N. K.; and Mendelson, J. H. Experimental Analysis of Drinking Patterns: Concurrent Psychiatric Observations. *Amer. J. Psychiat.* 124:1063, 1968.

33. Meerloo, J. A. M. Artificial Ecstasy: A Study of the Psychosomatic Aspects of Drug Addiction. *J. Nerv. Ment. Dis.* 115:246, 1952.

34. Menninger, K. *Man Against Himself*. New York: Harcourt, Brace, 1938.

35. Moore, R. A., and Murphy, T. C. Denial of Alcoholism as an Obstacle to Recovery. *Quart. J. Stud. Alcohol* 22:597, 1961.

36. Murphy, G. E., and Robins, E. Social Factors in Suicide. *JAMA* 199:303, 1967.

37. Nathan, P. E.; Titler, N. A.; Lowenstein, L. M.; Solomon, P.;

and Rossi, A. M. Behavioral Analysis of Chronic Alcoholism. *Arch. Gen. Psychiat.* 22:419, 1970.

38. Paffenbarger, R. S.; King, S. H.; and Wing, A. L. Chronic Disease in Former College Students: IV. Characteristics in Youth that Predispose to Suicide and Accidental Death in Later Life. *Amer. J. Pub. Health* 59:900, 1969.

39. Palola, E. G.; Dorpat, T. L.; and Larson, W. R. Alcoholism and Suicidal Behavior. In *Society, Culture, and Drinking Patterns,* ed. D. J. Pittman and C. R. Snyder, p. 511. New York: Wiley, 1962.

40. Philip, A. D. Traits, Attitudes, and Symptoms in a Group of Attempted Suicides. *Brit. J. Psychiat.* 116:475, 1970.

41. Pitts, F. N., and Winokur, G. Affective Disorder: VII. Alcoholism and Affective Disorder. *J. Psychiat. Res.* 4:37, 1966.

42. Rado, S. The Psychoanalysis of Pharmacothymia (Drug Addiction). *Psychoanal. Quart.* 1:1, 1933.

43. Report on 2nd Annual Medical and Scientific Conference of the National Council on Alcoholism, California, April 14, 1971. *Recovery* 5, no. 2, 1971 (Ayerst Laboratories).

44. Rosen, A. C. A Comparative Study of Alcoholic and Psychiatric Patients with the M.M.P.I. *Quart. J. Stud. Alcohol* 21:253, 1960.

45. Rotov, M. Death by Suicide in Hospital. *Amer. J. Psychother.* 25:216, 1970.

46. Rushing, W. A. Suicide and the Interaction of Alcoholism (Liver Cirrhosis) with the Social Situation. *Quart. J. Stud. Alcohol* 30:93, 1969.

47. Schilder, P. The Psychogenesis of Alcoholism. *Quart. J. Stud. Alcohol* 2:277, 1941.

48. Schildkraut, J. J. The Catecholamine Hypothesis of Affective Disorder: A Review of Supporting Evidence. *Amer. J. Psychiat.* 122:509, 1965.

49. Sclare, A. B. The Female Alcoholic. *Brit. J. Addict.* 65:99, 1970.

50. Simmel, E. Alcoholism and Addiction. *Psychoanal. Quart.* 17:6, 1948.

51. Sourkas, T. L. Twenty-five Years of Biochemical Psychiatry. *Canad. Psychiat. Assoc. J.* 15:625, 1970.

52. Tamerin, J. S., and Mendelson, J. H. The Psychodynamics of Chronic Inebriation. *Amer. J. Psychiat.* 125:886, 1969.

53. Travis, J. C. Use of Iproniazid in Treatment of Alcoholics. *JAMA* 172:909, 1960.

54. Vega, A. Cross-Validation of Four M.M.P.I. Scales for Alcoholism. *Quart. J. Stud. Alcohol* 32:791, 1971.

55. Vogel, G. W. *REM Deprivation:* III. Dreaming and Psychosis. *Arch. Gen. Psychiat.* 18:312, 1968.

56. Weijl, S. Theoretical and Practical Aspects of Psychoanalytic Therapy of Problem Drinkers. *Quart. J. Stud. Alcohol* 5:200, 1944.

57. Williams, J. H. Characteristics of an Alcoholic Sample. In *Alcoholism: The Total Treatment Approach*, ed. R. Catanzaro. Springfield, Ill.: Charles C. Thomas, 1968.

58. Williams, J. H. Characterization and Follow-up of Alcoholic Patients. In *Alcoholism: The Total Treatment Approach*, ed. R. Catanzaro. Springfield, Ill.: Charles C. Thomas, 1968.

59. Winokur, G.; Cadoret, R.; Dorzab, J.; and Baker, M. Depressive Disease. *Arch. Gen. Psychiat.* 24:135, 1971.

60. Winokur, G.; and Clayton, P. Family History Studies: II. Sex Differences and Alcoholism in Primary Affective Illness. *Brit. J. Psychiat.* 113:973, 1967.

61. Winokur, G., and Pitts, F. N. Affective Disorder: VI. A Family History Study of Prevalences, Sex Differences, and Possible Genetic Factors. *J. Psychiat. Res.* 3:113, 1965.

62. Witkin, H. A.; Karp, S. A.; and Goodenough, D. R. Dependence in Alcoholics. *Quart. J. Stud. Alcohol* 20:493, 1959.

63. Zung, W. W. K. A Self-Rating Depression Scale. *Arch. Gen. Psychiat.* 12:63, 1965.

64. Zwerling, I. Psychiatric Findings in an Interdisciplinary Study of Forty-six Alcoholic Patients. *Quart. J. Stud. Alcohol* 20:543, 1959.

65. Zwerling, I., and Rosenbaum, M. Alcohol Addiction and Personality. In *American Handbook of Psychiatry*, ed. S. Arieti, chap. 31. New York: Basic Books, 1959.

19

Psychedelic Drugs and Masked Depression

It is far too simplistic and naive to search for a single reason or motivation for psychedelic drug use. People may prefer one or a variety of these drugs or use them in combination with other categories of drugs, such as stimulants or depressants. They may take these drugs for a wide variety of reasons, including curiosity, rebellion, escape, relief of emotional distress, and social or religious purposes. They may use these drugs in a wide variety of contexts, including solitary or social settings, and view the drug experience as something apart from their daily lives or as a way of life in itself. It must also be recognized that psychedelic drug use, albeit illegal, need not always be regarded as psychopathological under all ircumstances. Some drug use may be viewed as healthy and adaptive when used for exploratory, educational, or experimental purposes.

It is not my purpose to present a comprehensive overview of psychedelic drug use and abuse in society. Nor, for that matter, do I intend to deal with the ethics of this type of drug use and some of the social-religious determinants responsible for labeling this behavior "bad." Instead, I wish to confine my remarks to a very special type of psychedelic drug use under very special circumstances by some very special types of people. I am referring specifically to circumstances in which continued psychedelic drug use may be viewed as a symptomatic expression or even smoke screen for an underlying depressive state.

In employing the term "depressive state," I am not referring to a classical situational neurotic depression or an endogenous psychotic depression. Although these depressive states may be associated with the occasional use of psychedelic drugs, they are less likely to play a role in its prolonged use than another type of dysphoric emotional state that tends to be of a mild, chronic, ingrained nature. As we shall see, the use of psychedelic drugs not only masks this basic dysphoric affectual state but also serves as a temporary specific antidote for it.

There have been many terms employed to describe this dysphoric affectual state, such as "anomie," "alienation," and even "existential depression." Individuals experiencing this state speak of a sense of ennui, difficulties in interpersonal involvement, emotional emptiness, lack of purpose or goal, and profound loneliness. There are no obvious external precipitating causes for these feelings, the origins of which often extend into childhood. Specific suicidal ideation is uncommon, although the desire to "turn on" and seek out drug-induced alterations in consciousness seems indicative of a need to escape from the pervasive psychic discomfort. Moreover, unlike neurotic and psychotic depression, it is difficult to uncover the existence of intense, internalized anger or object loss as a basis for these feelings. Anger may be present, but it is diffuse, global, and attenuated, not directed toward any specific persons or persons. In the place of personalized guilt is a pervasive disillusionment with social values and standards.

There has been considerable speculation that this type of affectual syndrome has arisen in response to the tremendous technological advances in society with an associated dissolution of the family structure and breakup of institutional (religious, educational, political) standards and values. Without internalized standards and goals, many modern youths find themselves in the frustrating position of wanting something other than what they have but not knowing what it is they want or how to achieve it.

If there are no external goals to be accomplished, then there can be no future, and without any future there can be no past. As a result, the present or *now* becomes all-important. Moreover, without external standards there can be no objective gauge to measure self-worth, and without a sense of self-worth there can be no true self-identity. In the place of self-identity, there is a frantic effort to experience the "self." As a result, a premium is placed on the subjective experience as the major avenue to truth and ultimate worth. It is only when the present is empty and the subjective experience shallow that a vague, uneasy, emotional disquiet may follow. Since individuals who experience this disquiet often behave in a depressed manner (i.e., withdrawn, uninvolved, expressed feelings of futility), we shall regard this affectual state as a species of the family of depressions.

Given the existence of such an affective state in a particular youth, it should not prove surprising that he will be drawn to certain psychedelic drugs. In actual fact, the clinical effects of these drugs, although socially maladaptive, may be viewed as psychological complements or specific antidotes to this underlying depression. When a person is emotionally depleted, unexcited by external social stimulation, disillusioned by social standards or traditions, and uncertain about who or what he is, it is no wonder that he is attracted to drugs that imbue his perceptions and thought processes with uniqueness, wonder, and a sense of newness, and which make him acutely aware of his subjective self through the internal panoply of extraordinary sensations. The drugs also confirm his long-standing suspicion of the instability and illusory nature of external reality, which vacillates and changes constantly in response to the pharmacological stimulation of his brain. With this accentuation of subjective reality, the individual begins to feel emotionally and intellectually alive again.

Of all the drug effects, perhaps the one representing the greatest "lure of the sirens" for the individual is the arousal of an increased sense of meaning or significance to his thoughts, perceptions, and behavior. In William James's words, things appear more "utterly utter." Ordinary objects or thoughts become extraordinary. The individual sees connections and implications in events that previously seemed disconnected or self-explanatory. Insights or solutions to imponderable or even insoluble problems or philosophical questions become plentiful. It is as though the individual is undergoing an attenuated eureka experience, whereby he is literally wallowing in insights. All human experience, no matter how trivial or mundane, becomes imbued with a new sense of importance and becomes interpretable within the context of this new subjective world view.

This sense of significance and meaning is also extended to the sphere of interpersonal relationships. The individual feels an emotional union and increased empathy with his compatriots. He believes himself *en rapport* with their inner, "true" selves, experiences a sense of communion with them and a meeting of minds. Whereas the basic depressive state accentuates his aloneness and isolation from his fellow man, society, and the world, these drug-induced effects not only produce a long-sought sense of closeness with others, but also, through the dissolution of ego boundaries, provide him with an experience of cosmic consciousness or merging with some greater unity or whole. The world no longer seems meaningless, the individual no longer seems alone. Everything becomes meaningful and all people become one and an integral part of an infinite nature.

There are two essential aspects of these particular drug effects which require elaboration. First, the very potential of these drugs for producing a transcendental experience may likewise produce panic and paranoia. It is only a small step from attributing profound meaning to one's thoughts and perceptions to having psychotic insight into the actions of others, so that the individual interprets the glances or gestures of other people as indications that they are planning to perse-cute or harm him. Moreover, when reality props begin to dissolve and when these subjectively experienced changes cannot be organized into some meaningful system, the resul-tant sense of loss of control may readily give way to panic.

Second, it must be recognized that the *sense* of signifi-cance or meaning or the emotional experience of insight can-not be regarded as synonymous with *real* significance or true insight. Although seemingly obvious, this distinction is sel-dom made by clinicians or patients. For every real insight, people have thousands of false ones. Moreover, the fact that someone subjectively regards an idea, perception, or conver-sation as meaningful does not mean that it is truly meaningful—in fact, it may prove to be trivial, mundane, insignificant, or false. Although the drug user tends to equate the actual emotional experience of insight with the proof of its truth, the insight will have little heuristic or practical value unless it receives intellectual elaboration and some sort of objective corroboration. The fact that someone feels attuned to the "inner being" of another does not mean that he truly knows what the other person thinks and feels. Moreover, many of these subjective truths must be regarded as examples of omnipotence of thought unless they can be applied, shared, and tested. It is unlikely that the insights of Buddha would have had much relevance had he remained under the bo tree, or that Jesus' precepts would have spread far if he had re-mained in the Garden of Gethsemane. What holds for the religious, philosophical, and aesthetic realms holds with even greater strength for science. Subjective insight without some cognitive elaboration and objective verification is nothing more than emotional autoeroticism.

On the basis of the foregoing description of drug effects, it should be apparent that the use of psychedelic drugs dovetails almost perfectly with the underlying depressive state. For people disenchanted with the external social world, feeling isolated and uninvolved, suffering from a sense of ennui, and reluctant to commit themselves to future goals, pharmacological agents that confirm their disenchantment, provide them with a sense of belonging, stimulate them with dramatic, unusual subjective sensations and experiences, and provide them with pleasure and meaning in the present are more apt to be regarded as emotional panaceas than as detriments. Only when the effects of these drugs produce more pain than pleasure, or when distraught parents or parental surrogates intervene, are these individuals likely to present themselves for psychiatric help. Even in these instances, however, the motivation for help extends only to a desire to relieve the unpleasant drug effects or to remove the noxious societal pressures —not to a desire to work for a drugfree existence.

The desire to live without drugs is more likely to come when the pressures of external reality become so great that the price of a drugged existence far exceeds the benefits experienced by the individual or when the individual can no longer deny his self-destructive behavior. Unfortunately, it is far more common to find that legal sanctions and the reality problems of surviving in the real world while in a drugged state are far more powerful motivators for change than sudden "existential insights" gleaned spontaneously or through involuntary psychotherapy.

Some Treatment Principles

Although clinicians adopt a variety of stances toward treatment, my own biases, evolved through many failures as well as some successes, dictate that certain treatment principles are essential for working with these patients.

First, I believe it is both unfruitful and unrealistic to set the goal of drug abstinence as a precondition of successful therapy. In a drug-taking society such as ours, abstinence from all psychotropic drugs, including alcohol, not only seems too stringent and rigorous a criterion to set for treatment outcome, but also tends to reflect a middle-aged, middle-class bias, if not frank hypocrisy. It is not necessarily the drugs themselves that are evil for the individual, but the misuse and abuse of them. Therefore, the focus of the psychotherapy should be directed more toward emphasizing the self-destructive and self-defeating aspects of the patient's drug-use pattern in terms of inhibiting the realization of his own individual potential through adverse psychological effects or the imposition of certain social sanctions. In other words, the individual must be made aware of the ways in which the excessive, inappropriate, or indiscriminate use of drugs will influence his life in the long run. Whether he chooses to avoid these problems through total abstinence or a limited use of drugs must remain his decision.

Second, in view of the chronic nature of the patient's underlying dysphoric affective state, his nonhistorical orientation, and his reluctance to postpone gratification, I do not feel that a classical insight-oriented approach, aimed at uncovering early life determinants of current behavior, will prove of much value. Since the patient seems much more predisposed to talk about his present difficulties and interpersonal relationships, an extensive discussion of the here and now tends to prove much more productive for the establishment of a therapeutic relationship than digressions into the psychogenetics of his behavior. Once this relationship is established, it then becomes possible to explore available options and alternatives to drugs to aid the individual in coping with his emotional dysphoria. Once the individual can begin to consider other options rationally, he has taken a first step toward liberation from his bondage to drugs.

Third, the issue of choice inevitably leads to a consideration of the matter of responsibility. Many of these patients somehow feel victimized by an alien society and view their drug-taking as the only way to escape. In a sense, they blame society for their predicament and feel unjustly treated when social sanctions are levied. At some point, what they must realize is that it is they who have chosen to opt out and that they are not hapless, helpless victims. If they do not like what exists out there, then they can play some role, albeit small or even seemingly insignificant, to change things. Should they choose not to become involved, they themselves are responsible for their predicament. Therefore, if these individuals do not like their predicament and feel unfairly treated, it is their obligation to behave in such a manner that these undesirable consequences do not occur. No one else is going to eliminate these unpleasant consequences for them.

I use the term "responsibility" in a special sense, meaning that individuals are the primary initiators of their behavior (and hence cannot blame others for making them do what they do), and as such are accountable for their own actions. Unless patients can come to understand and accept this type of responsibility fully, the outcome of psychotherapy is likely to be poor. Responsibility without accountability is a hollow concept.

Fourth, a vigorous educational approach within the context of therapy is also necessary to alter the solipsistic orientation of these patients, which is compounded by the drug experience. Patients must be brought to realize that there is a vast difference between the sense of significance and real significance, between subjective insights and objective insights.

Most patients are willing to debate this philosophical issue at length with therapists, but they eventually find great difficulty in reconciling their viewpoints with the fact that most of their esteemed heroes who have espoused similar philosophies have engaged in the arduous task of organizing them, writing them down, or at least communicating them. Moreover, through many therapeutic hours of amicably discussing or occasionally heatedly arguing this issue, a meaningful relationship is formed and patients become much more aware of the saliency of another viewpoint. In actual fact, their very behavior in debating this point speaks against their solipsistic stance and induces them to test out their subjective insights against a representative of objective reality in the person of the therapist.

Fifth, I have also found it helpful to discuss at length the issue of whether the search for "true" meaning in life is a hopeless, impossible quest without drugs. Simply because patients do not experience emotional meaning in social activities or reality situations does not mean that they cannot experience some degree of meaning if they make a commitment toward involvement. I believe it is unlikely that human beings ever can know with absolute certainty that anything they do or do not do is truly meaningful in the ultimate scheme of things, even though they have a need to believe that their lives are meaningful. This viewpoint has received considerable attention in the writings of Alan Wheelis. Nevertheless, the fact that we cannot know with certainty whether our actions are truly meaningful should not prevent us from behaving as if they are. If one makes a commitment to become involved in certain activities, that very process of involvement carries with it the implicit belief of significance and meaning. Living and doing are at least partial remedies for despair and aloneness. In other words, one aim of therapy is to get the patient to move from the either-or position of credulity versus nihilism to the as-if stance, which may offer some degree of emotional satisfaction.

Sixth, I do not believe it is sufficient for the therapist to expect that the patient can gratify all his needs for human closeness within the context of the therapeutic relationship. If the individual is to function in the real world, he must become involved in the real world, and involvement means working together with others. I have often found it helpful to encourage the individual to join any one of a variety of self-help groups, such as Encounter, so that he may derive the benefits of group support within the context of a common group goal. It is difficult to feel isolated and alone or even unique in a setting where others share similar problems and where automatic acceptance is possible simply by virtue of group participation.

In the final sense, the goal of therapy should be to wean the patient from the artificial confines of a doctor-patient relationship to a situation in which he is working out his dilemma with others. It is unlikely that the full impact of any psychotherapy will be realized without constant social reinforcement by peers, family, and the community at large. For these reasons, it is essential that provision be made for the patient to become involved with others in real activities in the real world.

These treatment principles are not exhaustive, nor can they be regarded as panaceas for a highly complex and often intractable sociopsychological condition. For patients who hurt but whose hurt has become a life-style, for patients who have found "canned meaning" through the ingestion of psychedelic agents but who are not drawn to the traditional social value system, and for patients who come to therapy not from personal choice but by happenstance or external pressures, it is unlikely that momentous changes in either attitude or behavior will result. Nevertheless, it is possible to attain some degree of success provided the therapist's goals are consistent with the reality expectations of patients and take into account the reality of the social context of their existence. In the last analysis, neither society, family, nor therapist can provide the patient's life with the elusive meaning he seeks: this is something only the patient himself can do. The therapist can, however, serve as a facilitative or catalytic agent in the realization of this goal.

Summary

There is a subspecies of depression, characterized by ennui, feelings of isolation, lack of purpose, and loneliness, which tends to predispose many young people to the chronic use of psychedelic drugs. In a sense, the clinical effects of psychedelic drugs are almost specific but temporary antidotes for this underlying dysphoric emotional state, since they provide the drug user with a sense of novelty, meaningfulness, and interpersonal rapport.

Because of this complementary relationship between the depressive state and psychedelic drug effects, these particular patients are extremely difficult to treat. Some basic principles, however, include *(a)* establishing realistic expectations concerning drug abstinence, *(b)* dealing with current rather than past behavior, *(c)* conveying the notion of responsibility to patients, *(d)* counteracting the solipsistic orientation of patients, and *(e)* utilizing constructive peer-group pressures.

20

Opioid Addiction as a Masked Depression

HOWARD WISHNIE

Introduction

The usual study of the opioid addict focuses upon his destructive actions rather than upon a useful psychodynamic understanding of the causes of his activities or their personal significance. This lack of a pragmatic concept regarding the origin of opioid addiction may result from several factors. Psychoanalytic thinking, while understanding the addict's regression and fixations, has not provided useful tools for treatment based upon these ideas (2, 8, 9). The addict's destructive behavior, while distressing to the observer or recipient, allegedly does not trouble him, and he therefore does not seek meaningful assistance. When confined to a prison setting, he continues to be uninterested in self-evaluation and preoccupied with projection of responsibility. His basic paranoid projections are reinforced by the reality of prison, or he may be docilely altered by the rigid external controls. In the traditional hospital setting, he does not share the goal of the staff members, who want to help him to try to improve his situation regarding drug abuse and criminality.

The issue then becomes control and elimination of this

behavior. The addict and his would-be therapist become enmeshed in his manipulative and self-destructive behavior and rarely get beyond this point. A consequence of this dilemma has been the development of self-help units, because the professionals essentially give up.

The theme of this discussion hinges upon the fact that the destructive behavior pattern is an effective mask for an underlying depression. The patient's actions have served to distract both himself and the observer from examining his chronic and pervasive painful internal experience.

As with other severe character disorders, the patient does not perceive a delineated issue. He does not suffer a character disorder, he *is* one. Thus to acknowledge the existence of the problem is to make an overwhelming admission. As one patient said, "My God, Doc, if what you're talking about is true, that's my whole life. That's me."

Like the manic patient who flees from depression through activity, the addict uses action to deny his affect. He becomes involved in rituals of sharing and preparation, "exciting" illicit activities, and prolonged verbal denials of any role in his problem. Where the manic works toward a mindless, trouble-free state of exhaustion, the addict injects his calm, trouble-free state of mind (5). If one gets him to relinquish his action solutions, the affect of depression emerges. It is not surprising that narcotics addicts show elevation of a psychopathic deviant, depressive, and hypomanic scale on the M.M.P.I. This is found whether he is institutionalized or in the streets (3, 10).

To speak of the addict as one type or person would be inaccurate. Addiction frequently represents a final attempt at self-treatment for depression after other means have failed. The addict arrives at this treatment modality from diverse origins. He may be a ghetto black who sees himself as hopelessly entrapped by a system, neighborhood, and family that are disrupted. His adult models, which to us are deviant, are for him normal. His addiction, while predicated on a sense of personal futility based upon his own personal experience, is supported by his environmental reality.

He may be a poor or middle-class white whose family attempts to maintain an outer facade of normality while internally giving vent to violence, alcoholism, and a free expression of primitive emotions. Caught between the espoused value system and the operative value system, he develops a sense of difference and distance from his social peers. The result is withdrawal and isolation. As depression emerges, he reacts with maladaptive behavior that fails to relieve his discomfort and leads to his selection of a narcotic analgesic solution.

He may be a middle class white with high ideals and an adolescent sense of disillusionment. This individual, however, tends not to use opioid drugs unless he has also experienced significant personal deprivation in his primary object relationships.

The men in this study demonstrated an accessible depressive affect, which when elicited altered their subsequent institutional behavior and became the focus of therapy. This depression was reported by the patients and observed in their behavior. A consistent pattern emerged. The initial issue was a partial or total primary object deprivation including both parents. This deprivation led to a sense of emptiness and futility. When the deprivation was total and occurred early in childhood, the drug-abuse pattern appeared more malignant. Reaction to the initial deprivation usually involved maladaptive activity aimed at achieving restitution or self-punishment followed by restitution. When this failed, the patient felt an increased sense of futility and hopelessness and gave up trying to achieve through his own efforts. He withdrew from personal relationships and established a relationship with his narcotic. It provided for him motivation and goal, both pleasure and punishment. Depending upon the onset of the primary object deprivation and his previously achieved ego skills, the addict ran the gamut of experience from marginal passive-dependent functioning to early death. This deprivation model is anaclitic in nature.

The Study Setting

The case material for this study is derived from an intensive investigation of sixty male opioid addicts who resided at the Clinical Research Center, Lexington, Kentucky, for a period of five to seven months between August 1970 and March 1971. All but three of these men were from the South. Thirty-two were white and twenty-eight black. Sixty percent of these men came in lieu of facing prosecution or prison sentences for drug related crimes. In general, they were unmotivated and hostile to any concept of treatment.

The Clinical Research Center is midway between a prison and a hospital. Until 1968 it was a medium-security prison. Since that time, all the external signs of prison have been removed. There are no more barred windows, barbed wire, weapons, solitary confinement, or armed guards. A door is always open and a patient may leave at any hour.

The patients live on a unit comprised of four wards containing from fifteen to twenty beds each. Each patient has his own room, which he can decorate to his own taste. There is modified self-government, which plays an active role in the unit's functioning.

The Addict

The average addict in this study is a twenty-two-year-old man with a tenth-grade education. Thirty-three percent of the men began heavy alcohol abuse at the age of fifteen to sixteen. By the age of 18.5, this group, plus an additional 8 percent, were using nonnarcotic drugs.

The average addict in this study was regularly abusing opioid narcotics by the age of 19.3 years. At the time of admission, the median period of consistent abuse was 3.5 years.

The economic background of the average patient is poor to lower middle class. Seventy-six percent had mothers in the home until age eighteen. Fifteen percent of these mothers were alcoholics, and 5 percent used opioid narcotics during terminal illnesses. Another 5 percent were seriously drug-dependent independently of any illness.

Only 41 percent of the patients in the study had fathers in the home until the age of eighteen. Thirty-seven percent of the fathers were severely alcoholic. Fifty percent of all the fathers were brutal, physically abusive men when they were in the home.

Only 10 percent of the patients had never been arrested. Seventy-six percent had been in jail.

The man in this study is the street addict, everybody's treatment failure. He has been to self-help programs and has either left or been thrown out. In methadone clinics, he sells some of the methadone in order to buy heroin, or shoots heroin with methadone. When he enters this institution, he sees himself as just doing another form of jail time. To him, everybody is a con man. There are those who have been caught and those who haven't. He projects all responsibility and argues vehemently when cornered. He takes pleasure in reciting tales of public officials caught embezzling and frequently asks the therapist if he has ever tried a particular illicit endeavor. Drugs are not his problem: the laws concerning drugs are his problem. Manipulation by word and deed is the major tool of his trade. Failure to achieve a desired end results only from not knowing the correct manipulation.

Any reasonable observer can see that this person uses his behavior to bolster a basic sense of low self-esteem, a sense of impotence in dealing with the environment in anything but a deceptive way. We can see his use of rationalization, distortion, denial, and projection; unfortunately, he can't.

Depression

The depression that this man suffers does not neatly fit into our current concepts. In the continuum of mental illness, it occupies the middle ground between neurotic reactive depression and psychotic depression. It borrows from both and has some unique aspects of its own. An individual may appear to have more neurotic traits than psychotic and also may shift along this spectrum.

The content of the depression contains hopelessness about oneself. The individuals have no belief in their ability to change, grow, or alter their life-style. This hopelessness does not represent a change from a previously hopeful state, but is viewed by the patient as lifelong and gradually worsening. As a result, he lives for the moment and is unable to plan realistically for events in the future. Plans may be made and actually embarked upon, but unless they are actively reinforced by the staff, the goal-directed activities will last two weeks at the most. Because there is no future, gratification must be now, immediately. Both physical and emotional distress must also be relieved at once.

There is a withdrawal from human relationships. Forty-seven percent of the men were divorced. Seventy-five percent of them described themselves as not being close to anyone and having never developed a significant friendship with anyone with whom they could share concerns or personal material. Mr. J. stated it this way: "It's funny, even the situation where it's a buddy, I know I should feel something, like sympathy or understanding. You know, I feel nothing, I just kind of go through the motions."

In this quotation there is another element of the general depression, the lack of internal feeling. Thirty-two percent of the men described themselves as feeling "empty," having "something missing," being "inadequate" and "inferior." Mr. H. stated the danger of closeness most clearly: "The only things that could make me weak are the things I'm strong for. Like a man's a really good pimp until he falls for one of his whores, then he's finished."

The patient does not verbally express negative feelings toward himself, but his appearance, behavior, and repeated self-destructive acts demonstrate his attitude clearly.

The patients consistently lack what Beck calls a "mirth

response"(1). Their jokes, when observed in the institution, are sadistically based upon making another individual look foolish in front of his peers. The lack of ability to express positive feelings was graphically demonstrated in the psychodrama group. One evening after the group members had pantomimed the feelings of anger and rage, they decided to try happiness. None of the eight men present could portray in a convincing way any of the feelings related to being happy. Their portrayals were tight and constricted. If one considers these patients according to Beck's cognitive manifestations of depression (1), depression is evident.

As I have said, the patients demonstrate low self-esteem. They are indecisive. They have negative expectations of themselves and a definite lack of motivation. They do not, however, openly blame themselves. They deny, distort, and project to avoid any sense of self-blame. The individual's sense of self-esteem is constantly being tested. As he has little beside this bravado image, all of his energies go into its maintenance. He has no accomplishments or other sources of pride that would allow him to tolerate criticism or self-observation. If at all possible, he will tend to avoid and escape uncomfortable situtations. He externalizes his role and blames others for his situation. He verbally denies suicidal wishes but constantly acts them out.

Physical manifestations of depression are seen in his activities even when he is withdrawn from drugs. In the hospital he is listless, sleeps poorly, watches TV, plays cards or pool. He will walk to meals but has trouble getting a team to play ball. He makes sick call for all minor ailments. His face is frequently expressionless; aside from flashes of anger, little else is apparent. His libido, while gravely diminished during the period of drug abuse, increases only moderately when drugs are withdrawn. Thus the depression includes many of the elements described for other depressive states.

Unlike the psychoneurotic depressive reaction, this depression does not appear to have current precipitants or loss. Frequently, however, there is a history of a turning point when the patient gave up working toward alleviation of his painful internal state. For example, Mr. H. was an eighteen-year-old high school dropout whose family had managed to maintain a middle-class facade. For as long as the patient could remember, his father had been a brutal alcoholic who had been hospitalized repeatedly for detoxification, but managed to work intermittently as a motel manager. As a child, the patient frequently tried to destroy his father's hidden liquor supplies, and his father would become enraged at him. When he was thirteen, the patient found a bottle hidden in the laundry, but left it there because he felt there was no longer any use in trying. He could not get his father to forget the bottle and pay attention to him. Feeling this way, the patient became increasingly involved in delinquent behavior, first alcohol and then drug abuse. The incident when he gave up trying—when he left the bottle in the laundry—was the turning point.

The neurotic patient uses depression as a defense against the anxiety associated with loss and its inherent ambivalent feelings. The more primitive addict patient must defend against the depression itself, as he has little to help him tolerate it. Mr. R. said, "My God, if I were to listen to you and think about that stuff, I couldn't like myself, I'd have to kill myself. It makes me feel like nothing."

The depression also contains a vague delusion that is ever present (5). This delusion involves an empty hope, based upon nothing but faith, lacking reality, and contradicted by the patient's words and actions. An example was given by Mr. V., a 24-year-old divorced high school dropout. He had had two previous admissions to this hospital. During his first three months of hospitalization he was unable to sleep and stayed up listening to the radio throughout the night. He failed to participate in therapy, spoke very little to anyone, peers or staff, and appeared listless at all times. During his first staff conference he said, "Drugs make me forget my problems, Doc. I honestly can't picture myself without them. I know I'll leave here, work for a few months, and that will be it. I'll be back on the stuff." He was unable to focus clearly on his problems beyond the pervasive sense of futility. During his five-month staff conference, he stated that the evening before he had thought of the questions that might be asked and the answers he would give. In evaluating his own answers, he said that he expected that people would conclude that he was still hopeless. (In fact, the review did lead to this conclusion.) He went on, "I know it looks that way. I know it sounds that way. My words say it, I say it, but that isn't the case! I know that it's different!" The delusion here involves the belief that there is a reality more important than that portrayed by words, actions, feelings, and behavior.

Twenty-eight percent of the men described themselves as isolated and depressed. They stated and gave evidence that the depression was the primary motivation and major issue in sustaining the use of drugs. The unique elements of this depression involve its lack of self-blame, its verbal suicide content, and the use of action where one would expect affect. The superficial affect is anger and complaints of depression are lacking. In a neurotic depression, the response appears to be out of proportion to the precipitants. In this instance, quite the reverse is true.

This depression relates to primary object relationship deprivation. Usually one parent was physically absent and the remaining parent emotionally unavailable. These patients were unable to find adequate substitutes. When substitutes were available, the patients were unable to form relationships with them.

The Addict's Mother

The mother of the addict has been described as an overindulgent woman who promotes an infantilizing relationship with her son or an overtly rejecting figure (6); a masochistic woman who indirectly expresses her rage at her husband through her male children (4); a depressed woman ambivalent toward the responsibility of caring for her own children (7). Fifty-four percent of the mothers in this study were described as overprotective, indulgent, and babying.

Fifty-eight percent of the mothers were described as incapable of setting consistent limits and expectations. In all these cases, the fathers were absent or nonparticipants in the raising of the child. Most of the addicts stated, in fact, that they could always get around their mothers. Twenty percent of the addicts described themselves as "mamma's boys" until early adolescence. By this they meant that they were forced to attend school and church, stay home and not play with neighborhood youths who were considered too tough and inferior by their mothers. During the adolescent period, all the addicts had engaged in passive-aggressive and self-defeating activities aimed at causing their mothers to react.

Because of the hostile-dependent and passive relationship with the mother, direct confrontation was too threatening to the patient. There were also individuals whose mothers not only provided the money for their drugs, but in some instances purchased the drugs for them so that the addict's "safety" would not be jeopardized. It was noteworthy that the addicts who had this hostile-dependent relationship with their mothers consistently avoided assaultive behavior in supporting their drug habits. They chose forgery, shoplifting, and stealing. On the unit these men were not the loud troublemakers. Seven men who initially used alcohol found that alcohol brought out their covert rage against their mothers and wives. Two tried to kill their mothers. When their behavior became too disturbing, they switched to narcotics, which provided relief but did not promote expressions of rage.

The question arises as to how this inadequate mother is also depriving. She does not treat the patient as a real or separate individual. He becomes an object used to work through her own hostility toward her husband or other men in her life. The patient is tied to her in a way that does not promote independence. In spite of the overindulgent aspect noted above, close investigation frequently revealed that the relationship lacked warmth and affection. Mr. J. told how his mother kept his delinquent behavior from his father. He spoke proudly of the way she defended him against school officials who would come to the home. She stood on the porch, cursing and swearing at them, insisting that what they said about her son could not be true. As soon as these people left, she slammed the door and failed to discuss any of the issues with her son. Her overt indulgence vaguely disguised her desire to take the path of least involvement.

Twenty percent of the mothers were described as aloof, distant, or uninvolved. Many of these women worked and maintained the family and had little time for the children.

The Addict's Father

As noted earlier, the fathers were either unstable and erratic or absent. In addition to the 50 percent who were consistently physically abusive when they were present, another 18 percent set unreasonable demands for achievement which the patient felt he could not satisfy. After repeated attempts to please such a father, the patient usually gave up and saw himself as a failure in comparison with his more successful father. This situation led to a sense of guilt and worthlessness.

Seventy percent of the fathers who were available at least until the patients were six were described as cold, cool, aloof, indifferent, or disinterested. When the father had never been present, he was longed for as a fantasied object of restitution. One-third of the patients focused exclusively upon their fathers in their evaluation conferences. The issue frequently boiled down to the statement "If only he had been there, I would be different."

More striking, however, were the 15 percent of the group who during adolescence began a search for the father who had never been present. Mr. P. was a 20-year-old single ex-Marine. He described his mother as "someone who never gives up on anything, even me." His father had never lived at home. The patient dropped out of high school and joined the Marines because "it would build me into a man." He explained that his mother had been a successful arranger of everything in his life (including his hospitalization). He had wanted to be more independent. He found the Marine training very difficult, but he stayed with it, even though he refused to seek promotions for fear of losing peer-group support. Upon discharge, he felt rejected, "like nobody, without the Marines." He then paused and asked why it was that whenever he talked with someone, anyone, he felt the other person had an advantage over him, had something he didn't possess. He paused again and stated that he was remembering that he had begun searching for his father when he was fifteen. When he found him, he saw a boy about his own age standing on the front porch. He went into the house and found his father asleep in the back bedroom. He remembered standing over him and silently looking, not knowing what to say. His father raised himself on one elbow, shook hands, and lay back down. Mr. P. could not describe what he had hoped for or anticipated, but his eyes filled with tears.

Wanting the Marines to make him into a man, feeling personally deficient and less adequate than his mother—all appeared to be related to his fantasies of what the presence of his father might have done for him. He sought out this man apparently looking for help in achieving his own sense of independence.

Clearly the father is longed for as an alternative to the overindulgent or distant mother on whom the patient is strongly dependent. The fantasied father is a combination of an independent man who functions without having to turn to a woman and at the same time is warm, understanding, and essentially maternal.

When the sought-after individual, mother or father, has never been present, idealization and identification occur. An example of almost total deprivation and identification with the lost person is Mr. F. G., a twenty-one-year-old high school dropout. He was an impulsive young man who rapidly shifted from rage and demandingness to a clawing dependency. His mother died when he was two years old.

Following her death, the patient became so difficult to manage that he was given to his maternal grandparents when he was four years old. He began stealing from teachers' purses during kindergarten to buy candy, although money and sweets were readily available to him. He spent two years in a school for delinquent and disturbed children from age thirteen to fifteen. At eighteen he had attempted suicide by shooting himself in the abdomen. At that time he had been on heroin for several years and was having no legal difficulty but found no relief from an increasing sense of futility.

Following the conference, he sought out the interviewer because of disturbing memories. The issue of his suicide attempt had been going around in his mind. He said, "It was very strange, Doctor. I remember thinking, now maybe I will see my mother." The patient then asked the doctor to write for records from the school for delinquents which he had attended. He indicated that it contained some information that he was vague about in regard to his mother. When the information arrived from the school, it stated that his mother had been a drug addict who had committed suicide. When the parent has been present for a period of time, there is an identification with many of the pathologic aspects of his or her behavior.

Mr. B. was a twenty-year-old high school graduate whose father left home when he was twelve years old. Prior to that time, the household had been chaotic. His father was described as an alcoholic who was always fighting with the patient's mother and beating the children. Mr. B. said he was a born loser who failed at everything and he was glad when his father left home. The staff noted that Mr. B.'s delinquent behavior began shortly after his father's departure. Further probing revealed that the patient began binge-drinking at the age of twelve. "All the kids drank a little, but I got loaded all the time."

He attributed his drinking to a feeling of inadequacy. When pressed for further explanation, he answered, "Something is missing. Hell, I don't know what it is." He had left home at the age of fifteen because he felt his behavior was adversely affecting his mother and he did not know how to control it. In discussing his delinquent behavior, Mr. B. said, "I always knew I would get caught. It's really strange." This self-destructive pattern was clearly demonstrated in several instances when Mr. B. unconsciously arranged for his own apprehension. His own failures, abusiveness toward his mother, alcoholism, and leaving home were replications of his father's behavior. In effect, he had replaced the loss of his father by becoming like him. The ambivalence toward the lost object appears in the identification followed by self-destructive behavior, as if to punish the internalized remnant.

Techniques

Beginning in July 1970 a plan was developed for confronting these patients with their current behavior and its psychodynamic antecedents. The first stage was to take the group of unmotivated, hostile, and isolated individuals and force them to work in a more cohesive fashion. The patients initially participated in the setting up of guidelines for behavior. Each time they failed to live up to their goals, an investigation of the failure was made and a new limit was set. Here is an example:

The unit is a U-shaped building with a wall at the end of an open courtyard. During the evening, small groups of patients would go over the wall to obtain drugs. These escapes required elaborate diversionary and lookout systems. The patients were told that the courtyard would be closed if this continued. At that they threatened riots and dire consequences. Finally they suggested that the barbed wire be replaced. They did not want the responsibility of applying group pressure to keep their comrades off the walls. Essentially, they wanted a privilege without any responsibility. To put back the barbed wire would have been to reinstitute the prison system, which externalizes all controls. After the courtyard was closed for two days, no one went over the wall for nine months. Similarly, a man going on pass had to be evaluated by the group. If he "messed up," then the group would lose its pass privileges.

In addition, each patient was required to work twenty hours a week and attend his group therapy regularly. Early discharge for good behavior was eliminated, as this had nothing to do with the clinical reality that treatment takes longer than the six months allowed by law. In addition, this discharge policy had supported the idea that the hospital was a prison. These changes resulted in a twelve-hour strike by the patients. The staff remained indifferent to the strike and the resistance evaporated. It was followed by a period of depression when the men realized that an individual's behavior, not his promises, would be the significant issue.

While all this was going on, the social worker was conducting intensive background studies on each individual. The general medical officer, in an overlapping fashion, was conducting psychiatric studies on each man. The nurses and aides were observing the men's behavior on the unit and in therapy. At two months and five months after admission a comprehensive staff conference was held. Past history and current behavior were reviewed with the patient present. This was followed by one and a half hours of psychiatric interview. There was a definite attempt to interpret defenses or bypass them to get to the painful issues and force the patient to experience and understand them consciously.

One example was Mr. G., who was twenty years old and single. He entered the conference with his usual air of provocative indifference: twenty minutes late, sloppily dressed, fly open. He said the staff would have to awaken him if they expected him to be up that early, nine-thirty A.M.

The social worker related that his mother had been a prostitute who had given him away at the age of eight to a man alleged to be his father. As other material about his impoverished background was related, he began shifting about uncomfortably, attempting to set up diversionary discussions with other staff members. He asked if it was necessary to review his background, because it was "unimportant." He recalled that his childhood had been fun and free; he could come and go as he pleased. When he was five or six he had been able to sneak out and be on his own for days at a time. He laughingly remembered a time when he had been caught in a storm drain and was rescued by the police. His freedom was interpreted to him as evidence that apparently his mother was too busy and perhaps didn't even care about him. His activity during the conference was interpreted as a way of avoiding the affect associated with his deprived background.

In spite of his verbal show of independence, it was pointed out that his behavior was aimed at promoting others' concern and protection: the police to rescue him when no one else cared, the nurse to awaken him if she cared enough to want him present, and someone to tell him to dress properly and close his fly. He became angry and tearfully exclaimed, "I want to get away from all that! I don't want to look at that stuff. I've been trying to run from that all my life. If I ever think about that I'll get depressed and that will make me feel bad." The pressure continued and he spoke of his mother's being too busy making ends meet. He referred to himself as an "accident," as being "unwanted." His means of avoiding these painful areas in the past had been his constant involvement in "exciting" illegal activities.

Frequently in these conferences, the important issue was found through a discrepancy in the information gathered by the various sources. Mr. W. initially described his father to a social worker as a "quiet, good man." Some discrepancies noted during the therapy sessions were investigated. The investigation led to the revelation that the patient's father was a brutal alcoholic whom the patient had tried to kill when the father was strangling his mother. The issue of denied rage and its control became a focus of the investigation and led to the emergence of depression.

Occasionally there is a need to strip away a defense. This

has precipitated severe depressions, and in two cases transient psychosis. These confrontations lead to overt depressions. As a result, thirty-five percent sought individual therapy because of memories, nightmares, sleeplessness, and lack of energy. It should be understood that for these men to seek help frequently meant breaking the prisoner's code that had initially been part of the unit structure. These men stayed in therapy and continued to be depressed, although their available energy increased. Their behavior was noticeably different. The conferences that were initially avoided were now anticipated as a place where one painfully but fruitfully observed himself. In addition to the group, milieu, and individual therapy sessions, evening therapy was developed. The patients spontaneously tripled the amount of time they spent in therapy. The issues became today's behavior, its relation to the past, and its personal meaning to the individual.

Summary

In an open setting where there are clear expectations and firm but reasonable limits, without bars, guards, weapons, and other objects that reinforce projection of responsibility, a group of sixty basically unmotivated criminal narcotics addicts were involved in a six-month program geared toward rehabilitation. By constant observation of successes and failures and confrontation with behavior, the men began to see the significance of their behavior. By correlating this with past situations and past experiences in a forceful, nonpunitive way, the men began to see their role in promoting their difficulties. This realization elicited a pervasive depression.

The individuals sought to avoid this painful internal state, but a consistent attempt to confront them in many instances led to a more extensive awareness of their current and past states of feeling. Dynamic understanding of the precipitants of the action was constantly used, but never allowed to excuse deviant behavior.

The depressions were chronic and pervasive. They were

related to early life experiences. Investigation of family background revealed consistent major disruptions and significant deficits. Mothers were overindulgent or aloof. Fathers were absent, alcoholic, unstable.

No claim is made here for cure. Frequently the depression emerged after four to six months of treatment and the gains made were not substantial enough to enable the staff to believe that drug abstinence would be sustained beyond the six months of treatment in the institution.

The experience thus far suggests that depression is a primary issue in narcotics addiction. Of greater significance is the fact that the depression is an issue that is available for use in therapy and rehabilitation. The previous focus upon the addict's disruptive behavior alone fits into his defensive structure whereby he attempts to distract himself and others from his internal affect by his actions.

References

1. Beck, A. I. *Depression: Clinical, Experimental, and Theoretical Aspects.* New York: Harper & Row, 1967.
2. Fenichel, O. *The Psychoanalytic Theory of Neurosis.* New York: Norton, 1945.
3. Hill, H. E.; Haertzen, C. A.; and Glaser, R. Personality Characteristics of Narcotic Addicts as Indicated by the MMPI. *J. Gen. Psychol.* 62:127, 1960.
4. Hirsch, R. Group Therapy with the Parent of Adolescent Drug Addicts. *Psychiat. Quart.* 35:702, 1961.
5. Lewin, B. *The Psychoanalysis of Elation.* New York: Norton, 1950.
6. Lewis, J. M., and Osberg, J. W. Treatment of the Narcotic Addict. *Amer. J. Orthopsychiat.* 28:730, 1958.
7. Mason, P. The Mother of the Addict. *Psychiat. Quart.* 32:189, 1958.
8. Rado, S. Narcotic Bondage. *Amer. J. Psychiat.* 114:165, 1957.
9. Savitt, R. Psychoanalytic Studies on Behavior: Ego Structure in Narcotic Addiction. *Psychoanal. Quart.* 32:43, 1963.
10. Wellisch, D.; Gay, G.; and McEntra, R. The Easy Rider Syndrome. *Family Process* 9:425, 1970.

INDEX

Index

Index